T0328887

Formula 4.0 for Digital Transformation

Formula 4.0 for Digital Transformation

A Framework Using Digital Enablers from Industry 4.0

Venkatesh Upadrista

Routledge
Taylor & Francis Group

A PRODUCTIVITY PRESS BOOK

First Edition published 2021
by Routledge
600 Broken Sound Parkway #300, Boca Raton FL, 33487

and by Routledge
2 Park Square, Milton Park, Abingdon, Oxon, OX14 4RN

Routledge is an imprint of the Taylor & Francis Group, an informa business

Library of Congress Cataloging-in-Publication Data
A catalog record for this title has been requested

ISBN: 978-0-367-74686-5 (hbk)
ISBN: 978-0-367-74684-1 (pbk)
ISBN: 978-1-003-15907-0 (ebk)

Typeset in ITC Garamond Std
by KnowledgeWorks Global Ltd.

Contents

SECTION III   FOUNDATION PLATFORM

SECTION IV   PEOPLE, PROCESSES, AND TOOLS

Foreword by Erik Verrijssen

Many books have been written about Digital Transformation, but so far nobody has been able to define a real good, pragmatic framework for success until this book is released.

Digital transformation is all about business transformation using technology. Quite in line with many corporate transformations, many digital transformations do fail. Though there are clearly very specific digital driven reasons for failure (e.g., technology complexity and readiness), most reasons for failure have to do with people skills and competencies, organization culture, right decisions, and governance, as well as lack of true and measurable tangible objectives. The key to digital transformation success is to work on many pillars at the same time, to make the holistic transformation a major success. It is not just about new IT technology, it is not just about data, and it is not just about cost efficiencies. All pillars of transformation need to be brought together and each one needs a clear focus and attention from business management and IT for digital transformation to be successful. IT is part of the business, NOT next to the business. The position of IT function is mission critical for success, but it is not the only thing that needs to be fixed. Mr. Venkatesh Upadrista has explained all these concepts exceptionally well in his book, *Formula 4.0 for Digital Transformation*, and has provided a clear approach on how to bring these concepts to action in real life.

In my experience as CIO of large corporations, I can only testify that we need to a holistic framework for digital transformation; we need a clear guide and cookbook for success. This book is a big step forward to such guide. It contains true pragmatic approaches that can be applied very widely. To those who are trying to crack the digital transformation nut, the Formula 4.0 framework as defined in this book is a recipe to sure shot success and is worth your reading time!

Enjoy!

Erik Verrijssen
Chief Information Officer—Sanofi

Foreword by Simon Hollins

This is a book about joy.

Browsing the chapter headings, "joy" is probably not the first emotion that grips you. Curiosity, anticipation, or trepidation maybe, but joy?

Businesses have been transforming using digital technology for many years. As customers, employees, and shareholders, we've all enjoyed the new products and services, the real-time customer experience, and the new efficient business models. Frankly though, as the leaders driving the transformation, it's been tough. It's not much fun when the early excitement of a compelling transformation vision has drifted into a complex web of systems, people, and process programs. The thrill of a customer-centric vision gives way to the despair of scope reductions, cost reforecasts, and strategy resets.

It doesn't have to be like this; my greatest professional joy has come from those digital transformations where the vision, the team, and the customers came together to create something extraordinary and enduring. I've seen some of the despairs as well, enough to realize that the difference between joy and despair mostly rests on how well you and your team have learned the craft of digital transformation before embarking on your journey.

Venkatesh Upadrista has written a book that outlines the practical approaches that any successful digital transformation will need. He has drawn on his own experience as a successful leader and his previous research and writing in this field. As I read his book for the first time, some chapters brought back the excitement of using similar techniques on successful transformations, and the effort it had taken to learn them. Other chapters gave me new insights into transformation challenges that still puzzle me.

For instance, why is creating a clear, detailed, and definitive business vision so hard? Too often, vision development only reveals the executive team's lack of understanding of their business. But the "vision statement" is a good one so we rush into delivery using simplified models and analogies.

As Venkat explains, our minds are just naturally better at dividing and simplifying than integrating. Faced with a complex problem, we break it down into small pieces that we can solve. Then we wonder why fixing all the small problems didn't transform our business. There is a smarter way to create an integrated vision for the business—not easy work, but Venkat has set out the recipe in a way that any executive team should be able to follow.

Sometimes I've found that executive teams refuse to simplify. I challenged one consultant on why she had created the "Nine Pillar Strategy" for my then-employer. She pointed out that there were nine divisional Presidents and no-one wanted to be left out. The strategy needed to be everything to everyone. As Venkat illustrates, early on you need to choose whether your strategy is driven from inside your business out to your customers or from your customers into your business. Cleverly, he then uses the Formula 4.0 model to explain the relationship between a Business Transformation Strategy and a Customer Engagement Strategy. Either can work, but failing to make a choice at the outset will guarantee that your transformation will fall apart under the tension of competing expectations. Interestingly, neither the Nine Pillar Strategy nor any of its successors have stopped that company losing a once-dominant position in its market.

Organization Design is one of the toughest transformation problems, often left to individual managers to determine toward the end of the program. They frequently use the traditional methods of "how do I give all my strongest people a decent new role" and "how do I afford new talent while continuing all the existing work." We've all become familiar with the language of Agile and Products: rapid prototyping, combined business/ IT teams, Minimum Viable Products, and the entrepreneurial spirit usually found in startups. Rarely do the early successes in the transformation team translate into a lasting change across the whole business. In time, the enterprise falls back on the familiar Project language: sales teams need committed dates for product features, production managers need capacity forecasts at least 18 months in advance, and finance teams are setting next year's development budget before the first products even go on sale. A truly successful Product organization, as Venkat describes, needs careful design across many areas of people skills, organization structure, and working relationships. I found this section one of the most enlightening— understanding the key metrics, why a diamond shaped organization delivers better than a pyramid, or even the role of outsourcing in accelerating your transformation.

Venkat has created a work full of insights, techniques, and practical examples. Taken together, they represent all of the core skills that a leader needs to drive a transformation that is successful, enduring, and joyful.

I wish I'd had this book to learn from when I started out as a CIO. I hope that you enjoy it as much as I have.

Simon Hollins
Group CIO—Informa plc (Retired)

Foreword by Satyanarayana Murthy

Thus far we have seen the most prominent effects of digital transformation in industries like retail, advertising, media, and music at the hands of digital age companies such as Microsoft, Amazon, Google, Netflix, and Spotify. Digital transformation has created whole new industries and business models such as transport services like Uber and lodging services like AirBnB. We are also seeing digital transformation in financial services with support from hundreds of fintech's backed by billions of dollars in venture capital. It will not be long when digital transformation becomes the only way for enterprises to survive in the market. However, there are more failures in digital transformation than successes. This is because digital transformation thought is a widely discussed topic, since the past several years the industry has lacked a clear methodology on how to achieve this transformation successfully. I have personally interacted with several IT service provider companies and digital leaders and have come across many different models on digital transformation, but none of them were clear enough or have provided me with the confidence that an organization could be successful by implementing one of these models.

Before reading the book produced by Mr. Venkatesh Upadrista, I was not convinced that a single methodology exists in the market that can guide an enterprise in their digital transformation journey. Mr. Upadrista has since proved me wrong with his unique methodology on digital transformation, which he calls Formula 4.0. He has articulated the importance of business-driven digital transformation as the way forward for enterprises to be successful. This is an amazing concept which needs to be adopted by every organization aspiring to transform their business using technology. The methodology not only speaks about the importance of business-driven digital transformation, but it also provides a very clear direction on how to do so. There are several case studies provided in the book which demonstrate Mr. Upadrista's vast experience in digital transformation. Formula 4.0 looks very easy to implement and provides me with the assurance that enterprises can be successful in their digital transformation journey if this methodology is followed.

Having worked closely with Mr. Upadrista on a very large transformation program few years back, I can say without hesitation that he has mastered the art of technology and is a thought leader in the digital transformation space. He has continually demonstrated his interest and aptitude for bringing value to us by utilizing his extensive knowledge of technology and business expertise.

Mr. Upadrista has now produced a book that articulates his digital transformation methodology and experience: *Formula 4.0 for Digital Transformation: A Framework Using Digital Enablers from Industry 4.0.* The methodology he endorses is a unique concept that should be adopted by every enterprise aspiring for digital transformation. The book provides a clear approach on how enterprises need to plan their digital transformation journey and execute it successfully. This setting creates a unique symbiosis that brings business strategy, execution power, and technology together to make digital transformation successful—and this book speaks all about it.

Few people are as well qualifies as Mr. Upadrista to help organizations understand and successfully navigate the challenges of digital transformation. Like all accomplished technology leaders, Mr. Upadrista is both a constitutional optimist, always seeing a world of half full glasses, and a person of vison and action. His goal is not just to help readers understand what digital transformation is but to provide actionable advice—based on proven experience—to help them move forward and achieve sure success.

My advice to all chief executives who aspire to excel in their business using technology: read this book and study its lessons. Take its advice to heart. There is no better guide than Mr. Venkatesh Upadrista to show the way to digital transformation success and this book speaks all about him.

Satyanarayana Murthy
Advisor to President—Microsoft Corporation
Board Member—Futurelight Technologies

Foreword by Raahil Burhaani

Over the past 30 years, working in corporate CXO roles for companies like Enron, Tata & Essar Group, I have come across many enterprises and individuals who spoke about digital transformation—most of the time it was about technology and less about business drivers. Business demand drives digital transformation and not vice versa—this is the most important point which every industry expert need to understand when they bring digital transformation agenda to their customers. Mr. Upadrista has been spot-on to this concept in the book which he named as *Formula 4.0 for Digital Transformation*.

Formula 4.0 clearly presents a model using which enterprises can identify business drivers for transformation and then use technology to achieve their business aspirations. Enterprises can disrupt themselves with new business models or by making modifications to existing business models or amplify their customer engagement strategy using Formula 4.0.

Another interesting concept which Mr. Upadrista speaks about in the book is the confluence of four major technological forces—cloud computing, big data, artificial intelligence, and Internet of Things, which is causing a mass extinction event in the industry, leaving in its wake a growing number of organizations that have either ceased to exist or have become irrelevant. At the same time, new age organizations are rapidly emerging, with a different kind of DNA born of this new digital age. This is a concept very easy to speak about, but bringing a solution to address this challenge is quite difficult—Formula 4.0 is a model that has sharply addressed this challenge.

During this time of digital acceleration, it is very essential for enterprises to have a proven and successful model towards business-driven digital transformation. The Formula 4.0 model created by Mr. Upadrista is undoubtedly the best one I have come across so far.

Treasure this book as you will need to be rereading this book repeatedly in your entire career, since digital transformation is a journey and not a destiny. This book has all the ingredients that can make enterprises successful in their digital transformation journey. If you are looking for a capability with the breadth and depth of business and technology to make your enterprises successful in digital transformation, there is no better person than Mr. Upadrista and no better model than Formula 4.0 to lead you to success.

Raahil Burhaani
Chief Information Officer
Essar Oil (UK) Limited

Foreword by Julia Sattel

Digital is changing the world with breath-taking speed. I have come across many transformations which are either centred around technology or around a business use case addressing a very specific problem using technology—in my experience, such piece meal transformations have seen very limited success. Transformation needs to be driven from the business vision and is the only way for enterprises to be successful. Easier said than done, there is not much guidance in the industry on how to achieve this. Mr Venkatesh Upadrista has now brought a very unique and compelling model to make this a reality and he calls it Formula 4.0.

Formula 4.0 is a powerful methodology for enterprises to embark on their digital transformation journey. Mr Venkatesh Upadrista provides a unique way to think about how business and technology need to come together and create value using the Formula 4.0 model. He provides a way for enterprises to plan and execute together, to innovate for their customers, and to win in the marketplace—to disrupt, instead of being disrupted.

Formula 4.0 proves to be a great guide for enterprises striving to reinvent themselves using digital. This book is a must read for everyone who wants to do business differently using the power of technology.

Julia Sattel
Senior Expert – Travel IT
Advisor for Airlines and Mobility

Acknowledgments

I have had the opportunity to interact with several managers and CIOs during my two decades of career in the IT industry. This book is, in a way, an outcome of the numerous challenges I have heard and experienced in the industry on digital transformation.

The successes I have had, the challenges I've heard, the extensive research and experiments I have carried out—all have a common thread, where, due to lack of a methodology to execute digital transformation, enterprises have failed to demonstrate the benefits of technology. This is one of the reasons why digital transformation is not perceived as being easy to achieve. Personally, I have seen enormous success in this area, which was the inspiration for me to craft this book. I thank all those people who have worked with me to achieve the common goal of bringing these efforts to success.

I am grateful to all the employers I have worked with. They have given me the rich experience that underlies this project. I am thankful to my sponsoring editor for providing me with important advice on formatting the book and managing the project smoothly. I also appreciate the efforts of the editing team for giving my flow and expressions a facelift and guiding me through the manuscript development process.

Most importantly, I would like to thank my guide, Siva, for helping me to complete this project. I hope his blessings are always with me throughout my life. My special thanks to my family for supporting me in this project—for giving up so many weekends and tolerating the late nights required to put this together, and for cheering me along through every step of writing this book.

About the Author

Venkatesh Upadrista is currently leading digital transformation for several clients across the UK and Ireland, BeNeLux and France regions for a large IT Services company. He has been recognized as an exceptional digital talent leader by UK Tech Nation and is the recipient of several national and international awards. He is a board advisor to digital start-ups and provides his guidance on technology trends to develop competitive products and service offerings.

Mr. Upadrista is a thought leader in the digital transformation space. In his career of more than two decades experience, he has had the opportunity to consult several Fortune 500 companies on large scale enterprise level digital transformations. Mr. Upadrista has also provided his guidance to several enterprises in areas of Cloud Transformation, IoT & Blockchain implementation, Project to Product Transformation, and Agile-DevOps set-up, and he used these varied experiences in crafting this book.

Mr. Upadrista began compiling technical encyclopedias as a high school student. He took the vast collection of experimental facts from various sources and the research that he had been accumulating for several years and began to deploy them throughout his professional experience.

He is an advisor to a number of digital initiatives in the UK and has been a partner to CIOs of several large organizations to help them define ways to improve their business using technology.

His experience moves across technology and sales leadership. He has worked in a blended mixture of the onsite/offshore model and, through his experience, he has helped many customers move their strategies to gain several qualitative and quantitative benefits.

Introduction

Digital transformation is the transformation of business and organizational activities, processes, competencies, and models to fully leverage the changes and opportunities of a mix of digital technologies and their accelerating impact across industries in a strategic and prioritized way, with present and future shifts in mind.

Digital transformation is not about technology, but it is a way for enterprises to do business differently to remain competitive and be disruptive in their market space. To achieve this change technology is utilized. In practice, end-to-end customer experience optimization, operational flexibility, and innovation are key drivers and goals of digital transformation, along with the development of new revenue sources and information-powered ecosystems of value, leading to Model Transformations and new forms of digital processes.

Digital transformation is the only way for enterprises to be relevant in the market; however, it is a well-known fact in industry that there are more failed projects in digital transformation than successes. This is caused because there is no standard definition of digital transformation and, secondly, there is no clear methodology existing in the market that can help enterprises in their digital transformation journey. Digital transformation is treated differently by different individuals and enterprises, and many of them think of digital transformation as a pure technology initiative. Some think with Data and Analytics they can become digital. Some enterprises use Artificial Intelligence and some introduce Cloud in their enterprise and consider themselves as digital. A staggering 70% of digital transformations have failed as per McKinsey in their report.[1] The key reason why enterprises are failing in their digital transformation journeys is because there is no standard methodology in the industry that enterprises can follow to transform themselves to digital. There are several books that speak about Cloud, Artificial Intelligence, and Data Analytics in silos, but no one provides a harmonized view on how enterprises need to embark on their digital transformation journey and be successful, with a combination of these technologies keeping Business Processes as the main driver behind transformation. Digital transformation is not about technology adoption. It is about bringing a change in business using technology as a byproduct.

An enterprise can achieve success in digital transformation only if it is able to redefine the existing Business Processes and think about new ways of doing business to increase revenues. Once such a business transformation roadmap is defined utilizing technology to meet these aspirations, it is what we call digital transformation. As an example, imagine how Amazon has been able to transition from "bookstore" to "everything store" with the online retailer selling music, movies, video games, home improvement supplies, and a little of everything else, and then, in 2001, it entered into a completely new business domain by selling on-demand Cloud computing platforms. Amazon was able to achieve this radical shift in their business model because they utilized technology to become super agile in adapting to new business models. This is what digital transformation is all about. It is about reimaging existing business models and creating new business models to do business better, and then utilize technology to adapt to any new and disruptive business models in the most agile way. With this as a standard definition of digital, the Formula 4.0 methodology has been defined.

The book is divided into six Sections and 16 Chapters.

The first section will introduce readers to the generic industry perspective on digital transformation. We will also briefly discuss the building blocks of Formula 4.0 methodology. Formula 4.0 is a Business-Driven Digital Transformation Framework Using Digital Enablers from Industry 4.0.

In the second section, we will discuss the business transformation model using which enterprises can define a business strategy to compete in their market space. Once a Business Strategy is defined, the Business Transformation Model helps in identifying existing and new Business Processes that differentiate the enterprise in their market space using a combination of Systems Thinking and Design Thinking. For all those differentiating Business Processes, associated systems which need to be transformed are identified for transformation. Typically, all Business Processes which are client facing or business generating become part of the digital transformation journey and need to be modernized. Once Business Processes are modernized, enterprises can adapt to any changing business needs in the most agile way.

In the third section of this book, we will discuss setting up a foundation for digital transformation. We will discuss Atomic architecture (e.g., microservices) that enables enterprises to develop software as a collection of loosely coupled lightweight and independent services. Atomic architecture applications have become highly maintainable, independently testable, and deployable. Atomic architecture eliminates the traditional challenge, which enterprises face due to application-to-application dependencies. Cloud infrastructure is the second element which we will discuss in this section. Cloud enables enterprise to adapt to any new technology, tool, or service in the most agile way without any upfront expenditure. We will subsequently discuss the importance of Application programming interfaces (APIs) as part of the digital foundation. APIs enable enterprises to have a standard interface of communication between all applications across the organization. APIs eliminate the challenges which enterprises are facing currently with peer-to-peer application interactions.

Section four will discuss people, processes, and tools. It is very essential for enterprises to move from a project-based enterprise to a Product Organization to reap the benefits of digital. However, this is a very complex transformation and involves a massive shift to the human resource function of an enterprise. In this section, we will discuss how enterprises can transform themselves to a product-based organization and how human resources function within an enterprise need to change.

We will also discuss the importance of DevSecOps, which is a set of practices that combine software development and IT operations with Security. DecSecOps eliminates the security concerns of traditional enterprises and brings in harmony between people, processes, and tools.

In the fifth section we will discuss Big Data and Analytics. Big Data is essential for enterprises that make business decisions from data, and therefore data and analytics play a very vital role in the success of these enterprises. In this section, we will discuss how to set up an efficient data platform using Formula 4.0 methodology that will enable enterprises to spend less money and efforts toward managing their data platform and focus more on actual insights to improve their business. In this section, we will also discuss the importance of automation using Robotic Process Automation and Artificial Intelligence that will deliver cost reduction, efficiency improvements, and customer delight for any enterprise. We will also discuss the importance of IT-OT Integration and how Internet of Things becomes a reality for enterprises with Formula 4.0. Subsequently, we will discuss the importance of moving to an enterprise-level governance from a business unit silos governance, which is a recipe of success for any enterprises embarking on their digital transformation journey.

Finally, the last section will bring all the Formula 4.0 capabilities together and provide a perspective on how Formula 4.0 needs to be implemented to transform a traditional enterprise to a digital organization.

Overall, Formula 4.0 is an enterprise digital transformation framework that enables organizations to do business better using technology.

This book is intended for all chief executives, software managers, and leaders who intend to successfully embark on a digital transformation journey with business as the core driver for transformation for their enterprises.

This book is an output from multiple successful engagements in digital transformation which I have led during the last 8 years. Not the least, this book is also an outcome from the learnings I had from failed digital transformation programs—a combination which had helped me to define a solid methodology to execute large digital transformation programs.

Before officially releasing this methodology into the market, Formula 4.0 was implemented in several organizations over the past 3 years. The methodology has demonstrated superior benefits when compared to any other guidance provided in the industry today. There are several case studies described in the book. All of them are from experiences with real companies, but their names have been changed to disguise their identity.

There are several good practices that are described in this book. The term "Good Practice" has been used instead of "Best Practice." A best practice is always considered to be the end state or the most mature state of a specific practice and there can be no better solution than the one stated. A good practice always has a scope of improvement, and hence I chose to use good practice because continuous improvement is one of the core fundamentals of Formula 4.0.

Note

1. https://www.mckinsey.com/industries/retail/our-insights/the-how-of-transformation

INTRODUCTION TO FORMULA 4.0

This section provides a perspective on the importance of digital transformation for enterprises, along with the successes and failures many enterprises have encountered from digital transformation in the last few years.

This section will also introduce readers to Formula 4.0 methodology, which is a framework for Digital transformation using digital enablers from Industry 4.0.

Chapter 1

A Generic Industry Perspective on Digital Transformation

Technology has been in existence for many years, and over the course of time, new-age technologies have completely revolutionized the Information Technology (IT) industry.

The modern age is referred to as the "Digital Age" since more and more technologies are stacking onto each other and developing into something greater. Consumers and businesses alike are expecting to see more opportunities for growth as future technology develops further.

For some enterprises, being digital is solely concerned with technology. For others, being digital is a new way of engaging with customers, whereas for a small minority, it represents an entirely new way of doing business. Although all these definitions of digital are correct in their own sense, often such diverse perspectives trip up leadership teams since they reflect a lack of alignment and common vision regarding the direction their business needs to go. This often results in piecemeal initiatives or misguided efforts that lead to missed opportunities, lackluster performance, or even false starts.

Enterprises and business executives need to have a clear and common understanding of exactly what digital means to them and what they want to achieve. As a result of this, they need to understand what it means to their business based upon which digital strategies or digital transformation initiatives should be defined to drive business performance. Digital transformation is all about doing business better using modern technologies.

Although digital is becoming mainstream for many enterprises, it is essential to understand that for many enterprises legacy is going to remain and cannot be completely eliminated. As an analogy, think about buying a house. If you buy a new one, it may be easier than renovating an old one. It is easier to start fresh and build from the foundation up. The issue is that this is not always possible, and a number of factors may point to keeping the foundation and improving on the existing house. This is exactly the case for traditional businesses: some have spent years building their reputation and their processes. Their employees are trained; they have an established customer database and proven products and services. They cannot change everything as this could be counterproductive and may not be required. They do, however, have to meet the demands of the digital world and adapt in their own way.

Being digital requires enterprises to be open to re-examining their entire way of doing business and understanding where the new frontiers of value are and how technology can play a key role in showcasing this value faster.

Digital for enterprises is all about rethinking how to use new capabilities, tools, and technologies to improve how customers are served whilst at the same time reducing IT costs and overall working more efficiently.

To understand how to better serve the customers, one needs to understand each step of a customer's purchasing journey—regardless of channel—and think about how digital capabilities can design and deliver the best possible experience, across all parts of the business. For example, the supply chain is critical to developing the flexibility, efficiency, and speed to deliver the right product in a way the customer wants. By the same token, data and metrics can focus on delivering insights about customers that in turn drive marketing and sales decisions.

On reducing the cost of IT, enterprises need to understand how the existing IT landscape stacks up on value versus cost and what drivers in the market exist that can reduce their CapEx and OpEx costs, with Cloud, for example, being the biggest opportunity to do just this. Aside from cost reduction, automation plays a pivotal role in ensuring that operational efficiencies are improving over a period of time. As more and more automation is enabled (be it in customer journeys, Business Process Flow Automation, operations, or development) enterprises will see more and more efficiencies in their business and the total cost of ownership. There will be less and less defects due to human errors and enterprises will move away from active monitoring to active auditing. Ultimately, this means there will be less efforts spent in day-to-day monitoring of services by humans and to ensure things are going right, more time will be spent in auditing.

DEFINITIONS

Active monitoring means that there is a full-time team that continuously monitor for errors. In contrast to active monitoring, *active auditing* means that checks are performed at certain predefined intervals for errors. Active auditing does not need a dedicated team since most of the checks are automated and performed by machines. If an error is identified, resolution is automated so that the same error does not occur in future.

Development is the process of creating a new software or product or an infrastructure. This goes through a process of planning, creating, testing, and deploying an information system.

Maintenance or *Operations* is the process of maintaining the developed software or product or infrastructure. Operations are not just about fixing defects but modifying a software product or an infrastructure after delivery to correct faults, as well as to improve performance. Small enhancements are also performed as part of operations.

Digital is not about delivering a one-off customer journey or a one-off improvement in total cost of ownership. It is about continuous improvements where processes and capabilities are constantly evolving based on inputs from the industry or the customer. This fosters ongoing product or service loyalty, and to enable this, enterprises need to create the right digital foundation that will allow the organization to achieve its business goals.

Digital foundation is all about utilizing technology and organizational processes that allow an enterprise to do their business agile and fast.

Designing Business for Future

There are four pillars that are critical to guide organizations thinking when they are assessing strategies for business transformation. These can be found as follows:

■ The right business model—becoming digital is not simply about taking existing products or customer interactions and experiences and putting them online. Enduring success in the digital economy means fundamentally rethinking how business is conducted today. The way in which organizations get products to market through centralized catalogues and move to deliver entirely new consumption models (such as pervasive digital services and subscriptions rather than one-off purchases) in addition to how consumers now purchase and use offerings is fundamental.

■ The right partners—businesses that work together with digital partners across industry borders achieve far beyond what any individual business could do on its own in the ever-changing digital world. To achieve this, businesses must now integrate with a myriad of existing and third-party systems, streamline and simplify Business Processes, and develop efficient improvements that decrease operational risk and expense. The sharing of knowledge and unique experiences to develop new applications, products, and services will become essential.

■ The right technology—not all platforms are created equal, and it will become painfully evident to those that do not choose wisely and bravely. The cost of legacy system infrastructure maintenance, integration, and operations will become prohibitive when digital competitors operate at a fraction of the cost. Not all legacies can be replaced however, and there is a right balance to be made between legacy and digital for every enterprise.

■ The right mindset—providing evolved customer experiences regardless of who those customers are, from consumers, to vendors, to partners— is vital to digital success, but it is only half the equation. To survive and (most importantly) flourish a digital culture must be integrated at all levels of the organization to instill the mentality of agility and continuous learning the digital economy demands. This requires a change to the enterprise workforce and operating model.

There is no one-size-fits-all approach to digital transformation; each strategy will be unique to each organization. However, a focus on balancing activities across these four pillars provides the compass to guide a successful transformation.

Digital Transformation—How Is It Being Driven Today

The way in which digital transformation is driving business is split broadly into four categories as depicted in Figure 1.1.

The first area is creating a digital foundation platform that will enable enterprises to achieve faster time to market, be able to adapt to the changing business needs quickly, and be cheaper. This brings a need for application

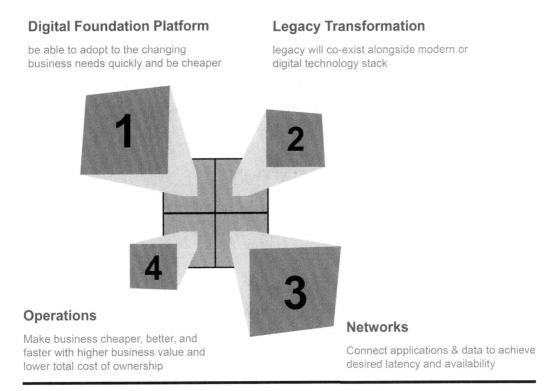

Digital Foundation Platform

be able to adopt to the changing
business needs quickly and be cheaper

Legacy Transformation

legacy will co-exist alongside modern or
digital technology stack

Operations

Make business cheaper, better, and
faster with higher business value and
lower total cost of ownership

Networks

Connect applications & data to achieve
desired latency and availability

Figure 1.1   Digital transformation focus areas

or businesses to have a loosely coupled IT architecture and a platform which
is agile, supports pay as you use models, and can be flexed-up and flexed-
down when required. The platform also needs to be highly modular, scalable,
and flexible.

> **DEFINITION**
>
> ***Time to market*** *is the length of time it takes from a product being con-*
> *ceived until it is available for sale.*

The second aspect is the whole legacy transformation piece. While the
digital foundation which is being spoken about in the industry is great, from
application perspective, it is not logical to say that legacy will not exist in
the IT estate. It is clear to any organization that legacy will coexist alongside
modern or digital technology stack. In the last 6 years dealing with digital
transformation initiatives, I have interacted with several executives, and
almost 80% of the enterprises either had a mainframe component or SAP
components or another legacy stack including Unix or Linux components in

their IT estate. For the next several years, legacy is not going anywhere, and enterprises need to find a way to separate legacy transformation or retention from pure digital initiatives. This could mean leaving legacy as it is or legacy migrating (not rewriting) to digital platforms that can drive increasing consumption on the digital foundation. One example is moving SAP from On-Premises to SAP on Cloud.

DEFINITION

An On-Premises system is installed and runs on computers on the premises of the organization using the software, rather than at a remote facility such as a server or a cloud.

The third component is the network which is all about how to connect applications and data with each other that will give the desired latency and availability of the applications after moving to the digital platforms.

The final component is all about operations. Once enterprises complete their digital transformation journey, how can they run their business cheaper, better, and faster that can provide business value and lower total cost of ownership to enterprises? An example could be how technologies, such as Internet of Things (IoT), robotic process automation (RPA), or automation, can be enabled in the enterprises that can provide business value.

The most appealing part in digital transformation for enterprises that have focused on the above four areas is that they have become very modular, independent, and flexible, thereby allowing themselves to adapt to any changes in the most agile way without impacting existing operations. The two most common areas where enterprises are considering digital adoption are cloud computing and data analytics. Digital transformation is not just about cloud and data, although these two are undoubtedly important.

Cloud Computing

One specific area in digital foundation platform is cloud computing adoption, which is a combination of a private and public cloud.

Cloud computing is the on-demand availability of computer system resources, especially data storage and computing power, without direct active management by the user. The term is generally used to describe data centers available to many users over the Internet. Typically, this is known as public cloud.

Cloud Deployment Models

Deploying models in cloud computing takes several different forms and, based on the need of an organization and the security requirements, one or a combination of these models can be selected.

Private Cloud

A private cloud is a model in which the infrastructure, services, and software are located within the organization. The cloud is maintained and managed in-house, by staff or by external providers working from within the organization. Capital expenditure and maintenance costs also remain in-house. Security features prevailing in this model go hand in hand with the organization's security requirements.

Public Cloud

A public cloud is mutually exclusive to the private cloud, where required services are hosted outside the organization. A public cloud is a platform that uses the standard cloud computing model to make resources, such as virtual machines (VMs), applications, or storage, available to users remotely. Public cloud services are offered through a variety of subscription or on-demand pricing schemes, including a pay-per-usage model. The cost advantages realized in this model are quite high compared to any other model.

Community Cloud

A community cloud is a service rendered by cloud providers to an enterprise of similar businesses or communities in a shared model, with the cloud itself residing on a public cloud. There are several examples where community clouds are created for marketing, banking products, and so on. The costs are spread across a community of users and the cost savings in this model are relatively low compared to a public cloud model, but higher than a private cloud. Security considerations can be relatively high in this model because security features are added to the cloud based on the enterprises that form this community.

Hybrid Cloud

A hybrid cloud is a combination of two or more types of cloud models such as a combination of a private cloud and community cloud or public cloud. It is a model that enables the use of multiple deployment models together. Many enterprises today are on a hybrid cloud where critical systems are deployed on a private cloud and rest on a public cloud.

Multi Cloud

Multi cloud is the use of multiple cloud computing services for multiple vendors for different cloud types. This also refers to the distribution of cloud assets, software, applications, etc. across several cloud-hosting vendors.

In the last 5 years, I have seen a significant increase in consumption of public cloud services by enterprises and this has now become almost part of the daily lives in 2020, which has been further accelerated by the COVID-19 pandemic. There are two reasons for this:

1. Enterprises are looking at faster revenue generation to sustain their business. By using cloud for product development, enterprises can increase the pace at which they want to adopt new technology and with cloud they can get access to the latest technology and tools in minutes rather than weeks and months enabling them to be prepared for the future. This enables them to develop products faster.
2. Enterprises are also looking at cost cutting, which is true for almost every industry. Cloud provides enormous cost savings if implemented properly. By using cloud for product development, enterprises need not maintain expensive, high-maintenance enterprise-level tools On-Premises.

When we talk about cloud, each enterprise is taking a different path but most of them follow a hybrid cloud strategy. Only a few enterprises have taken a 100% public cloud strategy, and these are small technology companies which have started in recent years. A lot of other enterprises are looking at hybrid cloud adoption. Some enterprises have taken a step forward and are adopting multi cloud strategy. For example, a few of the enterprises I worked for have migrated their SAP to Google cloud and Java-based applications to Amazon Web Services (AWS), but they also have a private cloud setup for their core business critical and compliance related applications.

Until recently cloud adoption has been hampered because of latency issues which enterprises face after moving to cloud. This gave an evolution to a concept known as edge computing.

Edge Computing

Edge computing is transforming the way data is being handled, processed, and delivered from millions of devices around the world. The explosive growth of Internet-connected devices—the IoT—along with new applications that require real-time computing power continues to drive edge-computing systems.

Faster networking technologies, such as 5G wireless, are allowing for edge-computing systems to accelerate the creation or support of real-time applications, such as video processing and analytics, self-driving cars, artificial intelligence, and robotics, to name a few.

Gartner defines edge computing as "a part of a distributed computing topology in which information processing is located close to the edge—where things and people produce or consume that information."

At its basic level, edge computing brings computation and data storage closer to the devices where it is being gathered, rather than relying on a central location that can be thousands of miles away. This means that data, especially real-time data, does not suffer latency issues that can affect an application's performance. In addition, companies can save money by having the processing carried out locally, reducing the amount of data that needs to be processed in a centralized or cloud-based location.

Edge computing was developed due to the exponential growth of IoT devices, which connect to the Internet for either receiving information from the cloud or delivering data back to the cloud. Many IoT devices generate enormous amounts of data during the course of their operations.

Edge computing is primarily about moving processing from the cloud, closer to the end-device or end-user. This also incorporates latency for time-sensitive applications, such as those within IoT which need real-time responses.

The key drivers for this are:

■ Network and bandwidth—Edge computing can minimize the cost of moving large amounts of data, plus reducing reliance on the network.
■ Data privacy and security—Edge computing approaches can help organizations comply with data sovereignty laws and make sure intellectual property remains On-Premises.
■ Adoption of edge computing is also being driven by a desire to make local computing—on devices or On-Premises—more cloud-like. Many applications are already being processed close to the end-user, but they run on traditional appliances that are not cloud-native. This fact makes it difficult to change applications, whether it be software upgrades or adding and testing new workloads.

On latency issues, edge computing has disrupted the complete market. So far peer-to-peer network connectivity are the only networks being used to connect data and applications, because they provide the required speed in the most consistent way. Cloud is all about accessing systems on the Internet which means data and communication need to be moved back and forth over the Internet. This gave a lot of importance to concept of edge networks, which is slowly mitigating the network latency issue.

DEFINITIONS

Edge computing *is a distributed computing paradigm that brings together computation and data storage closer to the location where it is needed, to improve response times and save bandwidth.*

Workloads *is a term used within this book, which is a combination of applications, connectivity, and data either in full or in parts.*

There are specialized enterprises that have come up with their own models known as Cloud Interconnect Fabric where cloud can overcome the latency issues. With Cloud Interconnect Fabric, servers are maintained and managed regionally that will ensure that enterprises do not need to move the work-load back and forth on the Internet, thereby committing the latency which the application and the business teams within an enterprise is looking from cloud. In addition, Cloud Interconnect Fabric goes further and also allows enterprises to connect applications and data spread across multiple cloud providers (e.g., AWS, Azure, or Google cloud) and across private and public clouds. This is especially important for larger enterprises that choose to setup their own private cloud in a colocation environment for mission critical or sensitive applications and data, and move the rest to a public cloud. The need to collaborate and communicate between private cloud and public cloud is enabled by Cloud Interconnect Fabric.

A number of private and public cloud providers are highly engaged in making edge computing a success.

Data Analytics

Data analytics is the science of analyzing raw data in order to make conclusions about that information. Data analytics techniques can reveal trends and metrics that would otherwise be lost in the mass of information. This information can then be used to optimize processes to increase the overall efficiency of a business or system.

The amount of digital data that exists is growing at a rapid rate, doubling every 2 years. An article by Forbes[1] states that data is growing faster than ever before. By the year 2020, about 1.7 megabytes of new information will be created every second for every human being on the planet, which makes it extremely important for enterprises to rely on data for their business.

There is a big gap in the industry between the aspirations which organizations have versus the reality on the ground with respect to data analytics. Organizations believe that analytics has the ability to dramatically increase profit. Almost all enterprises I have spoken to agree that data is absolutely crucial to their decision-making and there is massive growth to be found in data solutions. However, in reality, what truly happens is that, unfortunately, enterprises are massively involved in preparation of data rather than spending time in understanding and creating insights from the data. This has potentially led to a loss of motivation for organizations as data preparation is a very time-consuming process and because of this many enterprises are not be able to get insights at the right time which potentially defeats the whole purpose of their data analytics program. In addition, scope and clear objectives and success criteria of data program have not been identified up front and because the cultural and people implications of that implementation have not been considered up front it means that unfortunately 70% of change initiatives have actually failed.

According to a new report from IBM Marketing Cloud, "10 Key Marketing Trends For 2017,"[2] 90% of the data in the world today has been created in the last 2 years alone, at 2.5 quintillion bytes of data a day. The report also states that with new devices, sensors, and technologies emerging, the data growth rate will likely accelerate even more. This brings one very important expectation in a data program which is to ensure that foundations are set right before embarking on a data journey. Enterprises should try to create the right data platform that is fully automated which can ensure that they spend less time in data preparation and more time on defining use cases and executing them to provide value to their business. As an example of a large insurance client, voice analytics was used to determine how call agents are dealing with customer complaints. For this client, using analytics client sentiments were monitored in real time. By understanding not just the words that are being said, but also the intonation and whether speakers are talking over one another, potential causes of tension were identified and a decision was made if the call has to be escalated to the next level in the organization, i.e., to a specialist team.

Summary

In summary, if you have understood the concepts discussed in this chapter so far, there is a tremendous impact digital is having on the IT industry. This starts by enabling enterprises to develop digital lead applications apart from providing flexibility to moving legacy systems to modern platforms to harness the power and benefits from digital platforms. This means that enterprises that do not wish to change the core legacy systems still can benefit by utilizing digital platforms such as Cloud. All these stack up quite well in the digital transformation roadmap for enterprises and it is essential that enterprises make best judgments in harnessing the power of technology with the right enterprise led strategy.

As we see digital maturing over a period of time, more and more enterprises are now looking at adopting digital. Whilst enterprises are focused on transition and transforming to digital they are also worried about how these new technologies will be managed and the benefits they will achieve in the long run. This is where operation management and automation comes into play, where development and operations tools, orchestration, and monitoring tools enable complete agility in the environment.

There are several benefits that organizations can reap out of digital, but key to this is ensuring that the right digital transformation strategy is followed with the right set of tools and technologies.

Notes

1. https://www.forbes.com/sites/bernardmarr/2015/09/30/big-data-20-mind-boggling-facts-everyone-must-read/?sh=40aca62a17b1
2. ftp://ftp.www.ibm.com/software/in/pdf/10_Key_Marketing_Trends_for_2017.pdf

Chapter 2

Business-Driven Digital Transformation Framework: Formula 4.0

Cost optimization had been a driving factor in the IT industry for a decade, and most enterprises are looking at ways to reduce their costs to the best of their abilities; without compromising the quality of services they provide. Today, with digital in the forefront, enterprises are not only achieving cost targets on optimizations but are also able to achieve speed of delivery and exceed customer experiences.

Though cost optimization is one of the driver enterprises consider for digital transformation, it is important to understand that digital transformation journey should not be embarked just for optimizing costs in an enterprise. Digital transformation journeys are embarked by a need for enterprises to do business differently and adapt to any changing business needs in the most agile way. Business transformation means changing the way enterprises interact with their customers or businesses.

As digital technologies dramatically reshape industries, many enterprises are pursuing large-scale-change efforts to capture the benefits of these trends, or simply to survive in the market. It is critical to embrace the dynamic landscape, as new economic opportunities are continually opening for organizations that need to quickly build and scale robust environments. Transforming the entire operations of an enterprise is extremely complex and can present a significant risk if not executed correctly. Without the right guidance and experience, it is all too easy to focus purely on technology adoption to drive the successful implementation of digital transformation strategy, overlooking the impact the changes will have on the rest of the organization. The result is high implementation costs, missed project deadlines, and an inability to see a return on investment. Formula 4.0 provides enterprises with the knowledge and direction necessary to deliver business strategy and lead the transformation. It has step-by-step and practical solutions to overcome complex problems encompassing people, processes, and technology, based on the Business Process Transformation required in an enterprise.

Formula 4.0 enables enterprises to use modern (digital) technologies to create new or modify existing Business Processes, culture, and customer experiences to meet changing business and market requirements. This reimagining of business in the digital age is digital transformation.

Let us now get into the details around what it means by a business strategy or business lead digital transformation.

Formula 4.0 (Business-Driven Framework for Digital Transformation Using Digital Enablers from Industry 4.0)

There are numerous IT services companies that claim to transform organizations to digital for work they are contracted to. Piecemeal digital transformations are quite dangerous, as they typically end up adding new complexities, thereby making the IT landscape much more cumbersome. On the other hand, many enterprises treat digital transformation as a pure technology stuff, whereas the real definition of digital transformation is thinking how an organization should use modern technologies, people, and processes to fundamentally change business performance.

A digital transformation journey is a top-down rather than a bottom-up approach and is successful only if it is done at an enterprise level. This does not mean that organizations need to embark on a digital transformation journey and make big changes to their already existing IT systems, tools, and processes. What this means is that digital transformation should be embarked by utilizing a well-defined enterprise-level digital transformation methodology. Without an enterprise-level methodology, enterprises cannot succeed in their efforts toward digital transformation.

Formula 4.0 is an enterprise-wide digital transformation framework that empowers all types of organizations to embark on digital transformation journeys, thereby allowing enterprises to achieve the full benefits of digital at scale by first understanding the business drivers behind the transformation and then enabling transformation. Formula 4.0 provides guidance at all levels of the enterprise that are actively engaged in using IT for their business growth. The results of Formula 4.0 implementation are achieving greater alignment and visibility across the organization, connecting the business strategy to execution, and enabling better business results faster and with a higher degree of predictability and quality; with a lower operational cost.

The end results by implementing Formula 4.0 framework are as follows:

- Improved customer experience and business satisfaction
- Faster time to market
- Ability to make business decisions from data
- Reduced OpEx and CapEx costs (with automation)
- Enablement to adopt any new technology anytime
- Increase ease and speed of doing business (i.e., with business automation)
- A high-caliber team that can adapt to changing needs of the enterprise

In the simplest sense, Formula 4.0 is a set of well-defined patterns, with an enterprise framework to scale organization from an "as it is" state to a digital enterprise, and such enterprises reap full benefits from digital technologies. Currently, digital transformation is a term used very loosely within the IT industry, which has led many organizations either to fail in their digital transformation journey or achieve very minimal benefits from their digital transformations. Formula 4.0 mitigates all such challenges.

Figure 2.1 depicts the Formula 4.0 framework, which is centered around Business Transformation Model. The model is the heart of Formula 4.0 framework, which determines the business drivers that will enable digital transformation in an enterprise. There are four horizontal capability areas and one vertical capability area all, which are governed by an enterprise, lead governance and centered around business transformation model.

Business Transformation Model

The first step for any enterprises embarking on digital transformation journey is to define a business strategy. Based on the business strategy existing and future business process that will differentiate an enterprise in their market space needs to be identified and a digital transformation roadmap needs to be defined. Business Transformation Model defines the four quadrants where differentiating and non-differentiating business process are

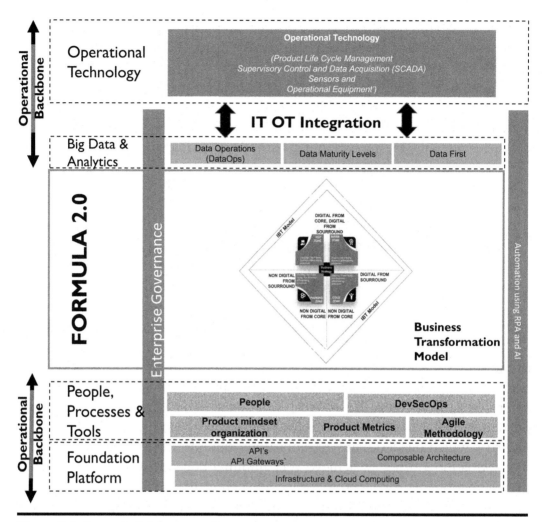

Figure 2.1 Formula 4.0 framework

placed based on which a digital transformation roadmap is defined for an enterprise.

A non-differentiating business process is a process which does not generate revenues for the enterprise. An example of a non-differentiating business process could be an HR system or a payroll system. However, this does not mean that the business process is not important for the enterprise.

A differentiating business process is a process (or part of the business process) which generates revenues for the enterprise. An example of a differentiating business process is an online banking application.

As depicted in Figure 2.2, the first quadrant in the Business Transformation Model is the Hot Zone, where existing client facing business processes that differentiate the enterprise in the market are placed.

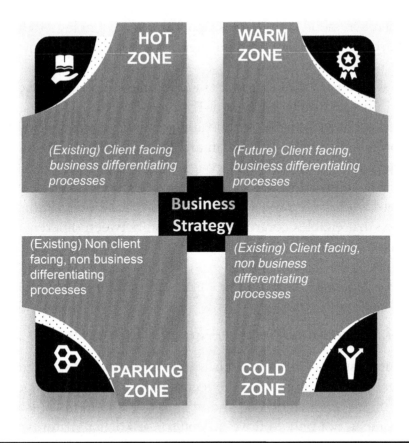

Figure 2.2 Business transformation model

The second quadrant is the Warm Zone, where future business processes and new business models are placed.

The third quadrant is the Cold Zone. In this zone, existing client facing business processes, which are non-business differentiating, are placed.

Finally, in the fourth quadrant called as the Parking Zone, non client facing and non-business differentiating processes Business Processes are placed.

Once all business processes are placed in one of the four zones, business problems and opportunities are assessed using a combination of systems thinking and design thinking and a digital transformation roadmap is defined at an enterprise level.

Formula 4.0 Horizontal Service—Foundation Platform

The second dimension of Formula 4.0 is setting up a technology baseline for embarking on a digital transformation journey. Setting up the right foundation is essential for enterprises to be successful in their digital transformation journey.

Formula 4.0 recommends three areas that form the technology foundation for any enterprise embarking on their digital transformation journey:

1. The first area is embarking on a cloud journey—this means adopting Cloud infrastructure to implement Formula 4.0.
2. The second is adopting to Atomic architectures—an Atomic architecture per Formula 4.0 terminology is an architectural style in which applications are separated into loosely coupled services.
3. The third is utilizing APIs for communications between systems within and outside the enterprise—an API is an application programming interface that enables controlled interaction between different software programs an enterprise is using.

Each of these capability areas will be discussed in more depth in Section III.

Formula 4.0 Horizontal Service—People, Processes, and Tools

The third dimension of Formula 4.0 is the people, processes, and tools.

People are just as important as the technology and tools. A huge part of this is the culture of an enterprise and what it offers in terms of learning and development, not only to drive an enterprise's digital maturity but also to demonstrate its investment in the future of its employees.

As the pressure to improve learning and development opportunities continues to intensify, those responsible with skills progression need to develop new ways to empower employees and offer opportunities for growth within the business.

When it comes to digital, the stage of mindset in the transformation process is about leadership, strategy, and culture, with the end goal of the business adopting a culture with digital threaded into its DNA.

Whilst the lack of buy-in from senior executives was once cited as the reason for the slow progression of digital transformation, it now has completely changed. New research by McKinsey[1] found that 84% of CEOs are involved in and committed to transformational change. This means a lot of executives at the top have already accepted that technology changes are the future of their business and have started adopting them. Challenges do still however lie at the bottom part of the pyramid, which is the execution layer, where the skill and cultural gap is much higher. This is the layer of developers, analysts, testers, and architects. It is a hard fact to digest but not all existing people within an enterprise will be required. After it is digitally transformed using Formula 4.0, enterprises will need to let go of staff who are unable to adapt to the new ways of working and technologies of a digital enterprise. The Formula 4.0 framework provides a strong methodology known as the Hackfest model, which allows enterprises to assess individuals within the enterprise and make appropriate decisions on retaining versus firing. In addition, enterprises will need to invest in hiring new talent from the market using the Hackfest model. Hackfest is a Formula 4.0 model which provides an approach on how Product Engineering Team needs to be identified and is discussed in detail in Chapter 9.

Product-Based Organization

Process forms a very essential element in digital transformation programs. Without a defined process, a digital transformation journey tends to not reap the benefits the enterprise would desire.

A recent survey of directors, CEOs, and senior executives[2] found that digital transformation risk is their number-one concern in 2019. It is worth noting that 70% of all digital transformation initiatives do not reach their goals,[3] and of the $1.3 trillion that was spent on digital transformation last year, it was estimated that $900 billion went to waste. Why do some digital transformation efforts succeed where others fail? Fundamentally, it is because most digital technologies provide possibilities for efficiency gains and customer intimacy, but if people lack the right mindset to change and the current organizational processes are flawed, digital transformation will simply magnify those flaws.

There is no single technology that will deliver "speed" or "innovation" as such. The best combination of processes, tools, and technologies for a given organization will achieve this vision.

Formula 4.0 recommends moving from a project-based structure to a product-based organization. In a product-based structure (also known as a divisional structure), employees are assigned into self-contained divisions according to the particular line of products or services they produce, the customers they deal with, and the geographical area they serve.

In a survey conducted by Gartner,[4] more than half of organizations (55%) surveyed said that they are moving from project to product delivery to continuously integrate and deliver new features and capabilities to the business.

Product-Based Organization Is the Lever to Achieve Speed

Successful digital transformations occur through continuous innovation. This means that enterprises need to change business models and capabilities per the market demands. This empowers organizations to launch, learn, and relaunch initiatives, swiftly reacting to changing market conditions and customer needs. Product-based organization enables the organization to be dynamic within the continuously changing environment.

Product-Based Organization Embraces Two Core Principles—Agile Methodology and DevSecOps

Agile methodology—Agile software development refers to software-development methodologies centered around the idea of iterative development, where requirements and solutions evolve through collaboration between self-organizing cross-functional teams. Many organizations adopted agile development practices a decade back to deliver goods and services to customers more efficiently and with greater reliability. Using this software-development approach across all business units and product groups, enterprises designed and built features quickly, tested them, and refined and refreshed them in rapid iterations.

Agile has been worked exceptionally well so far. Enterprises are producing software faster and creating more cross-functional and collaborative teams than ever before. It is worth noting however that a lot of enterprises are now experiencing diminishing returns on their investment to go Agile; this is because enterprises have already achieved the benefits of Agile and have come to a point where returns are now linear.

Product-driven organization to build a system of delivery is the receipt of success in getting more mileage out of the investments in Agile. This is one of the key reasons why Formula 4.0 instills in a product-based organization following Agile practices to the fullest.

Development and operations (DevOps) for accelerating product development—DevOps is a set of practices that combines software development and IT operations. It aims to shorten the systems development life cycle and provides continuous delivery with high software quality. When implementing a product-based organization, DevOps accelerates the complete product development process. A DevOps culture is fundamental to adopting a product IT operating model. DevOps ensures high-quality products are delivered within short deployment lead times, along with the ability to fix production issues with low mean time to recover (MTTR) and ensure a minimal to zero failure rate.

DEFINITION

*Mean time to recovery, or **MTTR**, is the average time that a device will take to recover from any failure. Self-service access to infrastructure is a principle in which teams can automatically procure new infrastructure such as servers, software systems, and tools when required.*

DevOps also enables new-age practices such as automated testing and self-service access to infrastructure.

DevSecOps is the term used when security is integrated into DevOps. It ensures security aspects are built into the process across the DevOps delivery pipeline, so the product development is not only fault tolerant but also foolproof. An experienced DevOps team builds and integrates security into their day-to-day DevOps processes to safeguard the organization. Embedding security into DevOps makes the proposition much more powerful.

DevSecOps accelerates the complete product development process and is a requirement for any enterprise embarking on the Formula 4.0 framework for digital transformation.

Formula 4.0 Horizontal Service—Data and Analytics

Data and analytics form one of the very important drivers for organizations to excel in their digital transformation journey.

Data analytics (DA) is the process of examining data sets in order to draw conclusions about the information they contain, increasingly with the aid of specialized systems and software. DA technologies and techniques are widely used in industries to enable organizations to make more informed business decisions.

There is a greater expectation that the DA methods not only provide insights into the past but also provide predictions and testable explanations. Leading organizations in every industry are wielding data and analytics as competitive weapons.

A leading financial services institution uses predictive data indicators that analyze historical transactions and variables to forecast potential churn and customer loyalty. The company believes that it can identify 54% of accounts that will close within the next 6–8 months. Knowing which accounts are likely to close allows management to make better business and marketing decisions to retain customers. Improvements in such predictions were achieved with a data and analytics platform. As machine-learning models absorb more data, they can relearn the scenarios multiple times and better anticipate what is the likeliest outcome.

Another case study is about closing deals, which is the key objective of any salesperson. Shorter sales cycles essentially enable salespeople to increase their sales volumes, although this is not always the case. Some deals may take a longer time to close than others but may be worth several times more in terms of profit. Using DA, a company was able to focus on deals that had faster closure rates. This was achieved by analyzing past data to estimate the likelihood of conversions as well as their potential values.

Formula 4.0 emphasizes on a data first philosophy for digital transformation. Data first means that for any enterprise, data is the first thing to look at to make any business decisions. Enterprises should adopt DA in their digital transformation journey, thereby enabling them to compete in their market space and be ahead of the competition.

Formula 4.0 Vertical Service (Automation and Enterprise Governance)

Finally, in this section we will be talking about vertical services that support all the above horizontal services we spoke about so far which provide a seamless digital integration from both IT and business perspectives.

Automation

> Automation plays a very important role for enterprises embarking on their digital transformation journey and is one of the most important elements of Formula 4.0. Automation is about changing the tasks that humans carry out so that they can focus on purposeful work, thus optimizing productivity.

Automation is one of the key capabilities that supports digital transformation. From a business standpoint, eliminating the need for manual (i.e., human) intervention in complex or repetitive Business Processes can have a positive impact on operations. By automating certain decisions, organizations can not only accelerate process workflows but also improve the accuracy and consistency of the results. From an IT standpoint, automating key processes in DevOps not only increases speed but also improves quality and efficiency.

Robotic process automation (RPA) is a form of Business Process automation based on software robots and is used to automate repetitive processes. In other words, RPA is a rule-based software that has no intelligence and automates repetitive tasks. RPA combined with Artificial intelligence (AI) brings life into automation.

AI is the simulation of human intelligence processes by computer systems, or "machines." These processes include **learning** (acquiring information and contextual rules for using the information), **reasoning** (using context and rules to reach conclusions), and **self-correction** (learning from successes and failures).

Formula 4.0 instills automation with RPA and AI both in Business Processes and IT processes to improve the enterprise operating model.

Enterprise Governance

> To succeed in their digital transformation journey, organizations need firm governance around the digital initiatives at an enterprise level.

During 2017, while I was working for a large IT Services firm, a couple of regional CIOs whom I interacted with and were in charge of digital transformation for their respective business units explained: "We do not have the budget to develop our own capabilities so the questions are: How are we to get the most out of the central platform? How can we leverage these capabilities as much as possible?"

Another set of regional CIOs said that they have initiated their digital transformation journeys for their respective business units. At the end, they were able to achieve benefits from the initiative at business unit level, but since these initiatives were not aligned to the organization level goals of digital transformation, after 2 years they were required to shed away all these initiatives leading to several million dollars of wastage.

There are several case studies which have clearly demonstrated that digital transformation conducted in business unit silos has a negative effect on the enterprise performance. The reason is quite obvious that siloed digital transformation introduces multiple inefficiencies, duplications, and complexities into the enterprise IT and business architecture, which at times becomes impossible to rectify. Due to this, some organizations have reached a state where they have to rewrite and rearchitect their complete IT landscape to digitally transform themselves. This is of course very complex and many of said organizations are just continuing with their current IT estate without any modernization. Such enterprises which are highly dependent on IT for their business are at the verge of bankruptcy and the only way for these enterprises at this juncture to survive is to completely rethink their IT strategy.

Digital transformation should never be considered a purely technological initiative. They should be business-driven programs designed to deliver a certain business outcome. This is one of the reasons why there is high level of collaboration required between all business functions within the enterprise, this allows the organization to drive the digital transformation forward, with a strong enterprise governance being required for enterprises to succeed in their digital transformation journey. Enterprise Governance of Formula 4.0 is defined just to achieve the core goal of governing digital transformation at enterprise level.

The key ask of Formula 4.0 methodology is to design an enterprise-level digital transformation strategy that can enable rapid adoption of any technology. The framework also provides a clear guideline on how and when to utilize these technologies to achieve maximum benefits in the new digital world.

Notes

1. https://www.mckinsey.com/business-functions/organization/our-insights/the-people-power-of-transformations?cid=other-eml-alt-mip-mck-oth-1702
2. https://blogs.wsj.com/riskandcompliance/2018/12/05/businesses-predict-digital-transformation-to-be-biggest-risk-factors-in-2019/
3. https://www.forbes.com/sites/forbestechcouncil/2018/03/13/why-digital-transformations-fail-closing-the-900-billion-hole-in-enterprise-strategy/#3be684c77b8b
4. https://www.gartner.com/en/newsroom/press-releases/2019-02-19-gartner-survey-finds-85-percent-of-organizations-favor-a-product

IDENTIFYING BUSINESS PROCESSES FOR DIGITAL TRANSFORMATION USING SYSTEMS THINKING AND DESIGN THINKING

II

In this section, we will discuss the Business Transformation Model, also known as the BT Model. This model will help enterprises identify the right business strategy that will allow them to differentiate in their marketspace. Once a strategy is identified, the BT Model supports enterprises in choosing the business processes that need transformation based on the business strategy.

We will further discuss the importance of "systems thinking" and "design thinking" models and how to apply them to solve problems or identify opportunities for improvements within a business process. Problems and opportunities identified in the business processes using these two models will define the digital transformation roadmap for the business processes.

Chapter 3

Business Strategy for Digital Transformation

Digital transformation is a very broad topic, and it covers a number of different types of initiatives. But what it boils down is that digital transformation is changing how a business interacts with customers and employees using technology. It also means utilizing technology to improve customer experience and internal processes, by making them more efficient.

Digital transformation is characterized by transforming business processes or replacing traditional processes with new ones that can help an enterprise compete in the marketspace and promote innovation, optimization, and growth. On the other hand, digital transformation is also transforming the go to market strategies to enhance customer engagements which is entirely different from transforming or replacing traditional business processes.

As we all know that there is an evolution of technologies in the market such as mobile, Analytics, Cloud, Internet of Things, and so on. Interestingly it is not a big deal to implement these technologies if it is implemented one at a time. With my two decades experience in the IT industry, I would say that these technologies are all nice and create some new opportunities, but the key reason for any enterprise to embark on a digital transformation journey is because they want to be seen as a great company. And to be a great company they need to get the basics right and then use these new technologies to make themselves more special. So along the way of these technology evolution, everyone needs to understand that it is not about individual technologies that make an enterprise great or different, but it is more about the confluence of these technologies that creates opportunities for business to change the way they had been doing business earlier and be more competent. With the technologies we have in market today, the technical limitations we had in the past are eliminated, and therefore enterprises can run their business much more efficiently.

The way I have seen many companies going about the technologies is that they recognize a new technology, and they think they can have a new strategy. So companies have introduced a mobile strategy, a big data strategy, a social media strategy, Internet of Things strategy, a cloud strategy, a cognitive computing strategy, and this is how many companies have operated so far in silos of each technology which is a very bad idea. It is a bad idea not because these enterprises want to onboard new technologies but because there is no business strategy underpinning these technologies—as an example, a mobile strategy will not make a business successful.

A business strategy is required to make an enterprise successful and this strategy should integrate all capabilities together using whatever technology makes the most sense to the enterprise and their business.

Digital transformation is all about changes to the ways in which enterprises have been doing business traditionally. This has resulted from the use of digital technologies by either new market entrants or established competitors—and those can be competitors that were never actually your competitors before. This could mean a grocery store entering into a clothing business or the same grocery store entering into a radically different business line such as cloud computing, e.g., Amazon. Such competitors undermine the viability of your product service portfolio or your go-to-market approach. In other words, they find ways to make your customers happier than you do, by either offering them new kinds of relationships or a new product service for portfolio or a better customer experience than you do. This is called business disruption.

What this means is that for enterprise to be remain relevant in the market, they need to have an integrated business strategy inspired by powerful technologies to enable them to be responsive to constant market changes. To achieve this, every enterprise needs to adapt a start-up mindset based on which they can start to think about a strategy that is differently from what they have currently, which can make their enterprise constantly respond to the changing market conditions.

This means that the traditional approach to define a strategy—where enterprise sets targets on earnings per share or decides which new markets

Figure 3.1   Business transformation model

to enter or what companies to acquire is not meaningful anymore. The business strategy in the new digital transformation world is to define how enterprises need to make themselves special in the market and how they can deliver value to their customers. This is the basic concept of BT Model which we will be discussing in subsequent sections.

Digital transformation, using Formula 4.0 methodology, revolves around the business strategy for an enterprise. Based on the business strategy transformation, roadmap is defined by identifying business processes that can differentiate the enterprise in the market (from their competitors) or which can improve the customer engagement for the enterprise.

In the current market conditions, there are only two types of business strategies for enterprises to adopt and remain relevant in their marketspace—one is Customer Engagement Strategy and other is Business Transformation Strategy. This is illustrated in Figure 3.1.

Customer Engagement Strategy

The customer engagement strategy, also known as Go-To-Market Strategy, emphasizes completely on enhancing relationship with customers. It emphasizes on customer relationship to be built on trust and loyalty—ideally built on passion. This means enterprises need to transform their go-to-market strategy and keep customer relationship and customer happiness as their core fundamental driver to do business and compete in their marketspace.

Let me explain this with a case study. The United Services Automobile Association (USAA) is a San Antonio-based Fortune 500 diversified financial services group of companies including a Texas Department of Insurance-regulated reciprocal inter-insurance exchange and subsidiaries offering banking, investing, and insurance to people and families who serve, or served, in the United States Armed Forces.

USAA's Net Promoter Score is more than four times higher than the average industry, and its customer satisfaction scores are leagues ahead of the competition. Customers are loyal and more likely to stick with the company and get additional financial products than customers at other companies. USAA's dedication to customer experience and serving each person individually keeps customers coming back and singing its praises.[1]

If you are a USAA customer, you are probably aware that on their website people write things like I love my bank, I am never leaving my bank, this is the world's best bank, and so on. This is what customer engagement is all about.

How did USAA achieve and promoted this level of relationship?

A number of years ago, USAA which was primarily a financial services company decided that they are going to enter into new line of business. They redefine their whole business model by saying that they are now going to start serving life events of their customers. Serving life event of a customer means supporting them in buying a car, buying a home, financing while getting married or getting retired. These are the events that have financial implications to every individual. USAA wanted to make sure that their members are served in the most efficient, trustworthy, and financial secured manner during these life events.

As they started embarking on this new business model, they started thinking about a different approach for their customer engagement and started organizing around life events in an entirely new way. As an example, if you want to buy a new car and are a member of USAA, you can go to USAA auto capability store and they will help you pick the car you need, they will get you the best possible price using their buying service department, they will help with finance, and they will get the cheapest and best insurance. The end-to-end business process is entirely automated and the customer just needs to print the documentation and go to pick up the car. That is the way USAA do business with their members and all along they are scanning the marketplace for new technology that might help them to serve their customers better. As another example, the goal for USAA car insurance service is to make sure that their customers are the first ones in their neighborhood to receive a check if a natural disaster occurs, so that they can call a contractor and fix their home immediately. They identify technologies that will make their customer life easier. These days they are exploring on how drones will help serve their customer better and faster. This is extraordinary customer engagement and it is a strategy that guides USAA every action.

This is what customer engagement strategy is all about. If customer engagement is not the enterprise business strategy, the next one to look at Business Transformation Strategy.

Business Transformation Strategy

Business Transformation Strategy means that enterprise should move away from just thinking about the products and services they are selling. They need to think about customer needs and problems and how these can be solved by redefining their business, and if required enter into new territories or business domains. Business Transformation Strategy is broadly split into Process Transformation, Model Transformation, and Domain Transformation as depicted in Figure 3.2.

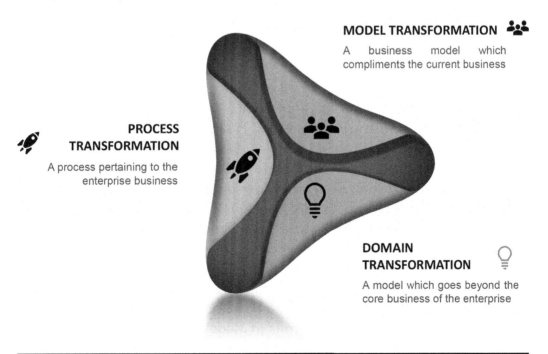

MODEL TRANSFORMATION
A business model which compliments the current business

PROCESS TRANSFORMATION
A process pertaining to the enterprise business

DOMAIN TRANSFORMATION
A model which goes beyond the core business of the enterprise

Figure 3.2   Business transformation strategy

Process Transformation

Process Transformation involves an examination of the steps required to achieve a specific goal in an effort to remove duplicate or unnecessary steps and automate as many actions as possible. The end goal is to improve customer satisfaction, be cheaper, and efficient.

We have already seen Process Transformation on the shop floor where companies such as Airbus have engaged heads-up display glasses to improve the quality of inspection by staff of airplanes. We have also seen Process Transformations in the customer experience, where Domino's Pizza, for example, completely reimagined the notion of food ordering, with the introduction of "AnyWare" which allowed customers to order their meals from any device. This innovation increased customer convenience so much that it helped push the company to overtake Pizza Hut in sales. We also see companies implementing technologies such as robotic process automation to streamline back office processes including accounting and legal, for example. Process Transformation can create significant value, and digital transformation in these areas is becoming increasingly popular. These Process Transformations tend to be focused efforts around specific areas of the business at an enterprise level, and therefore are often successfully led by a combination of CIOs, CBOs, or CDOs.[2,3]

Model Transformation

While Process Transformation focuses on finite areas of the business, Model Transformations are aimed at the fundamental building blocks of how value is delivered in the industry. Examples of this kind of innovation are well-known, from Netflix's reinvention of video distribution, to Apple's reinvention of music delivery (iTunes), and Uber's reinvention of the taxi industry. This kind of transformation should however be occurring in every industry, and digital can support such a transformation. Insurance companies such as Allstate are using data and analytics to unbundle insurance contracts and charge customers by the mile which is a big change to the auto insurance business model. Although not yet a reality, there are also numerous efforts underway to transform the business of mining to a wholly robotic exercise, where no humans would be required to travel below the surface.

Another of the most aggressive firms in Model Transformation is General Electricals (GE). GE moved away from financial services to their core competency around big assets such as building turbines, aircraft engines, and medical equipment. They are not limiting themselves selling these assets because it carries a high risk of economy volatility, as when the economy goes down people stop buying these products. Instead GE started thinking about the owners of these assets and what do they need after they buy an asset. They understood that owners need effective management and maintenance of these assets, and based on this understanding GE started looking at ways to service these assets to help their customer manage them better. So they started collecting data through the sensor that are attached to these assets, they started analyzing the data to find out how their customers are using these assets and based on the usage they are constantly providing inputs to their customers on how to manage their assets more efficiently. GE also started providing new services around asset performance management and maintenance, and as a step further they have started thinking about the whole ecosystem of partners who will support their customers and make their customers happier. In summary, GE started their journey toward a new business process, i.e., from a financial services company back to a manufacturing company, and subsequently extended their model to asset servicing and maintenance.

The complex and strategic nature of these opportunities requires involvement and leadership by strategy and/or business units. By changing the fundamental building blocks of value, corporations that achieve model transformation open significant new opportunities for growth.

Domain Transformation

An area where we see little focus in the industry today, which offers enormous opportunity, is the area of Domain Transformation.

Domain Transformation means entering into markets where enterprises were never present before, i.e., new or adjacent markets.

New technologies are redefining products and services, blurring industry boundaries, and creating entirely new sets of non-traditional competitors. Many enterprises do not appreciate the real opportunity for these new technologies to unlock wholly new businesses for their companies beyond currently served markets. Often, it is this type of transformation that offers the greatest opportunities to create new value. A clear example, how Domain Transformation works, is the online retailer Amazon. Amazon expanded into a new market domain with the launch of Amazon Web Services (AWS), now the largest cloud computing/infrastructure service, in a domain formerly owned by IT giants such as Microsoft and IBM. What made Amazon's entry into this domain possible was a combination of the strong digital capabilities it had built in storage, computing databases to support its core retail business coupled with an installed base of thousands of relationships with young, growing companies that increasingly needed computing services to expand. AWS is not a mere adjacency or business extension for Amazon, but a wholly different business in a fundamentally different marketspace.

Choosing between Customer Engagement and Business Transformation Strategy

Each enterprise needs to choose between one of the two business strategies discussed earlier based on which digital transformation journey needs to be defined. Once enterprises choose a business strategy, existing and new business processes need to be identified for transformation, after which technology is applied to make that strategy work. Technology is the operational backbone to deliver business results using Formula 4.0 methodology. Operational backbone will ensure that end-to-end business processes are run efficiently, reliably, securely, and are predictable. This means that enterprises have great systems as well as standardized processes that can achieve the desired business outcomes. And based on this, enterprises can enter new markets or create new products and services and enhance customer experience.

Operational backbone ensures that basic things do not go wrong, and new services are added addressing new problems and opportunities of customers. To elaborate a bit further on this, we will discuss about a company I have worked in the past.

The company we will talk about here is Nordstrom, Inc., which has chosen customer engagement as their business strategy.

Nordstrom, Inc. is an American luxury department store chain which was founded in 1901 by John W. Nordstrom and Carl F. Wallin. It has originated as a shoe store and evolved into a full-line retailer with departments for clothing, footwear, handbags, jewellery, accessories, cosmetics, and fragrances.

While I was living in the United States, this was my favorite store and the reason is because this company for years has been known for outstanding customer service. Nordstrom is centered around best customer service since the start and no other company is able to compete with them on customer service. Let me give you an example.

About 3 years ago Julia went to Nordstrom with her daughters. There was a sales representative by name Steve who started helping her while she was checking out. Julia said that she was glad that she brought her two daughters to the store as she was not aware of their dress sizes, shoe sizes, and so on. However, Steve told Julia that even if her daughters are not available, she can still visit the store and he will help her. After few months Julia went back to Nordstrom and by this time to buy some clothes for her elder daughter, who this time was not around with her. Julia remembered her last interaction with Steve and called him. She told him that she is looking for some trousers for elder daughter and after 30 minutes Steve came back with few clothes. Steve brought dark blue trousers. Dark blue is her daughter's favorite color and the size was exactly what her daughter wears which was a surprise to Julia. Steve was able to do that because of the capabilities that Nordstrom has created in him. Nordstrom created a complete transparent supply chain capability where Steve has access to all the events, and purchases that Julia and her daughters have performed in the last few months, based on which he was able to retrieve dress size and shoe size of Julia's elder daughter. Based on the insights that were made available by Nordstrom, he was also able to find out Julia's elder daughter's favorite color. This is the kind of customer experience we are talking about that is enabled via technology at Nordstrom.

To the other extend, if a particular item is not available at Nordstrom, the company and their sales representatives go to an extent to buy items from other stores and ship it to their customers. I personally ordered 20 items online from Nordstrom store once and they arrived in six different packages from six different stores—I know this because they were still on the hanger and they have a price tag on them. When I want to return few of the items I purchased online, I went back to one of the Nordstrom store and was looking for return desk. There was no return desk at that store. A sales representative comes over to me and asks me to shop for other items in the store while he completes the return. As I complete my shopping, he finds me at the payment counter and hands over the return slip to me. So, this is the whole philosophy at Nordstrom around customer engagement and this was completely enabled by the technology they use.

Nordstrom introduced their iPhone app in 2013 and they had Mobile Checkout at their app stores by 2014 and further they created the customer experience around Pinterest. By 2015, they recognized the opportunities to sell through Instagram and if you look at that list you will realize that Nordstrom had been simply adding more and more capabilities around mobility and around social media to improve customer experience. They analyze a lot of customer data using big data and analytics to make personalized customer experience. They extend their supply chain not just to their own stores but to partners as well. This is possible because of the capabilities they have built which are the power of business strategy driven by technology.

Notes

1. https://www.forbes.com/sites/blakemorgan/2020/06/01/5-customer-experience-lessons-from-usaa/#4fe9ca5b7e54
2. Venkatesh Upadrista. (29 Jun. 2017). The Art of Consultative Selling in IT: Taking Blue Ocean Strategy a Step Ahead Hardcover.
3. Venkatesh Upadrista. (1 Sept. 2008). Managing Offshore Development Projects: An Agile Approach Paperback.

Chapter 4

Business Transformation Model and Intelligent Business Transformation Model

In the current world, which is increasingly complex and interconnected, changes in the future will occur faster than ever before. There is a clear need to realize how the decisions that we are taking now will affect us in the future. Identifying future challenges and understanding how businesses will need to adopt to these should be a participatory process.[1] Extrapolating from current trends, enterprises must explore different scenarios that will be able to cope with some of the known restraints of our future, which will essentially be an interconnected world with people doing the most valuable jobs and machines doing the manual tasks as well as helping humans to make the right decisions.[2]

While historically our ability to prepare for the future has been dependent on our ability to predict how the future might look, this is further complicated today by an additional question: what is the future and is it worth preparing for? As a result, in business management we can almost see an evolution in the need to predict, prepare, and now design new business models.

This brings us to the most important need: having a clear vision for the future. This is not as simple as it sounds, and therefore we need to talk about our tendency to reduce. This is a natural process, and therefore necessary for our understanding of the world. We are used to reducing, in other words simplifying things in order to understand them and naturally our tendency to divide is stronger than our capacity to integrate. This is the way our minds usually work. Traditional reductionist applications and management practices have been ingrained within the command and control paradigm which has historically dominated our policies. This is based on the assumption that addressing individual elements or components could lead to an improvement in the system. Such practices have been widely acknowledged to provide limited results in a dynamic and continuously evolving world, emphasizing the need for improved inclusivity and multi-actor participation to provide a greater understanding of the plurality of processes associated with such complex problems.[3,4]

Managing business in the current market requires understanding it first; looking at system interactions and conditions rather than focusing simply on solutions. For example, the perception that technological developments and advances will provide the end solution to every problem is increasingly proving false, as new kinds of constraints are forcing businesses to rethink previous assumptions about technology, planning, and types of development. This is where systems thinking comes into play.[5]

The application of systems thinking is increasingly being considered in view of the limitations above, focusing on acquiring a more complete understanding of business problems through the study of interactions within a business process. Fundamentally, systems thinking embraces the union of interdisciplinary, integrated and holistic principles to create a mindset that addresses whole problems and not just parts.[6]

Systems Thinking

Systems thinking is a holistic approach to analysis that focuses on the way that a system's constituent parts interrelate and how systems work overtime and within the context of larger systems. The systems thinking approach contrasts with traditional analysis, which studies systems by breaking them down into their separate elements.

As depicted in Figure 4.1, a system is any entity that is made up of parts which interact together—these parts and their interconnections create a whole system and this system in turn produces results.

As per systems thinking, system behavior results from the effects of reinforcing and balancing processes. A reinforcing process leads to the increase of some system component. If reinforcement is unchecked by a balancing process, it eventually leads to collapse. A balancing process is one that tends to maintain equilibrium in a particular system.

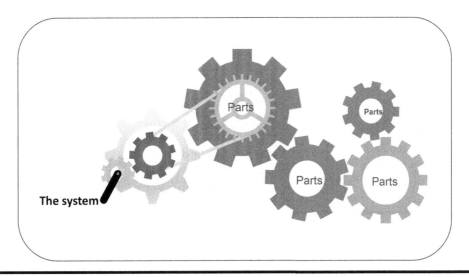

Figure 4.1 A system constituting of multiple parts

Attention to feedback is an essential component of systems thinking. For example, in project management, prevailing wisdom may prescribe the addition of workers to a project that is lagging. However, in practice, that tactic might have actually slowed development in the past. Attention to that relevant feedback can allow management to look for other solutions rather than wasting resources on an approach that has been demonstrated to be counterproductive.

Using the systems perspective is important because it helps us to better understand what helps or hinders the success of interventions.

The Iceberg Model for Systems Thinking

The iceberg model is one of the most popular ways to understand systems thinking. The iceberg model was invented by Peter Michael Senge, and I have taken the liberty to modify parts of the model to make it more easily understandable for readers.[2]

There are five elements of an iceberg model as depicted in Figure 4.2:

- Events—what is happening right now. Those single items that occur within an organization or within a society.
- Patterns—what has been happening over time and what are the trends. These are recurring events that make patterns.
- Structures—what is influencing these patterns and where are the connections between patterns.

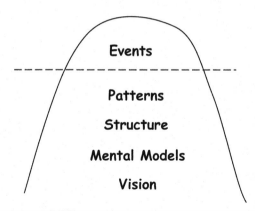

Figure 4.2   Iceberg model

■ Mental models—what values, beliefs, or assumptions shape the system. Mental models are visual representations that one may make an assumption about. As an example, the suggestion that short people cannot play basketball may be a mental model that you have.
■ Vision—what needs to be achieved.

Let me explain the relationship between all these five elements with a simple example. James is the fire chief for Slough Borough Council and has five fire departments underneath him. As fires occur, each one of these fire stations goes and puts out the fires relative to their location. These are the **events.**

After analyzing past data, James understands that 80% of all fires are happening near fire station B—this is a **pattern**. With this insight, James takes out some resources from other stations and deploys them to fire station B. That is a normal response that we see in day-to-day life. However, as per the systems thinking approach, what I would like to demonstrate is the fallacy of this response.

The main objective for James is to reduce the number of fire incidents occurring close to fire station B, which needs to be addressed by the **structures** and not the patterns. This is because all patterns are caused by structures. As we begin to look at the structures, we analyze the area of fire station B and look at elements such as:

■ Which areas do fire station B serve?
■ Within this area, do buildings have adequate fire suppression systems?
■ Does this area have proper trash removal systems?

- Do buildings have enough fire extinguishers?
- Do smokers throw lighted cigarette butts on the streets?

All of these structural elements are causing these patterns to occur, which cause this fire station to be exorbitantly busy compared to others. James' main goal is to ensure that he fixes the problem from a structural angle rather than from the patterns. As an example, he can recommend to the council that better trash removal systems need to be in place, if that is the main structural problem causing these fires.

We may however need to go deeper if we want to change a large system, which is addressing this issue at the **mental** model level. The mental model in context of this case study is to bring a change within individuals of this community and those who serve it. As an example, imagine each individual within this community makes sure that there are enough fire extinguishers in their buildings or smokers use designated areas. As we move through this, ultimately, we begin to change the **vision**, this vision being that as a community that they need to put in additional resources to bring about this change of ultimately reducing the large amount of fires they are having in their area. In the long run this will be far cheaper than James having to respond to 80% of all fires in one particular station.

The above example is a clear representation of the systems thinking iceberg model. In the case study if James only addressed the issue he was facing at the pattern level, he could redistribute his resources to fire station B but he will never be able to change the fact that 80% of the fires are happening at this station. Until he eradicates the problem at its source, which is at the mental model and vision levels, the problem will not be eradicated.

Design Thinking

We discussed about systems thinking so far which is meant to manage change and integration based on "top-down" big picture view, i.e., acting on vision and structures to prevent events to occur.

Design thinking is meant to innovate new solutions based on "bottom-up" human-centered approach.

Systems thinking approach complements with design thinking, instead of replacing it altogether. Systems thinking and design thinking are very closely related and Formula 4.0 mandates using both these together to arrive at the best possible solutions for digital transformation and solving business problems.

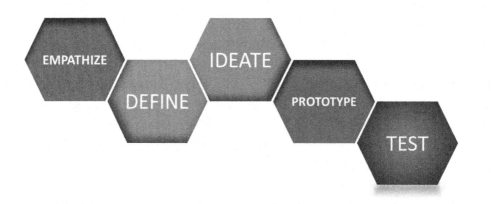

Figure 4.3   Design thinking stages

Once the big picture is arrived using systems thinking, design thinking should be applied to solve a specific problem. Design thinking is a non-linear, iterative process that teams use to understand users, challenge assumptions, redefine problems, and create innovative solutions.[5] Design thinking involves five phases as depicted in Figure 4.3, which are the following: Empathize, Define, Ideate, Prototype, and Test.

Over the past decade there have been case studies of successful applications using design thinking applied in businesses, non-profits, and government agencies.

Enterprises such as IKEA uses design thinking in its product development process and showroom experience. AirBnB, a unicorn startup, started to use design thinking in its early days. The Ministry of Manpower in Singapore uses design thinking to onboard the registration of new foreign employees. These are just some successful applications of design thinking.

What is superior about design thinking is its capability to transform designers' creative problem-solving into a structured innovation approach by providing the methods and tools to empathize with people, create human-centered solutions, and de-risk failure through prototyping.

Stage 1: Empathize—Research Your Users' Needs

In this stage, design thinkers gain an empathetic understanding of the one single problem they are trying to solve, typically through extensive user interacting and research. During this stage, design thinkers interact with the users to understand their challenges, issues, and risks and what the users think they want. Empathy is crucial to a human-centered design process such as design thinking because it allows the thinkers to set aside their own assumptions about the problems and gain real insight into users and their needs.

Stage 2: Define—State Your Users' Needs and Problems

In this stage, design thinkers define the problem and interpret the results. Based on the data gathered during the empathize stage, design thinkers analyze observations and synthesize them to define the core problems users have stated. These definitions are called problem statements. Design thinkers also create personas to help keep efforts human-centered before proceeding to the next stage.

Before we go into what makes a problem statement, it is useful to first gain an understanding of the relationship between analysis and synthesis that many design thinkers will go through in their projects. Analysis and synthesis are equally important, and each plays an essential role in the process of creating options and making choices.

Analysis is about breaking down complex concepts and problems into smaller, easier-to-understand constituents. We do that, for instance, during the first stage of the design thinking process, the empathize stage, when we observe and document details that relate to users. Synthesis, on the other hand, involves creatively piecing the puzzle together to form whole ideas. This happens during the define stage when design thinkers organize, interpret, and make sense of the data they have gathered to create a problem statement.

Although analysis takes place during the empathize stage and synthesis takes place during the define stage, they do not only happen in these distinct stages of design thinking. In fact, analysis and synthesis often happen consecutively throughout all stages of the design thinking process. Design thinkers often analyze a situation before synthesizing new insights and then analyze their synthesized findings once more to create more detailed syntheses.

Stage 3: Ideate—Challenge Assumptions and Create Ideas

Now that the problem is apparent, it is time to brainstorm ways to address those unmet needs. The ideation stage marks the transition from identifying problems to exploring solutions. Here we prioritize breadth over depth as we look for a diverse range of ideas to prototype and test with real people.

The ideation stage flows between idea generation and evaluation, but it is important that each process remains separate from one another. When it is time to generate ideas, design thinkers do so quickly without focusing on the quality or feasibility of the idea for the time being. You never know whether infeasible ideas can inspire somebody else. Design thinkers consider activities like sketching during the ideation process to communicate an idea.

Stage 4: Prototype—Start to Create Solutions

This is an experimental phase. The aim is to identify the best possible solution for each problem found. Based on the ideas and sketches developed during the ideation phase, teams produce some inexpensive, scaled-down versions of the product (or specific features found within the product) to investigate the ideas generated by the design thinkers. This could involve simple paper prototyping.

Stage 5: Test—Try Your Solutions Out

Evaluators rigorously test the prototypes. Although this is the final phase, design thinking is iterative and teams often use the results to redefine further problems. You can return to previous stages to make further iterations, alterations, and refinements—or to find or rule out alternative solutions.

Design thinking is as simple as stated earlier; however, it is hard to master and takes time for enterprises to adapt. In many cases, while designing a new product or a service, we think about a certain segment of the market and then design it for that specific market or enterprise. Design thinking in my definition is more about solving a particular user problem rather than creating a solution that will satisfy multiple users. The reason is because a lot of times when we try to design or create solutions that will fit larger groups and address multiple problems, we start making a lot of concessions and ultimately design something that has a lot of features but does not appeal to users. This is because the features of the product are compromised in many ways.

Let me explain this with an example. Figure 4.4 depicts two different peelers. One is an old vintage peeler and the other is the OXO Good Grips peeler.

The story behind the Good Grips peeler is that Sam Farber, the founder of OXO, once saw his wife Betsey having trouble holding her peeler due to arthritis. This got Sam thinking: why do ordinary kitchen tools hurt your hands? Sam saw an opportunity to create more thoughtful cooking tools that

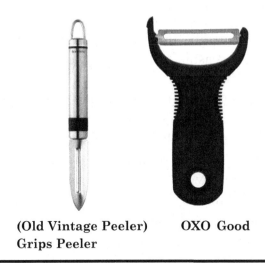

(Old Vintage Peeler)   OXO Good
Grips Peeler

Figure 4.4   Old vintage peeler vs modern peelers

would benefit people (with or without arthritis) and promised Betsey that he would make a better peeler. He then came up with OXO Good Grips peelers.

Aside from the new peeler, Sam also created 14 OXO Good Grips products that were initially launched with a wide, oval-shaped handle that was easy to hold and control no matter the size or shape of your hand or strength of your grip. OXO Good Grips are on all kinds of kitchen utensils these days and almost every utensil utilizes this kind of grip. By focusing on an extreme user with an extreme need, a specific product was built. The needs of this extreme user were amplified for a better reach. In the example, as discussed, the need for the user requiring a better grip peeler because she is suffering from arthritis has been amplified for all individuals requiring a better grip utensil. Ideally when we are working on a new product or service, we should figure out the extreme users in the marketspace and design products for these users after amplifying the user base, but at the same time address specific problem statements.

Applying Systems Thinking and Design Thinking Together—A Case Study

Let us now apply systems thinking and design thinking together to a banking case study. This was my third consulting assignment in showcasing impact of a combination of systems thinking and design thinking to my customer business. The case study is for a major bank named ABC bank, which provides a number of products and services including wholesale banking, retail banking, treasury, auto loans, two-wheeler loans, personal loans, loans against property, and credit cards.

During 2007, in the retail side of the business, the bank started losing customers tune to 7.5% every month and customer started complaining of poor customer service desk. The bank has outsourced their customer service desk to an India business process outsourcing company (named Company A). ABC Corporation initially saw the project as straightforward and was of the opinion that replacing Company A would be the solution and they did that. Even after a new service provider came in, the quality of the customer service desk remained the same and this time the Bank replaced the complete team and brought in senior customer service agents, who they believed can interact with their customers in a more collaborative way, thereby reducing customer churn rate. However, even after this change, the customer churn remained the same. Few leader from ABC bank got together and felt that they were just focusing on the events (iceberg model) and are employing a very narrow solution to the customer churn problem. They then invited a specialized design firm to come up with a solution to the problem. I was part of this design firm and took the assignment to apply systems thinking to the bank's problem.

We defined four phases for the program namely the discovery phase, define phase, develop phase, and roll out phase.

Discovery Phase

During the discovery phase we analyzed all customer data such as their onboarding date, their level of interactions with the bank, their spending patterns, and so on. We then specifically analyze the users who were leaving the bank. We wanted to understand the structures and mental models with a vision which is to reduce the customer churn.

It came as a surprise to all of us and the bank after realizing that around 80% of the customers who were leaving the bank were senior citizens. This brings in a very important perspective to understand the reasons why these categories of customers were leaving the bank. I created two teams to discover the needs, pain points and problems of sixty selected senior citizens (we will call them seniors henceforth). Out of the sixty seniors some were former customers and other were the banks current customers. We did extensive interviews both formal and informal and gathered several insights from the customer data the bank has stored. The interviews focused on day-to-day lifestyle and habits of the elderly, their social relationships and networks, their financial attitudes, and lastly their pains and gains using the digital platforms and debit cards. The final aspect was to understand what they feel about the bank, their challenges, and delight factors.

The key finding from these interviews was that senior are unable to perform banking using their ATM cards as it is hard for them first remember their personal identification number (pin) and secondly they cannot key their pin easily. Some even said that they write their pin on a piece of paper and there were few cases where fraudsters have stolen their money. And finally, when they call helpdesk, it is hard for them to reach the operator and if they are able to reach the operator they are asked with several questions quoting security, which again is hard for them to remember and tell because of their age factor. This was one of the consistent feedback from all seniors that were interviewed.

Define Phase

After understanding the user sentiments, the second phase called as Define phase was embarked. In the design phase, the Bank along with me and my team gathered for an ideation workshop to identify the opportunity areas. We brainstormed the events, patterns, structures, and mental models of the problem collectively rather than in silos. The conclusion was that key issue was the ATM card and solution was to make banking easier for customers. At the end of the workshop, we identified four smart value propositions to overcome the problems which the seniors faced. The value propositions had nothing to do with the customer service deck and were centered around making banking easy for senior citizens.

We understand during the interview that seniors use their money major for bus travel, for groceries and food, to recharge their phone cards, and for their fitness classes. Based on these four usage patterns we created a program called Smart system program where four propositions were identified called as smart payments, smart transport, smart communication, and smart fitness centered around the four usage patterns of the seniors. We decided that these four smart features will be designed into a card sleeve, worn around the neck, as we observed elderly wearing similar lanyards in the past and would face less implementation barrier as compared to a format they are less familiar with using the card. The card was built with a feature called

"Tap to Pay" where seniors would not need to enter the pin for selected transactions at selected terminals and shops.

Develop Phase

In the Develop phase, user testing was conducted to understand if the four key features were aligned to what seniors wanted. Selected seniors were presented with a concept board, with write-ups of the features in different languages (Dutch, French, Malay, and English) and different versions of how the wearable devices could look like as depicted in Figure 4.5.

Based on the inputs captured during the user testing sessions, the elderly wanted to have a more flexible format that could be worn in different ways. Apart from format, the respondents also gave various inputs on the effectiveness of the pedometer, use cases of a full-fledged cashless payment (instead of limiting to the four usage patterns) which were all captured for subsequent considerations.

Taking all the feedback into considerations, the bank issued an RFP (Request for Proposal) and identified a partner to help manufacture the devices. Once the device was manufactured, 54 participants were selected to take part in the 3-month pilot. The selection criteria include several senior citizens and few others in age range of 50–65 years. The program was initiated to allow the bank to understand if elderly would switch to Smart system program and if the behavior would remain after the program concludes. The results from the pilot was determined very inspiring and the bank decided to rolled out Smart system program across all its customers.

Figure 4.5   Wearable devices

Rollout Phase

The Smart system program was officially launched on 5th May 2018 and in just 2 months it provided the bank with a rich opportunity to understand and observe the cashless usage of the elderly. The outcome of Smart systems was very encouraging. The customer churn rate reduced from 5% to 0.8% in just 4 months and 32.2% of the customer who left the bank reengaged with the bank within 12 months.

After the conclusion of the Smart system program, the Innovation Management team of the Bank conducted a series of in-depth interviews with key stakeholders who participated in the program to discuss the learnings and takeaways, and the process of Journey Thinking was mentioned in several instances:

Strong Focus on Customers

As compared to the usual problem solving framework of the bank, where customers were rarely consulted and decisions were driven by business profitability and technology feasibility, systems thinking provided two opportunities where all the stakeholders would have to engage the customers in an in-depth way.

First of all, while the Product Managers from the bank had years of experience engaging the senior citizens, there were blind spots in their understanding and assumptions that they have formed up over the years. The focus groups and test gave them an opportunity to clarify their doubts and most importantly listen to the seniors instead of coming in as an expert to solve their problems.

Secondly, the experiments also gave the team added confidence on the robustness of the insights and helped the Product Managers adjust the value propositions before launching products into the market. This gave the team assurance on the desirability of the product, which was absent in traditional decision-making process.

Rigorous Process for Analyzing and Communicating Insights

While surveys were conducted in the past, the product team of the bank often did not have the tools to conduct more in-depth analysis of the data captured. The channels of engagement also did not afford the team such an opportunity to dig deeper. By embracing the approaches of design thinking, the team felt that the interviewing process of writing verbatims, clustering them according to patterns and structures, and the writing of insights statement is a much more rigorous process as compared to relying on superficial survey data.

Experiments and Iterations

The running of experiments to test value proposition is a completely new way of working for most stakeholders on the project. Prior to Smart systems program, the Product Managers in Bank were exposed to the concept of running User Acceptance Testing (UAT), which centered around user interface, experience (UI/UX), and less of the core product value proposition itself. Those tests were built on the assumption that the product was what the customers wanted, which is a huge risk the Product Mangers had to bear. The rapid iteration model introduced by design thinking required the Product Mangers to make quick decisions or tweaks for the next round, helping them see a difference in desirability within a short turnaround time, with no additional investment.

Conclusion

By improving the entire customer experience, design thinking clubbed with systems thinking enhanced customer relationships and reduced customer churn for the bank. As illustrated in the reviewed case studies, establishing systems thinking and design thinking as a pivotal element in business strategy can strengthen any enterprise position as it ensures that customers' needs and expectations are addressed.

With this case study I hope it is clear that systems approach clubbed with design thinking holds the most promise for addressing complex problems. The same concept is used in almost every industry to enable insights in solving complex problems.

The Intelligent Business Thinking (IBT) Model

As discussed so far, Design thinking is meant to innovate new solutions based on a "bottom-up" human-centered approach, while systems thinking is meant to manage change and integration based on a "top-down" big picture view.

Systems thinking is the approach beyond design thinking, and the BT Model fully embraces systems thinking combined with design thinking to make business driven digital transformations.

Just as we discussed in the case study of Bank ABC, the problem statement was not about the customer service desk, but was with complexity of performing a transaction by seniors. Once the bank identified the real problem using systems thinking, it next applied design thinking to solve the problem by defining the Smart system program. Had it have not understood the real problem, they would have been frustrated applying different solutions to solve service desk problem.

Utilizing a combination of systems and design thinking to solve a business problem is known as Intelligent Business Thinking (IBT) as per the Formula 4.0 methodology.

IBT is an approach which brings together the practices of systems thinking (top-down) and design thinking (bottom-up) to understand business problems, design, and systemize (deliver), the flow of value from various aspects of the organization across the value chain to ensure synchronicity, consistency, and integration as well as maximization between people, activities, processes, policies, places, and resources.[1]

Consider how IKEA operates using IBT. Not only is its product development process and showroom experience thoughtfully created and centered around people, but also the whole organization system is designed and operated using IBT. After visiting the showroom, customers are guided through to purchasing in a warehouse setting where items are sourced and procured not by IKEA employees, but by themselves. Customers also have the option to have their purchased goods delivered. This is the very notion of embarking on digital transformation initiatives to digitize their value proposition, and design thinking is at heart of this experience. It is systems thinking clubbed with design thinking that allows the implementation of value proposition, connects front-end experiences with back-end operations, and orchestrates the value between stakeholders and metrics to run a much better organization. This is what is known as IBT.

Business Transformation Model (BT Model)

Figure 4.6 depicts the four quadrants of BT Model. After a business strategy is chosen next step is to identify existing core business processes which differentiates the enterprise in the marketspace and aligns to the chosen

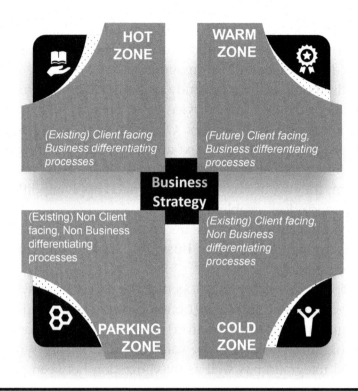

Figure 4.6   Business transformation model

business strategy. All such processes are placed under the Hot Zone for transformation.

Business processes that are not yet implemented but are part of the enterprise roadmap for future implementation are known as future processes and all such processes are classified in the Warm Zone. New models that can support an enterprise in achieving customer engagement strategy or business transformation strategy are placed here.

As an example, Mart A is a retailer corporation that operates a chain of hypermarkets, discount department stores, and grocery stores. The core business process for a Mart A is:

■ Receiving orders from eCommerce systems via a web application
■ Processing order information
■ Shipping

Let us assume that Mart A has chosen Business Transformation Strategy. A future process transformation model for Mart A could be to receive orders from eCommerce systems via new channels such as a mobile device or an iPad.

A future business process transformation model could be to bundle the sale of a watch with an insurance product. This new business model compliments the traditional business of Mart A by partner with insurance service providers. Mart A may aspire to enter into the transport sector to delivery products to their customer using their own trucks. This would redefine the complete business of Mart A and such processes are called domain transformation models. All such future processes transformation models, business process transformation models, and domain transformation models are placed in the Warm Zone.

There may be several business processes within an enterprise that are client facing but do not differentiate the enterprise in the marketspace. In other words, these business processes do not generate revenues for the enterprise but still are necessary for day-to-day functioning. Systems such as payroll and HR systems are two examples. All such business processes are placed in the Cold Zone.

Finally, existing business processes which are not client facing and do not generate any revenues for the enterprise and are non-essential for day-to-day operations of the business are classified under the Parking Zone.

Applying IBT Model on the Business Processes

Once business processes are classified into one of the four quadrants of BT Model, IBT Model is applied on selected business processes within the Hot Zone and Warm Zone. A team is created for all such selected business processes which constitutes of business users and IBT experts. The goal of this team is to find business solutions based on the problems and opportunities identified and make the business processes efficient, cost effective, and enjoyable for end users.

The definition of a problem is something that must be solved or an unpleasant or undesirable condition that needs to be corrected. The definition of an opportunity is an occasion or situation that makes it possible to do something that you want to do better.

To make the analysis simple, BT Model recommends that enterprises split the problems and opportunities and apply IBT Model on each of the problems and opportunities. It is not necessary that all business processes, part of the Hot Zone and Warm Zone, will have problems or opportunities to improve.

From my experience, business processes that are part of the Cold Zone and Parking Zone are not typically recommended for transformation, and therefore IBT is not applicable on these business processes. However, enterprises need to make this decision on a case-by-case basis.

Business Transformation Model Treatments

Using BT Model, we have classified all business processes into one of the four quadrants. We have also applied IBT on selected business processes and defined business solutions.

The next step is to identify all IT systems that are part of the business processes and identify technology solutions to enable digital transformation.

BT Model recommends two types of treatments to IT systems that are identified for digital transformation. One is called "digital from core" and the other is "digital from surround." Systems which are not part of the transformation are left as they are.

Digital from Core

Digital transformation from core (digital from core) in context of this book means that systems on legacy platforms are refactored (rewritten) using digital triplets to address the problems or opportunities within the business process.

Digital triplets means that systems are developed using cloud architecture, atomic architecture, and APIs. We will discuss digital triplets in further detail during Section III.

DEFINITIONS

A **legacy system** is an old method, technology, computer system, or application program. The implication is that the system is out of date or in need of replacement. Typical characteristics of a legacy system are the following:

1. Skills are hard to find in the market
2. Technology is not in use for new developments
3. System is hard to extend with new features and takes a long time to develop a new feature
4. Limited in-built automation capabilities

Refactoring also called **Rewriting** or **Modernizing** means that the complete applications need to be redesigned and rebuilt. Often it means that you may have to rewrite the application logic completely and develop the Cloud native version from scratch.

Digital from Surround

Digital transformation from surround (digital from surround) means that the core functionality of the system is retained as it is and new functionalities, capabilities, or technologies are added to the surroundings of the system that will address the problems or opportunities identified for the business process. This allows the system to benefit from modern technologies. The term digital for surround is used because the core functionality is not modified, but the system adopts modern technologies from the outside.

Digital surround means that these systems can undergo the following:

1. Modernizing front end for a better user experience wherever necessary. As an example, consider a mainframe application with green screens. The green screen can be replaced with an interactive UI that enables a superior user experience for specific use cases. This treatment is typically given for legacy applications which are part of non-core business processes
2. Automate a system using RPA and AI keeping the core functionality unchanged. An example could be automating business processes using AI and machine learning
3. Moving commercial off the shelf (COTS) applications to Cloud or Software as a Service (SaaS) based models
4. Implementing monitoring tools which can identify bottlenecks in a business process flow. Afterwards, RPA and AI can be used to automate these business process flows to overcome the bottlenecks
5. Mainframe or SAP system migration from On-Premises to Cloud. Here these applications harness the power of Cloud technology to become cheaper and perform more efficiently

DEFINITION

Software as a service[7] *is a software licensing and delivery model in which software is licensed on a subscription basis and is centrally hosted. It is sometimes referred to as "on-demand software" and was formerly referred to as "software plus services" by Microsoft.*[8]

Treatments for Systems under Each Zone of the BT Model

Figure 4.7 depicts the treatment that would generally be applicable on systems that are identified for a change.

Treatment for Systems under the Hot Zone

As a general rule, all systems identified for transformation for the business processes within the Hot Zone need to be digitally transformed from core, if they are on legacy platform. For Business Processes where problems and opportunities are identified, IT systems need to be transformed from core based on the business solution.

There could be exceptions as some systems classified within the Hot Zone cannot be rewritten using digital triplets or the return on investments

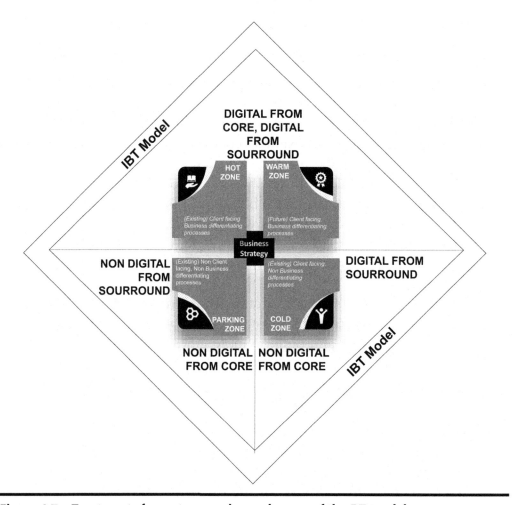

Figure 4.7 Treatments for systems under each zone of the BT model

from rewriting these systems using digital triplets are minimal. All such systems are digitally transformed from surround.

Treatment for Systems under the Warm Zone

The Warm Zone constitutes of business processes, business models, and domain models which are to be developed in future. However, it is essential for enterprises to understand the existing IT systems that form part of these future processes, business models, and domain models and need to be transformed from core.

IT Systems, part of Business processes where problems and opportunities are identified, need to be transformed from core in correlation to the business strategy and should mandatorily be part of the enterprise's digital transformation roadmap.

Without digitally transforming related systems from core that will be part of future models, it is impossible for enterprises to develop new business or domain models.

Treatment for Systems under the Cold Zone

The Cold Zone constitutes of systems which do not differentiate an enterprise in their marketspace, and therefore these systems are never digitally transformed from core.

There may however be client facing business processes which enterprises may decide to digitally transform from surround on a case-by-case basis.

Although they are not part of core business processes, they still can be client facing applications. Some examples of these are HR systems, payroll applications, finance systems, and so on. In large enterprises these could be COTS applications as well. These systems are not only hard to decommission and rewrite using digital triplets, but at the same time the return on investment achieved from rewriting these systems are not worth the effort.

Treatment for Systems under the Parking Zone

The Parking Zone constitutes of non-core business processes which mean they are not client facing or business differentiating. All systems within this zone are left as they are or are retired. My personal experience has been that systems within the Parking Zone are hard to digitally transform from core or surround even if this is desired by the enterprise. Examples of systems within this zone include hardware devices and network controls.

Notes

1. Venkatesh Upadrista. (29 Jun. 2017). The Art of Consultative Selling in IT: Taking Blue Ocean Strategy a Step Ahead Hardcover.
2. Venkatesh Upadrista. (24 May 2011). Distributed Agile: DH2A: The Proven Agile Software Development Approach and Toolkit for Geographically Dispersed Teams Paperback.
3. Monkelbaan, J. (2015). Experimentalist Sustainability Governance: Jazzing up Environmental Blues?. Public Participation and Climate Governance Working Paper Series.
4. Sabel, C.F. and Zeitlin, J. (2012). Experimentalism in the EU: Common ground and persistent differences. Regulation & Governance, 6(3), pp. 410–426.
5. Venkatesh Upadrista. (15 Dec. 2014). Managing Your Outsourced IT Services Provider: How to Unleash the Full Potential of Your Global Workforce Paperback.
6. Voulvoulis, N. (2012). Water and sanitation provision in a low carbon society: The need for a systems approach. Journal of Renewable and Sustainable Energy, 4(4), p. 041403.
7. Panker, Jon; Lewis, Mark; Fahey, Evan; Vasquez, Melvin Jafet. (Aug. 2007). How do you pronounce IT? TechTarget. Retrieved, 24 May 2012.
8. Microsoft describes software plus services. (26 July 2007). InfoWorld. Retrieved, 7 February 2017.

FOUNDATION PLATFORM

This section will discuss how enterprises need to set up a foundation for their digital journey using Atomic architectures, Cloud infrastructure, and Application Programming Interfaces (APIs).

With Atomic architectures enterprises are able to develop software as a collection of loosely coupled lightweight and independent services, thereby making applications highly maintainable, independently testable, and deployable.

- Cloud infrastructure enterprises can adopt any new technology, tool, or service in the most agile way, without any upfront expenditure
- APIs enable enterprises to have a standard interface of communication between all applications across the enterprise

Together, Atomic architecture, Cloud, and APIs form the foundation of a digital enterprise and are called Digital Triplets.

Chapter 5

Creating a Foundation Platform with Digital Triplets (Atomic Architecture, Cloud Infrastructure, and Application Programming Interface)

Digital transformation is not about adopting emerging or modern technologies. It is about creating a platform and architecture that is scalable to adopt any current and future technologies that will help enterprises to perform their business digitally and at the same time support them to achieve faster time to market and reduce costs.

The key objective is to minimize the complexity of corporate software systems by segregating design and development into multiple independent sections with minimal dependency on each other.

From the point of view of architecture, many large companies are facing immense challenges in their software development processes. This is because in the last several years, application development for many enterprises has been centralized using multitier architecture to create entire applications on a single codebase. The client-server model was an excellent choice when desktops ruled IT, but with the rise of mobile devices and the cloud, back-end data must now always be available for a wide range of devices. The old, monolithic architecture will no longer cut it, as a small change to the system will have an impact on the overall system, opening up the possibility of new bugs every time a new feature is added or the system is adjusted to fit a new situation. Even worse, if everything is tied to a single codebase, enterprises will not be able to scale-up a specific function or service without scaling up the entire application, leading to much higher costs.

DEFINITION

Multitier architecture or *multilayered architecture* is a client-server architecture in which presentation, application processing, and data management functions are physically separated.

Change is happening at a very fast pace in the IT industry based on the new technologies, tools, and models being invented which are known as the Digital Ecosystems. Eighty-five percent of enterprises feel they have just 2 years to make significant inroads on their digital transformation before suffering financially, and/or falling behind.[1] It comes as no surprise that, as Forbes has reported,[2] 90% of global businesses have kicked off a formal digital transformation initiative of some form.

The important aspect for any digital transformation is to ensure that the right foundation is set that can enable enterprises to embark on their journey toward digital transformation, based on which tools and technologies can be adopted. If the foundation is not strong enough or well thought out, digital initiatives fail to reap the benefits.

From a digital platform point of view, with the development of numerous new technologies and tools each providing their own benefits, enterprises need to be ready to adopt any new technology in the quickest way possible. This does not mean that new technologies should be adopted by companies without an evaluation of how they might benefit their business as a whole; rather than it is essential that the enterprise platform should be able to support the adoption of any new technology with minimal internal or external dependencies. The way to realize this aspiration is by creating the right digital platform that revolves around three core pillars as depicted in Figure 5.1.

1. The first is the application architecture that needs to be defined at an enterprise level. Within an enterprise, there will be several applications that need to continue to exist as they are, some will be legacy applications. There may also be other legacy applications which may need to be rewritten to achieve the digital goals of an enterprise.

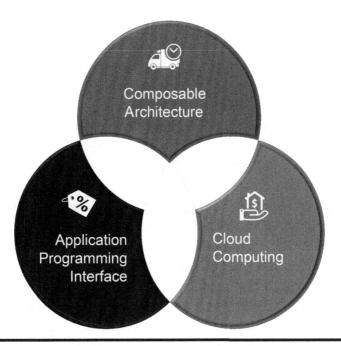

Figure 5.1   Digital triplets

Application architecture for all such rewrites and new application development should follow an architecture with loosely coupled services. **Atomic architecture** is therefore the right choice for organizations transforming themselves to digital.

2. Legacy application within an enterprise will continue to coexist, and new applications will be built using Atomic architecture. Communication between applications within the enterprise needs to be decoupled. What this essentially means is that peer-to-peer communications should be replaced with a common software intermediary, with **Application Programming Interface** being the solution.

3. The third principle is the digital enabling infrastructure also known as digital infrastructure. This means enterprises should have an infrastructure that will enable digital transformation in the most efficient and agile way and support adoption of any new tools and technologies. In the context of this book, **Cloud Computing** addresses this infrastructure need.

The above three areas are called Digital Triplets in context of Formula 4.0 and support the creation of a base digital platform for enterprises embarking on their digital transformation journey.

Atomic Architecture

Atomic architecture is an architectural style in which applications are separated into loosely coupled services. With loosely coupled services and lightweight protocols, Atomic architecture offers increased modularity, making applications easier to develop, test, deploy, and (most importantly) change and maintain.

In Atomic architecture, code is broken down into independent services that run as separate processes. Output from one service is used as an input for another in an orchestration of independent, communicating services. This type of architecture is especially useful for businesses that do not have a fixed idea of the array of devices that its applications will support. By being both device and platform agnostic, Atomic architecture patterns enable companies to develop applications that provide consistent user experiences across a range of platforms, spanning the web, mobile devices, and Internet of Things (IoT). Microservices is an example of Atomic architecture. Organizations that embark on a digital transformation journey need to mandatorily adopt the Atomic architecture framework in their application development; there are several benefits to them doing so, which is depicted in Figure 5.2 and explained below:

Figure 5.2   Benefits of Atomic architecture

Increased resilience—with Atomic architecture, the entire application is decentralized and divided into services that act as separate entities. Unlike the old, monolithic architecture (wherein a failure of the code would affect more than one service or function), when using Atomic architecture any failure would have a minimal impact. This applies even when several systems are brought down for maintenance; you can make sure specific users do not notice it.

Improved scalability—scalability is a key aspect of Atomic architecture. Since each service is a separate component, you can scale-up a single function or service without having to scale-up the entire application. Business critical services can be deployed on multiple servers for increased availability and improved performance without impacting the performance of other services.

The ability to use the right tool for the right task—with Atomic architecture, companies are not tied to a single vendor. Instead, they have the flexibility to use the right tool for the right task. Each service can use its own language, framework, or ancillary services whilst still being able to communicate easily with the other services of the same application.

Faster time to market—because Atomic architecture works with loosely coupled services, enterprises do not need to rewrite their entire codebase to add or modify a feature. They can make changes to one specific service and test it with complete confidence that other parts of the code will not be impacted. By developing applications in smaller sections that are independently testable and deployable, enterprises can get their products and services to market quicker.

Easier to debug and maintain—Atomic architecture also makes it easy to debug and test applications. With smaller modules going through a continuous delivery and testing process, your ability to deliver error-free applications is vastly improved.

Continuous delivery—unlike monolithic applications, in which dedicated teams work on discrete functions such as UI and database, systems built using Atomic architectures uses cross-functional teams to handle the entire life cycle of an application using a continuous delivery model. When developers, operations, and testing teams work simultaneously on a single service, testing and debugging become easy and instant. With this approach of incremental development, code is continuously developed, tested, and deployed. Code can also be reused from existing libraries.

Separation of Concerns

Implementing Atomic architecture, such as microservices, is a good start. There are however several companies that have failed in their product development journey because the design of their microservices was not optimized to achieve the desired results.

There are various questions architects need to consider before designing a system. Questions such as how many microservices need to be developed for a given product, how their granular functions need to be broken down, and which functionalities need to be consolidated under one microservice. If these points are not addressed, the product development could just lead to chaos.

As an example, Netflix estimates that it uses around 700 independent microservices to control each of the many parts that make up the entire Netflix service. One microservice stores the shows a user has watched, one deducts the monthly fee from credit card and one examines the watch history of a specific user and applies algorithms to predict what else he might like to watch in future. This is just the tip of the iceberg. Netflix engineers can make changes to any part of the application and introduce new changes rapidly without changing rest of the services. This is achievable because each microservice that Netflix uses is fully independent of others.

It is worth noting however that the Netflix example cannot be used to determine the number of microservices an individual application will need, neither should it be taken as an example of the granularity of the microservices required.

The whole concept of Atomic architecture effectively lies in determining the separation of concerns (SoC).

DEFINITION

SoC is a design principle for separating a computer program into distinct sections, so that each section addresses a separate concern. A concern is information or a set of functions that affect the code of a computer program.

Imagine that you and your team successfully release an application and you are getting great feedback from the users; then a requirement for a new feature comes in. What would be the potential risks when you add this feature?

We could cite a lot of them, but it ultimately all boils down to two things. First, it is possible that the feature could be difficult to write because you would have to write a lot of code in many different places. Secondly, you run the risk of breaking current features that are already working.

Keeping your concerns separate will decrease the above risks. If all the code related to a certain concern is kept together (e.g., in the same layer) it becomes easier to change it; you do not have to make a myriad of changes scattered throughout the code base, and you do not have to search for where a certain feature has been implemented since the code is organized according to its concerns. This means that you do not risk breaking functionalities that are not related to the functionality of what you are currently implementing.

This is one of the areas where most modern application designers, architects, and developers make mistakes that cause ongoing problems with their project. It is a much greater issue in large transformation projects, as mistakes made early in the process can be too expensive to rectify later. It is essential that SoC are identified whilst defining the application designs using microservice architecture.

Cloud Infrastructure

Infrastructure for digital enterprises may mean different things to different people. In context of the Formula 4.0 framework, a digital infrastructure is an infrastructure where systems and applications will reside. The infrastructure should be flexible enough to quickly scale-up and scale-down and adapt to any new technologies emerging in the market. An example of a digital infrastructure is a cloud platform. A system built on cloud will be able to achieve all the aspirations that enterprises expect from digital, which includes:

■ Scale-up and scale-down of any type of services in minutes rather than weeks or months. Services could be servers, storages, networks, tools, or technologies
■ A self-service and on-demand capability to manage scale-up and scale-down services, so that services can be procured in minutes, typically with just a few mouse clicks. This gives businesses a lot of flexibility and takes the pressure off capacity planning

- A self-service capability for operations such as restarting servers or monitoring infrastructure or application
- Improvement on availability, performance, and network latency
- Achieving higher reliability, for example making data backup, disaster recovery, and business continuity easier and less expensive
- The ability to adapt to any of the latest technologies, tools, and services
- Improved security, which means an infrastructure that provides a broad and better set of policies, technologies, and controls that strengthen enterprises security posture overall. This will help to protect their data, applications, and infrastructure from potential threats

Gartner[3] recommends that organizations continue to mature their cloud-first strategies—where the cloud is primary, prioritized, and promoted. According to Elias Khnaser, VP Analyst at Gartner: "If you have not developed a cloud-first strategy yet, you are likely falling behind your competitors."

IT organizations have moved past asking whether applications can be deployed or migrated to the public cloud. Instead, they are commonly accepting the pace and innovation of cloud providers as foundational to their business strategy.

Application Programming Interface (API)

An API is an interface that enables controlled interaction between different software programs an enterprise is using. In other words, it is a way for developers and software packages to integrate with the other systems within or outside the enterprise.

APIs are key in a digital transformation journey for enterprises. Using APIs, enterprises can connect to any systems seamlessly, be it a legacy system, a COTS application, or a new digital application. The challenge for enterprises is to implement a digital strategy against a background of increasingly complex day-to-day IT operations, which often involve managing both cloud and On-Premises IT infrastructure in a combination of legacy and modern technologies. APIs are an essential component of merging the old and the new IT platforms, capturing vast amounts of data, and ultimately achieving enterprise digital transformation strategy.

Secondly, as companies develop new applications, they are also creating new digital endpoints. An endpoint is any device that is physically an end point on a network. Laptops, desktops, mobile phones, tablets, servers, software applications, and virtual environments can all be considered end-points. Every time companies add a new digital endpoint, they must ensure the endpoint is connected to others in the network. With APIs enterprises can ensure this connectivity and maintain greater agility.

The most common description of an API is a set of functions and proce-dures that allow applications to access the features or data of an operating system, application, or other service to extend its capability or even create an entirely new feature.

A 2016 report from Deloitte[4] claims that 44% of IT decision-makers believe building and managing APIs is fundamental to their ability to be able to complete digital transformation projects quickly. The same number said API reuse would significantly speed up digital transformation. This report also states that APIs are increasingly moving from tactical develop-ment techniques to a business model driver, with companies frequently find-ing opportunities to reuse them, share them outside the organization, and ultimately monetize them.

In the report "A Developer's Guide to Forrester's Strategies For API Success," Forrester has named APIs as critical elements for all for digital transformation journeys. Beyond architectural role in application integration, APIs enable new business strategies, rapid business change, broad ecosys-tem connectivity, and improved customer engagement. To help application development and delivery (AD&D) enterprises need to establish and evolve a well-grounded API strategy. APIs are among the most important and man-datory elements for any enterprise that wants to embark on a digital trans-formation journey.

Notes

1. Are businesses really digitally transforming or living in digital denial? Progress Global Survey, May 2016.
2. Forbes, Diorio. (2017). Three Reasons Why CEOs Need To Be More Vested In Digital Transformation.
3. https://www.gartner.com/smarterwithgartner/6-steps-for-planning-a-cloud-strategy/#:~:text=Cloud%20has%20become%20the%20foundation,differentiate%20and%20gain%20competitive%20advantage.&text=Gartner%20recommends%20that%20organizations%20continue,is%20primary%2C%20prioritized%20and%20promoted
4. https://deloitte.wsj.com/cio/2016/06/27/apis-help-drive-digital-transformation/

Chapter 6

Cloud Infrastructure

Information technology infrastructure is defined broadly as a set of information technology (IT) components that serve as the foundation of an IT service. These are typically physical components (computer, networking hardware, and facilities), but also various software and network components.

According to the Information Technology Infrastructure Library's (ITIL) Foundation Glossary, IT infrastructure can also be defined as: "all of the hardware, software, computers, servers, networking, data, storage, physical and virtual facilities that are required to develop, test, deliver, monitor, control or support IT services. The term IT infrastructure includes all of the information technology but not the associated people, processes, and documentation."[1]

Enterprise IT infrastructure typically refers to components required for the existence, operation, and management of an enterprise IT environment. It can be internal to an organization and deployed within owned facilities, deployed externally, or a combination of the two.

In summary, infrastructure services within an IT world are the basic physical and non-physical structures that support IT. The term suggests basic foundation services on which information technologies and services are built. The common types of IT infrastructure services are:

Fiber-optic communication—the basic communication cables that connect cities and regions including submarine cables

Network hardware—the hardware such as core routers that connect networks to create larger networks, such as the Internet

Computing hardware—collocation or cloud computing hardware such as physical servers that form the basis of Internet computing capabilities

Facilities—where infrastructure lives, including data centers and telecom facilities

Software—fundamental software components that support services such as operating systems and web servers

Platforms—platforms that host a wide variety of services such as cloud computing platforms

Last mile infrastructure—the network infrastructure that connects locations such as homes and offices

End user devices—devices directly used by users such as laptops, desktops, and mobile devices

Internet of Things—devices such as sensors which are network connected

DEFINITION

Colocation *is a data center that rents space, computing hardware, and related services such as bandwidth, cooling, power, security, and onsite support services.*

Infrastructure Role in Digital Transformation

Digital is revolutionizing the complete IT industry, and new technologies are infiltrating every part of an organization, increasing productivity and efficiency. New applications are digitizing existing processes, making staff more productive, and allowing businesses to make better decisions that open up entirely new revenue streams. In essence, digital transformation is a megatrend characterized by automation and the best use of technology.

The backbone for this revolution is IT infrastructure and it is impossible for organizations to harness the benefits of digital transformation without establishing the building blocks that make it possible. The new-age digital solutions in IT infrastructure space are disrupting the complete IT industry.

DEFINITION

A ***product-based organization*** *is a structure in which teams are formed based on specific product lines or services, keeping in mind the customers they deal with and the geographical area they serve. For each product line, the entire business and IT teams specific to the product report into a single Product Organization structure. We are going to discuss product-based organization in more depth in Chapter 8.*

If you look at the expectation of an IT industry in an infrastructure space, from keeping lights on in hardware and network management space, the expectations have grown, especially in this age of digital transformation. Enterprises are looking at infrastructure services as drivers to enable agility that can help them adapt to new ways of working and new business models in a very agile way. As enterprises are moving themselves into new models, such as product-based organizations, it becomes far more important for IT infrastructure to be able to support this model. As an example, in a product-based organization new products or enhancements are built approximately every 2–3 weeks. With the need to create new products in such short timeframes, there is a requirement to provide new services such as operating systems (OSs), software, tools, and connectivity in hours rather than days. IT infrastructure should be capable enough to meet the demand of a product-based enterprise; else it will lead to enterprise failures in product development. This essentially means that IT infrastructure needs to have the ability to reconfigure and recalibrate the underlying hardware and network stack to allow enterprises to adopt using new capabilities, new development approaches, and new technologies. Highly automated and dynamic provisioned IT infrastructure services are becoming the need in this digital world.

Another example is the disruptions we saw during the COVID-19 pandemic. Working from home (WFH) became the norm for many people. To enable businesses continuity, enterprises were forced to relax several constrains they had in the past to enable WFH. This model led to almost zero business disruptions, most notably in the IT industry.

Even as the world recovers from the pandemic, WFH will reportedly become the new norm for 80% of organizations. A few IT services organizations have already announced that roughly 75% of the workforce may continue to WFH even after offices reopen. There are of course many other business areas which Covid-19 has impacted, and several industry verticals such as the pharmaceutical, retail, and hotel industries are reacting very differently. As an example, hotels are looking into the possibility of renting their rooms for short-term office spaces where individuals can book (rent) a hotel room for couple of hours on a pay-as-you-go basis.

New business avenues are being thought of throughout numerous industries, and both from an application side and IT infrastructure side enterprises must be ready to support these business changes. In order to meet the requirements of these new demands, IT infrastructure services need to be highly automated and flexible, which is essential for any enterprise to adapt to the speed of the new digital world.

Data Center

A data center is a building, dedicated space within a building or a group of buildings used to house computer systems and associated components. It is a network of computing and storage resources enabling the delivery of shared software applications and data. In the world of enterprise IT, the data center supports business applications.

The core components of a data center are:

■ Network infrastructure that connects servers, storage, and external connectivity to end-user locations
■ Storage infrastructure that stores the data
■ Computing resources which are the servers that provide processing, memory, local storage, and network connectivity for applications

All of these elements reside in one place, where physical racks and cabling are used to organize and interconnect them.

The facility itself provides power distribution and subsystems including electrical switching, uninterruptable power supplies (UPS), and backup generators, as well as adequate ventilation, environmental controls, and fire suppression. It also provides physical security, including access control.

Infrastructure Evolution—From Data Centers to Cloud

Computing infrastructure has experienced a wave of evolution in the last few decades, which includes:

- The first wave which saw a shift from proprietary mainframes to ×86-based servers, based On-Premises data centers and managed by internal IT teams.
- A second wave which saw widespread virtualization of the infrastructure that supported applications. This allowed for an improved use of resources and mobility of workloads across pools of physical infrastructure.

DEFINITIONS

Virtualization is the process of running a virtual instance of a computer system in a layer abstracted from the actual hardware. It is an act of creating a virtual version of something, including virtual computer hardware platforms, storage devices, and computer network resources.

*A **workload** is a collection of resources and codes that deliver business value, such as a customer-facing application or backend process.*

***Multitenancy** is a reference to the mode of operation of software where multiple independent instances of one or multiple applications operate in a shared environment.*

- The third wave finds us in the present, where we are now seeing the move to cloud services such as public, private, and hybrid clouds.

Cloud Computing

In the traditional world of enterprise IT, the data center supports business applications. These range from simple email and file sharing, through to customer relationship management (CRM), enterprise resource planning (ERP) to Big Data, communications, and collaboration services.

As discussed in Chapter 1, Cloud computing is the on-demand availability of computer system resources, from applications to storage and processing power, typically over the Internet and on a pay-as-you-go basis.

Rather than owning computing infrastructure or data centers, enterprises can rent access to anything from applications to storage from a cloud service provider. The key benefit of cloud is that enterprises can procure any new tools, software, servers, or environments in minutes rather than waiting for weeks or months. Another benefit of using cloud computing services is that firms can avoid the upfront cost and complexity of owning and maintaining their own IT infrastructure, and instead simply pay for what they use, when they use it.

As the name indicates, cloud has its origins from the network topology that represents connection to services over the Internet. Cloud computing involves computing over the Internet where users or programs can connect over a network to applications, software, hardware, data, etc. without knowing exactly where the applications, software, or hardware are located. The connection is established via a communication mode such as the Internet, Intranet, a local area network (LAN), wide area network (WAN), or other means of communication.

Instead of using a personal computer or a dedicated server every time to run an application or install software, enterprises can now run the application or use software from anywhere in the world by their preferred mode of communication and, in several cases, over the Internet.

With cloud, users now store data not on their own PC but somewhere at a remote location. It may be an internal private cloud where the servers are located within their own organization, or a public cloud where the servers are located outside the organization. Another example, which has been in existence for decades, is the use of thin client computers. In this model, local computers have very limited storage and processing capacity, but they can give the feel of a supercomputer. This is because users work on applications and software that are placed in a highly efficient and capable environment, which is located elsewhere and shared by several users. They provide access to applications and remote storage via a (web) browser. A thin client is therefore nothing more than an information viewer that seeks to connect via a network to the server, in order to perform the desired task.

With these examples, it is clear that cloud computing is not a new technology but has been in existence for decades. There have been several advancements to the technology, which have helped enterprises to leverage the technology in the best possible ways.

Several cloud models have come into existence in recent years; this makes cloud computing one of the most attractive options for organizations to adapt. Some advantages of cloud computing are:

■ Scalability and flexibility—Organizations can start small and increase the power of computing on a rapidly increasing on-demand basis.
■ Switching to any new technologies—With pay as you use models, enterprises can switch to the latest technologies without incurring any

capital expenditures. With the emergence of new technologies on a daily basis, this feature makes cloud adoption very appealing to enterprises.

■ Reliability—Organizations based on the type of requirements can get support on demand for their business continuity and disaster recovery needs.

■ Faster and quicker—Organizations need not wait weeks or months to get the services up and running. Several cloud providers have services in place that can be procured in just a few minutes.

■ Anytime and anywhere service—Users can access services on a public cloud simply with an Internet connection, thereby improving user experience.

■ Cost savings—Enterprises can reduce their maintenance costs and capital expenditures, aside from maximizing the effectiveness in specific areas.

There are several advantages of cloud computing; however, until recently cloud was less attractive to several enterprises because of security constraints, and despite the hype surrounding it, enterprises were skeptical about deploying their business in the cloud. Security issues in cloud computing have played a major role in slowing down its acceptance; in fact, security ranked first as the greatest challenge and issue of cloud computing a few years ago. This concern is however no longer as valid, as cloud providers have improved their security features to such an extent that cloud is now seeing widespread adoption across almost all enterprises and the technology has overcome all the major security concerns which enterprises used to have earlier.

Cloud Delivery Models

There are three cloud delivery models which comprise a natural provisioning hierarchy, allowing opportunities to procure services of combined models.[2] These are listed here.

Infrastructure as a Service (IaaS)

In this mode, hardware or virtual machines (VMs) are provided by cloud providers as a service. Users can install the required OSs, software, databases, etc. based on the needs in the hardware provided by the cloud providers.

In this model, the cloud user patches and maintains the OSs and application software.

This provides the most visibility into the stack. You can build whatever you want almost from the ground up because only the hardware is virtualized. I refer to this as bare metal. IaaS allows users to create their own VMs, load OS or databases, app servers, web servers, development tools, and build whatever type of applications they like. This is intended for IT developers and in many cases is offered with software as a service (SaaS, this will be explained further later). IaaS greatly minimizes the need for significant initial investment (capital expenditure) in computing hardware such as servers, networking devices, and processing power; and subsequently reduces hardware maintenance costs.

Platform as a Service (PaaS)[3]

In this service offering, cloud providers deliver a computing platform as a service—this is a step ahead of IaaS. The platform ranges from providing servers, software, OSs, programming language environments, database services, application servers, web servers, portals, and the like. Application developers can develop and run their software solutions on a cloud platform without the cost and complexity of buying and managing the underlying hardware and software. In this model, the VM and OS layer are hidden from users, and they are given an environment in which they can create their own custom application.

Organizations using PaaS achieve many more cost advantages (compared to IaaS) in terms of capital expenditure and maintenance costs, but there may well be a degree of lock-in with the cloud providers.[3]

Software as a Service (SaaS)[3]

Finally, this cloud service hides all the messy OS, application layers, and development tools. Most often, a complete "business service" is provided as SaaS to end users. There is some customization available, but the level will depend on how the SaaS provider has designed its platform and how it is handling multitenancy. Most often, you will be able to customize things like workflows and reports. Currently, there are offerings in the market for CRM, project management, human resource management, office tools such as email, messengers, calendar, etc., to name a few. Although there is an advanced cost benefit of using this model (compared to IaaS and PaaS) for critical application functionality, these will almost certainly induce a heavy lock-in with the cloud providers, and custom applications are not available.

The security constraints on this service can sometimes override the benefits because data resides on a public cloud and security measures in this model completely depend on the type of cloud provider chosen.

Cloud Deployment Models

We have discussed in Chapter 1 about the different cloud deployment models.

A private cloud is a model in which the infrastructure, services, and software are located within the organization.

In a public cloud services are hosted outside the organization and can be accessed via Internet.

A community cloud is a service rendered by cloud providers to an enterprise of similar businesses or communities in a shared model.

A hybrid cloud is a combination of two or more types of cloud models such as a combination of a private cloud and community cloud or public cloud.

Cloud Migration Approach/Treatment

The use of cloud computing for enterprises continues to grow, as enterprises are migrating to cloud and are pursuing multi-cloud strategies to generate lower costs, increased agility, and greater flexibility. Most enterprises today are in the journey toward cloud migration. Many cloud deployments have not however delivered the benefits, as we have discussed in this chapter so far, and many IT leaders have faced failed cloud migration projects. A recent study[4] from security provider Fortinet, conducted by IHS Markit, found that most companies have moved a cloud-based application back On-Premises after they failed to see anticipated returns. In a survey of 350 global IT decision makers, 74% reported that they had moved an application back to their own infrastructure.

The reason why cloud projects tend to fail is because of a simple reason, which is that migrations are not planned well. Aside from planning, many enterprises do not understand what treatment mechanism (migration approach) should be applied on each system. Another reason why cloud migrations fail is because the complexity of migration is always underestimated. Migrating to the cloud is a complex process that must be customized to address the technical, functional, and operational needs of the enterprise. A successful migration strategy should address short-term goals, like decreasing hosting costs, as well as longer-term goals like better alignment between IT and business objectives.

The six cloud migration approaches are depicted in Figure 6.1.

Lift and Shift Migration or Rehosting

A lift and shift migration is exactly what it sounds like. It means lifting an application out of its current hosting environment and shifting it to another environment—for example, from On-Premises hosting to a public cloud. Lift and shift migration means an exact copy of the top three layers: application, database, and OS layer. Some also call this rehosting, because it involves moving your stack to a new host without making extensive changes.

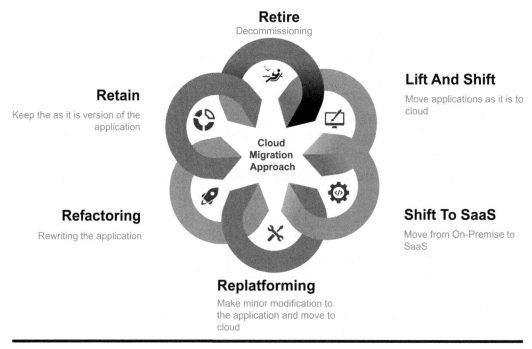

Figure 6.1   Cloud migration approach

This enables a rapid, cost-effective migration, minimal disruption, and quick Return on Investments (ROI).

Lift and shift migration is carried out many times via image backup. Image-based backup is a backup process for a computer or VM that creates a copy of the OS and all the data associated with it, including the system state and application configurations. The backup is saved as a single file, called an image, and then moved to cloud directly.

The primary advantage of this approach is that teams can migrate systems quickly, without modifying their architecture. This can however also be a disadvantage at times, as features of cloud infrastructure, such as scalability, will be missed.

Many failures in cloud migration are because enterprises have estimated that anything and everything can be moved to cloud by applying a lift and shift treatment, based on which cost of cloud migrations and timelines are arrived. Since this is not the right approach, it has led to severe frustrations within an enterprise. Although lift and shift migration is a possibility for moving from On-Premises to cloud, one needs to understand that there is a high chance that the application will be unable to achieve similar level of nonfunctional requirements such as scalability, availability, reliability, performance, and maintainability after migration. Another disadvantage is that enterprises cannot use cloud-unique services that cloud providers offer such as auto-scaling and dynamic load balancing.

DEFINITIONS

Auto-scaling is a way to automatically scale-up or down the number of computer resources that are being allocated to an application based on its needs at any given time.

*In computing, **load balancing** refers to the process of distributing a set of tasks over a set of resources, with the aim of making their overall processing more efficient.*

__Dynamic load balancing__ is the term used when load balancing is performed automatically by machines.

Lift and shift migration should be very carefully planned based on the enterprise needs, as only specific cases or applications qualify for lift and shift approach.

Shift to SaaS/Repurchase/Drop-And-Shop

Shifting to SaaS means moving applications to a cloud provider that specializes in managing those applications. Enterprises need to make this decision on a case-by-case basis, application by application, and only shift the applications they need to. Moving applications to SaaS also means that enterprises need fewer licenses for business tools. It is extremely important when shifting an application to SaaS that enterprises pick the right service and the right SaaS provider. Enterprises also need to understand the support model from the SaaS provider, especially when customizations are made to the product.

For some products a drawback of shifting to SaaS is that, while enterprises can personalize it, customizations can lead to problems. Interjectory code added to a SaaS product can cause a loss of the support and update models provided by the SaaS company. In some cases, enterprises that start shifting applications to SaaS can lose the customizations they have made on a product.

Moving applications from On-Premises to SaaS models should be carefully validated. There are products available in the market, have matured SaaS offerings and many of these products even support customizations. SAP products are one such example. Another relatively simple example of shifting to SaaS is for routine functions, email is a good example of a routine business function that can be shifted to SaaS e.g., Office 365.

Replatforming or Lift-Modify-Shift

Replatforming is essentially a variation of lift and shift, involving some further adjustments to the application that allows the benefits of a cloud environment to be utilized. Replatforming can be treated as a minor modification to the application and then hosting on cloud empowers businesses to accomplish important goals beyond rehosting, without greatly expanding the scope of the project.

In replatforming, enterprises modify applications during the migration process to take advantage of key cloud capabilities such as auto-scaling and dynamic load balancing. It could also be as sophisticated as utilizing serverless computing capabilities such as AWS Lambda for portions of the application. It may also involve using a cloud-specific data store such as Amazon S3 or DynamoDB.

DEFINITIONS

Serverless computing *is a method of providing backend services on an "as used" basis. Servers are still used, but enterprises that get backend services from a serverless vendor such as a cloud provider are charged based on usage, not a fixed amount of bandwidth or number of servers.*

*****AWS Lambda*** *is a serverless computing platform provided by Amazon as a part of Amazon Web Services.*

Amazon Simple Storage Service (Amazon S3) *is a scalable, high-speed, web-based cloud storage service designed for online backup and archiving of data and applications on Amazon Web Services.*

Amazon DynamoDB *is a fully managed database service that provides fast and predictable performance with seamless scalability.*

In the replatforming process, enterprises may make a few cloud (or other) optimizations in order to achieve some tangible benefit but are otherwise not changing the core architecture of the application.

Refactoring/Rearchitecting

A refactoring approach is driven by a strong desire to improve the product and represents the opposite to a lift and shift migration. It assumes that a specific business target will be set from the beginning e.g., in terms of availability or reliability of the application performance and that the complete applications need to be redesigned and rebuilt. Often it means that you may have to rewrite the application logic completely and develop the cloud native version from scratch.

DEFINITION

Cloud native computing *is an approach in software development that utilizes cloud computing to "build and run scalable applications in modern, dynamic environments such as public, private, and hybrid clouds."*

This is typically driven by a strong business need to add features, scale, or performance that would otherwise be difficult to achieve in the application's existing environment. Examples could be migration from a monolithic architecture to a microservices-based architecture to boost agility or improve business continuity.

Retain

Retain means doing nothing for now and leaving the application in an "as it is" state in an "as it is" location. These are applications which do not make sense from business perspective to migrate to cloud either because they are too complex to migrate, or the cost of migration is not worth the business value.

Retire

As the name indicates, retire mean applications which are not in use anymore and can be decommissioned or turned off. Several of my cloud migration experiences have shown that almost 10–12% of applications can be retired at an enterprise level.

Cloud Migration Strategy

A cloud migration is when a company moves some or all of its data center capabilities into the cloud, usually to run on the cloud-based infrastructure provided by a cloud service provider such as AWS or Azure.[2]

One of the first steps to consider before migrating to the cloud is to determine the use that the public cloud will serve. Is migrating to cloud being done to completely move out from existing data centers? Or is it for consolidating fewer data centers? Will it be used for core applications or non-core applications hosting? Or will it be for disaster recovery or development and operations (DevOps)? Will it be fully public cloud migration? Or will use hybrid cloud approach? All of these questions need to be answered to determine the cloud migration strategy.

Once we have the above answers, it is important to assess the enterprise environment and determine the factors that will govern the migration, such as critical application data, legacy data, and application interoperability. It is also necessary to determine enterprise reliance on data with two key questions: does data need to be resynced regularly? And what are the data compliance requirements? Determining these aspects will help enterprises charter a solid plan for cloud migration and the appropriate tools to be used during migration.

As an example, there are tools which will scan all IT applications in an enterprise and provide a heatmap on which applications can be moved to cloud and which cannot. These tools also provide a view on application dependencies and application complexities. CloudScape from Flexera is one such cloud assessment solution, designed to simplify the planning, costing, and execution of cloud migrations.

Another example in a data area is Azure AWS, a migration tool used to identify which data needs to be migrated (and when), if the data needs cleaning, the kind of destination volumes to use, and whether you will need encryption of the data, both at rest and in transit.

The first step in a cloud migration project is the assessment. For cloud migrations especially to public cloud, enterprises start with cloud assessments where each application within an enterprise is assessed for their portability to cloud, their connectivity with other applications, complexity of the application itself, and so on. This assessment is also typically broken down based on custom and bespoke applications to analyze which applications can go to cloud, what migration approach to be applied for each application, as well as when they should move to cloud. For enterprises that are migrating from data center to cloud, the time when an application can move to cloud is largely determined by their data center exist strategy.

Many enterprises do not have application portfolio view; neither do they have a structured configuration management database which stores information about all hardware and software assets within the enterprise. This provides an additional challenge to enterprises to arrive at their cloud migration strategy since not all applications are easily discoverable.

DEFINITIONS

A ***configuration management database*** *is used by an organization to store information about hardware and software assets.*

A ***resource*** *in cloud computing can be any service which can be consumed by cloud users or cloud consumers. It could be an OS, software, tool, or a combination.*

Bespoke software development *is an approach in which applications or other solutions are developed specifically for customer needs, unlike off-the-shelf products where applications are built for the wider audience.*

For a robust cloud migration strategy it is important to understand the level of maturity of an enterprise in terms of their applications, networks, data, and so on based on which cloud migration strategy is defined.

Another angle which many enterprises fail to understand is the side effects in a pure lift and shift or replatforming strategy. An application can undergo a pure lift and shift, but it is key to find out if the application is able to utilize the capabilities offered by a cloud provider. If applications cannot utilize the cloud capabilities such as auto-scaling or load balancing, then the benefits that enterprise can achieve from cloud migration are very minimal.

There are eight key considerations in cloud assessment to arrive at cloud strategy, which are listed below:[2]

1. Data gathering and analysis—which means creating an inventory of all applications within an enterprise and then understanding application to application interdependency and infrastructure dependency mapping. There is no one tool which can do this analysis in a fully automated way. There are areas where enterprises need to work with the application or infrastructure SME to get insights into areas where tools do not provide the information. From my own personal experience, the larger the COTS products in the IT estate of an enterprise, the larger the complexity. All such cases need to be very carefully analyzed to arrive at the treatment approach. Another area which also needs to be analyzed is version upgrades during migration, which many cloud migrations will typically undertake hand in hand.
2. Second is crunching of the data based on the analysis performed in Step 1 above to get some meaningful output on how each application or group needs to be migrated.
3. Next is the data center exit strategy. In some cases, enterprises look to consolidate data centers and in other cases enterprise want to fully exit their data centers with certain hard dates in mind. Some prefer moving to public cloud and some to a new private or hybrid cloud. The cloud migration strategy is also influenced by these considerations, both on data center migration and cloud deployment models. Moving 100% to cloud is a key ask for many enterprises these days and is one of the toughest and tedious tasks to achieve. There will be several applications within an enterprise that will not be compatible with cloud and as such refactoring is the only option for these applications.
4. The fourth key aspect that determines the success of cloud migration is assessment on connectivity and the latency requirements apart from security requirements. These factors form part of the cloud migration

strategy enabling enterprises to choose the right cloud provider based on the specific needs of the enterprises.

5. The fifth key aspect is the current version of the enterprises OS, software, and tools. Most cloud providers support only the latest version of software and OSs. However, many enterprises may not always have the latest version within their existing IT landscape. Migrating to newer versions as part of cloud migration introduces lot of risks and needs to be carefully planned out.

6. The sixth aspect is to look at external factors such as the complexity of the application. Whilst moving complex applications to cloud, enterprises need to analyze the complexity of dependencies for such applications. It is important to look at network readiness in terms of the cloud interconnect and whether the right mechanisms from the cloud provider are in place that can perform application routing based on the enterprise's specific policies and needs. If these aspects are not ready, then the migration should be delayed until after these dependent aspects have been rectified.

7. The seventh aspect is to determine the level of automation required once applications move to cloud. Enterprises can automate almost everything, starting from provisioning and deprovisioning of a cloud resource to deploying a code using DevOps pipelines or even conducting automation testing with zero human interventions. For one of the customers I worked for, automation was enabled to an extent where servers were scaled up automatically on a Monday and scaled down again on a Friday. The amount of automation required will determine the effort and price of cloud migrations, which cannot be underestimated.

DEFINITIONS

Cloud Interconnect *provides low latency and highly available connections that enable a business to reliably transfer data between On-Premises and cloud networks.*

   Dedicated Interconnect *provides a direct physical connection between On-Premises and cloud networks.*

8. The eighth aspect is to look at the multi-vendor cloud strategy. Each cloud vendor has their own merits and limitations. A careful analysis needs to be performed to understand which cloud provider is best suited for an enterprise. Many enterprises adopt a multi-vendor cloud strategy which means that more than one cloud provider is chosen

In summary, a cloud assessment output should determine:

1. Why an application should remain On-Premises. Applications with the following characteristics can remain On-Premises:
   a. Plans of decommissioning in next 6–12 months
   b. Any application falling under compliance norms that restricts its data movement
   c. An application dependent on another On-Premises application which cannot be moved to cloud
   d. Applications with licensing or support issues that mandate remaining On-Premises
2. Which applications need to be migrated using which treatment mechanism i.e., lift and shift approach, replatforming or refactoring approach
3. Whether version upgrades and tools consolidation need to happen as part of the cloud migration
4. Whether 100% movement to cloud or partial is required
5. The amount of automation required
6. The best suited cloud provider

Cloud Benefits Cannot Be Realized If It Is Not Managed Properly

There are several benefits of moving to cloud; however, the assumption that a public cloud will reduce costs compared to existing data centers, or private clouds is simply a myth. Once applications are migrated to cloud, the best cost advantages come only if cloud operations are managed well, else cloud will be as expensive as or more expensive than a data center.

Enterprises need to ensure that cloud provisioning (cloud management) is carried out in a controlled way. Cloud provisioning is the allocation of a cloud provider's resources and services to a customer. Cloud provisioning is a key feature of the cloud computing model, relating to how a customer procures cloud services and resources from the provider. Cloud providers will charge enterprises on the usage. Today, many organizations do not have proper governance for cloud provisioning which in many instances can cause cloud costs to be far higher than expected.

In one case study for ABC Hospitals, cloud provisioning was managed by developers and testers with approval from their line managers. Whenever a developer needed a new operating system or a tool, he would ask his manager who in turn would place a request with the cloud provider. Neither the developer nor the manager were aware of the costs associated with cloud and how to optimally use cloud. Due to lack of such awareness, for just one business unit out of seven within this enterprise, the cost of cloud instances increase to £120,000, and after analysis it was discovered that 50% of these instances were not being used for 90% of the time and can be decommissioned.

DEFINITIONS

*A **cloud instance** is a virtual server instance in a cloud computing environment. It is built, hosted, and delivered using a cloud computing platform, and can be accessed remotely.*

***Cloud operations** encompass the process of managing and delivering cloud services and infrastructure to either an internal or external user base. This involves ensuring peak performance and maintaining availability in order to satisfy the needs and expectations of customers, as well as meeting service level agreement standards.*

Creating and deleting of cloud instances should be dynamic and automatic. Kill an instance when it is not required, even if it is for 1 day.

For the same client in another example, moving from On-Demand to reserved instances in AWS (Amazon Web Services) reduced monthly costs by 40%.

DEFINITIONS

*An **On-Demand Instance** is a purchase of resources and capacity at a fixed rate per hour. For On-Demand Instances, enterprises pay for compute capacity by the second with no long-term commitments. There is no long-term commitment required when you purchase On-Demand Instances. However, this model can prove to be expensive than reserved instances if not managed properly.*

*A **Reserved Instance** is a reservation of resources and capacity, for a fixed duration (either 1 or 3 years). Cloud providers provide a significant discount on Reserved Instance as compared to On-Demand instance pricing.*

Cloud management is one of the critical elements required in order to keep cloud costs optimal. There are several cloud cost management and cloud spending management tools which are designed to help enterprises create detailed reports that point out what they are spending versus what they are using.[2]

Automation of policies to do basic cloud management is the need for many organizations to achieve maximum cost benefits from cloud provisioning. However, at many places this is still manual which causes many enterprises to bleed on cloud management costs. Tools such as Redhat, cloudForms, and RightScale can do the job.

Choosing the right service provider for cloud hosting based on the kind of work performed is essential to benefit from moving to cloud. As an example, for enterprises working on Microsoft technologies, it makes sense to go for Microsoft Azure as their cloud provider, as Microsoft will offer huge discounts if the organization is already using their technologies.

As a number of multi-cloud providers are growing, they form a competitive market that strives to offer optimal pricing for different resource capacities whilst remaining attractive to the majority of cloud users. This is known as multi-vendor cloud strategy. With this in mind, organizations should enjoy the freedom of comparing different providers and securing the best available rates based on their specific IT needs.

Since enterprises are not restricted to any single cloud provider's terms, they can select the best vendor based on its offerings such as payment flexibility, adjustable contracts, customizable capacity, and other important elements. Multi-vendor cloud strategy is not only cheaper, but also it overcomes the traditional problem of vendor lock-in.

Manual multi-cloud management process is another major area where cost leakages are certain to happen if not planned correctly. To automate the task and optimize costs, enterprises need a robust multi-cloud management platform. The rising need for adoption of multi-cloud management platform makes it important for enterprises to ensure that they automate the multi-cloud management process to effectively coordinate disparate applications, manage hybrid workflows, and integrate processes across multiple cloud providers. Automation ensures efficient orchestration of data, applications, and infrastructure across multiple cloud environments. Tools such as Flexera (RightScale) Cloud Management Platform can do the job.

Preparing to Migrate to Cloud—The Eight-Step Cloud Migration Checklist

It is essential to know that a cloud migration program is not as simple as many think, and only well-planned cloud migrations have seen the light of success. There are essentially eight key areas where enterprises need to focus for cloud migrations as depicted in Figure 6.2.

Right Planning

Migrations need to start without a clearly defined, well-researched, and coherent strategy. The first step in creating a robust functional plan for cloud migration is to examine the current infrastructure.

An organization needs to look at how they work now and think about what applications and which parts of their infrastructure need to move to the cloud. Having a master inventory of all applications is an important element in planning a cloud migration deal.

It is essential that a master inventory list is prepared during the start of an engagement at an accuracy level of at least 90%.

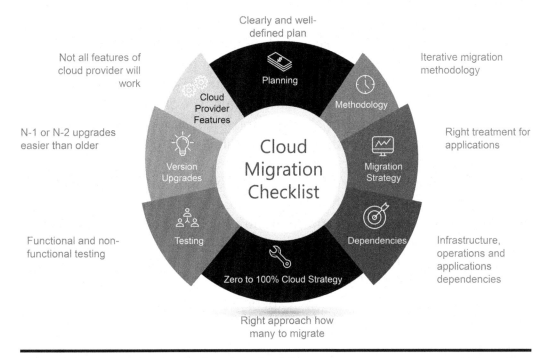

Figure 6.2 Eight-step cloud migration checklist

The organization needs to be thorough in preparing the master inventory list or use a tool to prepare the inventory. Missing dependencies at this stage can cause major issues during migration. It also needs to be considered whether any parts of the infrastructure will need to be integrated with other services. A note of all current KPIs should be made, such as page load times, CPU usage, and memory used percentages. Targets should also be set for improvement post migration.

A reasonable timeline needs to be created for migration to take place, considering any significant "buffer" time to account for any deviations or roadblocks. It also needs to be considered how applications will be migrated and which ones need to be rearchitected.

Too many system integration service providers or even cloud providers claim that cloud migration is as simple as dragging an application from data center servers and "dropping" it into the cloud. This is the biggest mistake that can be made during cloud migration. Lift and shift is not a silver bullet to cloud migration.

Typically for many enterprises I have worked for in cloud migration, I have seen that 40–50% of the applications fall under replatforming (upgrade to latest software or OS version and migrate), 20% fall under refactoring, with the rest into other categories. Only a very small portion qualifies for lift and shift. The only reason when lift and shift can be embarked on a large scale is when data center exit dates determine a cloud strategy, but this is a very risky approach and can only be carried out for very specific applications. As an example, I have come across an enterprise which has 2 months to exit a specific data center and because of this 70% of their applications were to be migrated using a lift and shift approach. However, since these were not core applications with no major scalability or availability requirements, the risk to the enterprise was minimal.

Cloud migration for the integration layer (integration transformation) is another major challenge which needs to be carefully planned. As an example, in one of my experiences, moving from IBM Web methods to Mulesoft was a mammoth activity since we had to understand functional specs for transformation, which is not an easy task.

Enterprises need to understand that a big bang deployment will ultimately be a recipe for failure. Based on my experience, applications need to be migrated to cloud every month (if not every week) in an iterative manner instead of waiting for a big bang deployment.

Dependencies between applications need to be carved out and dependent applications need to be moved to cloud in one shot.

Application groups need to be formed where dependent applications are identified and moved from On-Premises to cloud in one go (known as cut over). Out of half of dozen cloud migrations program I have led, there was never a single instance where we had a big bang deployment. This indicates that although there may be several dependencies between every application, the possibility of iterative deployment is always an option. It is just that dependencies need to be well thought out, and deployment plans need to be clearly defined.

Non-functional requirements need to be well planned before embarking on a cloud journey.

One needs to understand that not many applications will have performance benchmarks. A clear baseline needs to be set for each application on performance during the planning stage. Performance issues case arise most of the time for replatforming and lift and shift type of migrations. Despite best efforts, enterprises are still likely to run into application performance issues after the migration has been completed. Since cloud platforms inherently reduce IT team's level of direct application control, before putting applications on cloud enterprises need to ensure they have the right network and application monitoring tools in place, before and after migration. Enterprises will otherwise be reliant on cloud providers to troubleshoot performance problems resulting in an increased number of tickets and a loss of productivity from lagging support response times.

Third party dependencies are another critical element that needs to be considered during the planning phase, and each dependency should have a plan to address. As an example for third party tools, support considerations need to be planned before migration.

Enterprises need to ensure that BAU projects do not come in the way of migration. As an example, new functionality may be added to an application which are planned to migrate to cloud with a replatforming approach. This may have a major impact on the timeliness and state of the application post migration since new features will not be part of the migrated application. Change management is one of the key aspects to be instilled in a cloud migration program, allowing cross team changes to be managed well.

Execution Methodology (Iterative Cloud Migration Factory)

It is essential for a cloud migration project that success results are demonstrated as early as possible so that business confidence is built. It is also essential that initial failures of migrations are retrospected and learning is applied in the next iteration of application migration. This is one of the key reasons why Iterative (Agile) methodology becomes essential for any cloud migration program.

An agile cloud migration factory approach breaks down the planning, execution, and optimization of a cloud migration into a series of iterations. Each iteration focuses on a specific set of applications and elements of the migration, with strong checks and balances at every stage. At the end of each iteration applications should be up and running on the cloud in production or production like environment. All steps, from blueprinting to migration and testing to data transfer, are performed within each iteration with a fail-fast approach to expedite transition to the cloud platform whilst improving migration quality from one iteration to another.

Typically, applications are classified into COTS Apps or Bespoke Apps, and based on the complexity and dependency on other applications, iteration needs to be formed. Each iteration is a collection of dependent applications for migration. The initial 2–3 iterations need to be with applications which are easy to migrate and can run on the cloud environment with minimal application to application dependencies i.e., standalone applications. Success from these iterations will help to build business confidence. After the first 2–3 iterations it is essential that medium to complex applications are planned for migrations. Many enterprises make the mistake of choosing to migrate all simple applications in the initial iterations and park complex ones for later. This introduces a significant risk in cloud migration programs as continuous learning needs to be applied from initial iterations to make subsequent iterations migration successful. It is therefore essential that a combination of simple, medium, and complex applications are picked in each iteration.

Migration Strategy/Approach

The lift and shift approach, replatforming, and refactoring are all popular methods of shifting applications to the cloud, and each has its place in migration strategy.

Many enterprises opt for the lift and shift approach, since it looks to be the fastest and least disruptive model and typically costs less. This works only in theory and many cloud migrations have failed, because of this assumption.

There will be several legacy applications within an organization which may not be fit to move to cloud. There may be several bespoke

applications that can move to cloud with a lift and shift approach but they will hit several performance bottlenecks. A careful analysis and proof of concept should be created to ensure these applications can work on cloud before migration.

The key to arriving at a reasonable cloud migration approach is by considering which cloud migration strategy will fit for each application. Some applications may need to be refactored, some may need to be replatformed, and some can undergo pure lift and shift. The efforts and timelines for each of these migrations will be determined not only by the cloud migration strategy but also by the complexity of each application.

Estimating the size of migration is an essential element of cloud migration success. Migration strategy for each application plays a major role.

The other aspect to be considered while estimating cloud projects is not only the number of applications that need to be migrated but how many servers, how much data (gigabytes, terabytes), and how many database and interfaces need to be migrated.

There are several tool vendors that promise automatic deployment to cloud. Some tool vendors also promise automatic data migration from On-Premises to Cloud. A one fit solution from these vendors does not fit cloud migrations and has led several cloud migrations to fail.

As an example for one of our clients, we planned AWS Snowball to move data from a datacenter to cloud but this did not work out since there were several security considerations that did not allow us to use this tool. In another example, AWS Database Migration Service (DMS) worked quite well for migrating data from On-Premises to the cloud for large data sets. Whenever AWS DMS was unable to do the job, manual data migration was performed.

Application Dependencies

Migrating application with dependencies is one of the major challenges during cloud migration programs.

Migration would be easy if it only involved applications not talking to each other, but unfortunately this is not the case. The supportive services and dependencies that applications have on each other complicate the process since the application environment is a connected mesh of interdependencies. Without its supportive ecosystem, an application will not operate correctly. Service dependency mapping goes far beyond the mere inventory of application or grouping and is no small undertaking.

Infrastructure, operations, and applications form the three key layers which organizations must consider when migrating, and dependencies between these layers can cause a range of complications if left unresolved and unplanned. For example, migrating an application that relies on operational management by an On-Premises system can cause serious performance issues if not planned properly.

Currently, 42% of enterprises moving critical applications to the cloud experience latency between On-Premises and cloud applications following their migration.[5] In extreme cases, applications fail to work entirely and have to be brought back to the data center which is again an expensive and time-consuming operation.

A careful analysis needs to be performed on each application and their dependencies need to be carved out for cloud migration planning. Tools such as Cloudscape from Flexera can carve out these application dependencies. Thought these tools provide the initial insights, manual analysis needs to be performed in order to arrive at the migration approach.

Zero to 100% Cloud Approach[3]

Cloud migrations can go awry not only because of how enterprises decide to make the move, but also what they choose to shift to the cloud.

Although cloud vendors have worked hard to make the switch to cloud computing as seamless as possible, migration is still a huge undertaking, requiring a lot of time, effort, and money. With that in mind, it is not always the best option to go from On-Premises to 100% cloud in one big bang way. In one of my experience for a large telecommunication company, the organization wanted to move to cloud from their existing data centers. Service provider A came in and proposed an 8-month program where all their applications will be moved to cloud in a big bang approach. After 6 months, the program was terminated because applications were moved to cloud but 60% of them had performance issues and 20% of them were not working the way they should. I took over this engagement in the 7th month and gave a plan for Data Center consolidation first and then a phase wise migration to cloud which was a complete 2-year program. Twenty-five data centers with more than 50,000 applications were consolidated to 12 data centers in a 1-year duration and in parallel applications were migrated to cloud in an iterative approach. Finally, after 2 years only data center was retained with

400 applications and rest all applications were migrated to cloud or retired. In 1 year, $200 million savings were achieved by the client due to DC consolidation and in just over 2 years Opex cost was reduced by 50% due to cloud migration.

Often, businesses can get swept up by the transformative promises of the cloud and take an across-the-board or 100% cloud approach to migration. The reality is that not everything has to be moved at once. Not every application, process, or pillar of infrastructure is a candidate for cloud migration. Some workloads just are not a good fit or are incredibly tricky to migrate.

An enterprise needs to kickoff their migration planning by analyzing their current usage and determining which applications are worth relocating to cloud and which functions best fit On-Premises or can be retired.

Testing

Testing is an extremely vital step toward a cloud migration strategy which many fail to understand. Often, organizations think that since moving to cloud is a migration activity, testing will be an easy job.

Testing is vital at every stage of a migration plan, allowing the organization to spot any potential issues at the earliest possible stage. The more enterprises test and weed out problems early on, the smoother migration will go. Many cloud migration programs fail to extensively or adequately test before and after migrating their entire infrastructure and applications to the cloud.

DEFINITION

Regression test suite *is the set of test scenarios that are designed to ensure that software is accurate and correct after undergoing corrections or changes.*

Many enterprises have applications built years ago and lack proper documentation or regression test suites that would cover end-to-end functional tests. Because of this gap, once an application moves to cloud, there is no guarantee that all functions within the application will work the same way as in the past and if it will be possible to test all functionalities in totality. A thorough function test strategy should be devised, application by application to ensure correct functional testing is performed on working of the application after migrating to cloud. Another challenge which is common across cloud migrations projects are scalability and performance issues which are an essential part to be planned pre migration to cloud, and tested post migration.

Version Upgrades

Version upgrades during cloud migration can also be a costly affair if not planned properly. As discussed earlier, many software and tools do not support cloud on older versions and in such cases it becomes imperative to upgrade to a cloud compatible version.

As a guidance, moving from N-1 or N-2 version to N version is always easier with less compatibility and migration issues. For sake of clarity, N-1 version is the previous version to N version and N-2 is the previous version to N-1. An example for SQL Server, N version could be SQL Server 2012, SQL Server 2008 R2 would be N-1, and SQL Server 2008 would be N-2 version.

This is one of the important considerations during the estimation of a cloud migration program. The older the existing version is, the larger the migration efforts will be to move to the latest version.

There are tools available in the market which perform version upgrades and migrate to cloud at the same time. As an example, RiverMeadow Cloud Migration Platform migrates workloads to AWS and at the same time, upgrades from older Windows 2008 environments to the latest version of Windows, or a version in between. Not every software or tool can be migrated automatically, and as such a careful investigation needs to be performed on version upgrades during cloud migration.

Cloud Provider Features (Not All Features of Cloud Provider Will Work)

Almost all cloud providers have their own tools for performing operations and maintenance of the application and infrastructure deployed on cloud, but in many cases not all these tools fit the enterprises requirements.

Many enterprises assume that once they move to cloud, all capabilities provided by a cloud provider can be utilized. This is not correct. Enterprises need to understand that features provided by the cloud provider would not be a direct fit and in such instances out of box functionality or tools need to be deployed on the cloud environment to meet the enterprise needs. As an example for one of my clients named WWW Financials, after their applications were moved to cloud, monitoring and backup services provided by the cloud vendor did not fit the client needs and for this client third party tools were deployed—in this case AWS snapshot was replaced with Commvault backup. Similarly, the monitoring of tools provided by the cloud provider (in this case AWS) did not suffice the enterprise need, and hence they had to go with Neusoft tool.

Case Study

One case study we will discuss is for a large insurance client who I worked for in 2015 called ABC Insurance. ABC Insurance wanted to perform a big bang exit from their existing data centers to cloud and the demand from the client was a 100% migration to cloud on Azure in a big bang way. We had limited experience in such large-scale migrations during this time. We underestimated the complexity of the migration as a service provider for which we had to pay a price which was 700% more than what we had estimated. I still remember the sales pitch which was "no touch migration." No touch migration was the term used during the sales cycle to indicate to our client that we can migrate applications to cloud with just click of a button or with very minimal changes. Once applications move to cloud it will work seamlessly meeting or exceeding all the nonfunctional requirements such as performance and scalability; this was the biggest mistake we made in this program. In my experience working on several cloud engagements in last few years, I have come across very few instances where applications can move directly to cloud in a lift and shift model and still perform the same way as it was performing in the past on the On-Premises data center.

Another area we underestimated was on COTS applications migration to cloud. Although many COTS provide assure migration to cloud with minimal changes, the amount of customization made on the products, non-functional requirements and connectivity to other applications determine the complexity of the migration. It is essential that each of the COTS applications are tested via pilots first on specific platforms before deciding the migration strategy, else it may lead failed projects.

Notes

1. "ITIL® V3 Foundation Course Glossary" (PDF).
2. Venkatesh Upadrista. (29 Jun. 2017). The Art of Consultative Selling in IT: Taking Blue Ocean Strategy a Step Ahead Hardcover.
3. Venkatesh Upadrista. (15 Dec. 2014). Managing Your Outsourced IT Services Provider: How to Unleash the Full Potential of Your Global Workforce Paperback.
4. https://www.fortinet.com/content/dam/fortinet/assets/analyst-reports/ar-2019-ihsm-fortinet-wp-q2.pdf
5. Virtustream, New Study: General Purpose Cloud Migration Playbook Falls Short when Moving Mission Critical Workloads, 2017.

Chapter 7

SAP Cloud Migration

With disruption on digital in the market almost all enterprises and legacy technologies are undergoing transformation. SAP is an area which is also not immune to such an impact and the benefits from digital transformation are quite enormous for enterprises. More specifically SAP on Cloud is becoming very prevalent in the market due to the cost advantages that public Cloud providers provide for SAP workloads.

In majority of the cases SAP runs mission critical processes where there is a massive demand for high availability, reliability, and performance, without which SAP workloads cannot really work. Digital transformation for SAP in context of this chapter is about SAP migration to Cloud.

SAP migrations are mission critical, hence they should be done within a specified timeframe with the minimum risk and maximum flexibility. This brings in great financial gains because there is a huge decrease in operating expenses and a reduction in the usage of infrastructure. However, it is very important for enterprises to carefully plan the migration else they end up paying more money after migration, rather than a good return on investment.

When migrating SAP applications to the Cloud, deciding on the right time is crucial. Some of the factors to determine the timing for SAP migration to Cloud could be:

- New product release—migrations are best suited when new products are being launched or new SAP modules are being added to existing stack.

■ Mergers and acquisitions—one of the most common time when SAP Cloud migrations happen is during mergers and demergers or acquisitions.

■ Contract renewal or end of life—end of life means a certain product will not be support by SAP anymore which means end of support and customers will no longer receive any updates, security, or otherwise.

■ Hardware refresh—hardware refresh happens whenever enterprises plan to move to new versions of hardware due to limitations on current hardware.

■ Embarking on the S/4HANA journey—many enterprises today have made plans to move to S/4HANA. SAP S/4HANA's primary differentiator is its unique architecture which is quite a contrast from the classic relational database. It runs in-memory, with data stored in columns, allowing for faster, near to real-time analytics and compute capabilities. We are going to discuss about S/4HANA in detail in subsequent sections.

■ Service provider consolidation—for enterprises that are operating with multiple vendors with infrastructure managed by one vendor and applications management by other; vendor consolidation provides the right opportunity to move SAP applications to Cloud.

A workload in Cloud terms is a distinct capacity or work function on a Cloud instance. It can be an application, a Web server, a database, an operating system among other things.

System conversion also known as the Brownfield approach enables migration to SAP S/4HANA without re-implementation and without disrupting the existing Business Processes.

Greenfield approach is a new implementation starting from scratch. Greenfield is perfect for companies new to SAP, if they are moving their data over from a non-SAP system.

SAP HANA supports multiple isolated databases in a single SAP HANA system. These are referred to as **Tenant Databases**. A SAP HANA system is capable of containing more than one tenant database.

High availability disaster recovery, or HADR, is a database replication method that provides a high-availability solution for both partial and complete site failures. With HADR, data from a primary database is replicated to the standby database, which is essentially a clone of the primary.

Software as a service is a software licensing and delivery model in which software is licensed on a subscription basis and is centrally hosted.

A **solid-state drive (SSD)** is a solid-state storage device that uses integrated circuit assemblies to store data persistently, typically using flash memory, and functioning as secondary storage.

Elastic Block Store (EBS) volume is a durable, block-level storage device that can be attached to devices and is much cheaper than SSD.

The term business **downtime** is used to refer to periods when a system is unavailable for business users.

A Bit of Background about ECC to Suite on HANA to S/4HANA

SAP ERP Central Component (ECC) is the previous generation of SAP enterprise resource planning software. ECC provides modules covering a full range of industry applications, including finance, logistics, HR, product planning, and customer service, linked together into a single, customizable system that use to run on a database of the user's choice.

SAP ECC was succeeded by SAP S/4HANA which is SAP's in-memory database. Since most companies were using ECC before HANA was introduced, they were running on a database built by other companies such as Oracle. SAP S/4HANA is what SAP calls their "next generation business suite." It is intended to replace SAP ECC and was designed expressly to work with SAP HANA database. Running SAP S/4HANA on HANA is the most current and innovative way to run an enterprise, as per SAP.[1]

SAP has traditionally been an On-Premises version of the software. With the adoption of Cloud gaining popularity, SAP has adapted to the Cloud computing revolution. There are several challenges with On-Premises version of SAP which Cloud version has mitigated, some which are listed below:

■ The first challenge with an On-Premises approach is that the infrastructure required to scale SAP services takes weeks or sometimes months. As an example, couple of years back, I was working for a large bank named Bank X where they were trying to implement the SAP disclosure Management module. Bank X requirements were so unique that we had to work with SAP directly to develop the module, and on the other hand work with the Bank X on their customized requirements. Since this module was being developed from scratch, infrastructure requirements were also very unique and after receiving recommendation from SAP, the Bank X procured the required infrastructure. Bank X was operating in a traditional Data Centre model where new infrastructure procurement takes minimum of 1–2 months. During development and testing phase, the application started throwing peak loads and then we realized that the SAP proposed infrastructure will not be adequate to cater to the project needs and since we realized this too late in the implementation, the project go live was delayed by more than 2 months. Had it been SAP on the Cloud platform, the time to scale up new environment would have been just in few hours and this is agility and speed almost every enterprise is now looking for.

■ The other key challenge with on-premises version of SAP is that the infrastructure utilization is not optimal and cost effective. Almost all On-Premises SAP landscapes are provisioned for peak capacity, but peak capacity only happens for example around weekends or quarter end or month ends. With this kind of set-up for most of the time the underlying infrastructure is grossly underutilized. For example, a payroll run starts around 5 days before month end and finishes 2 days after month start which are the peak periods where SAP infrastructure is utilized to the maximum. What this means is that peak infrastructure is utilized only 7 days in a month and rest of the time it remains underutilized. However, with on-premises versions enterprises are forced to retain the full peak infrastructure through the life of the application. With SAP on Cloud, Cloud providers have defined commercial models that offer a true consumption-based or on-demand pricing which unlocks enterprises from legacy constructs where they had fixed CapEx and OpEx costs. Enterprises can procure new infrastructure during peak periods and release it during non-peak periods, which provides massive cost savings to enterprises. Apart from infrastructure, SAP investments are always very expensive such as license cost which are required to operate the SAP landscapes. Cloud providers provide on demand allocation of new licenses which reduces the costs significantly.

■ The other two reasons of moving to Cloud is that security and compliant requirements are taken care directly by the Cloud provider and enterprises need not worry as they had been in the past when they were on the traditional Data Centre or On-Premises platforms.

■ Usage of multi-Cloud strategy in SAP landscape is another reason why SAP on Cloud is becoming very popular. There are SAP applications that can go on one public Cloud and others can remain On-Premises or move to a second Cloud provider.

From the discussion above it is very evident that enterprises can overcome several shortfalls that exist with On-Premises version of SAP by migrating to Cloud. Below listed some of the key benefits of moving to Cloud:

■ Pay for what you use with consumption-based pricing. As an example, add 10 app servers 7 days before month end for the monthly payroll run. Turn them off on Day +3.

■ Spin up new SAP environment when you need and release them down when not required. As an example, increase compute and storage capacity to support new SAP products when you need them or turn on new severs for the overnight batch and then turn it off when not required.

■ Achieve cost effective HADR plans by paying for what you use. Almost all enterprises that run SAP On-Premises that I have come across have created HADR environments which are hardly utilized, and enterprises incur lot of costs. With Cloud, enterprises can optimize those capital expenses much better on public Cloud platforms.

■ Decrease time to market for procuring new capabilities. With SAP on Cloud any new service or workload can be procured in minutes.

■ Rollback to a clean and precise test system in just couple of hours with no BASIS effort—typically in an On-Premises environment it takes lot of efforts by the SAP Basis team to roll back systems to the original state after testing is performed. Cloud providers have automated this step and enterprises can rollback to a clean and precise test system in 60–90 minutes.

Initially SAP stayed away from public Cloud providers like Amazon Web Services (AWS) and Microsoft Azure because of several reasons including SAP wanting to have larger portions of the infrastructure revenues to themselves. However, with the popularity and benefits Cloud providers offer, SAP has embraced the Cloud technology and started offering several distinct options for enterprises that want to run some or all of their SAP landscapes on the Cloud. These include SAP Cloud platform, SAP S/4HANA Cloud as Software as a Service (SaaS), The SAP HANA Enterprise Cloud (HEC) and public Cloud hosting of SAP (e.g., on AWS).

The SAP Cloud Platform

The SAP Cloud platform is not an ERP suite on the Cloud. Rather, it is a Platform as a Service (PaaS) offering designed around SAP development.[1] It provides valuable tools for development and customization of HANA landscapes.

SAP Cloud platform can also play a crucial role in the SAP Cloud migration and upgrade processes. For example, by using the SAP Cloud PaaS, developers and SAP admins can extend the capabilities of their SAP legacy applications into the Cloud. It also allows developers to build applications without requiring an investment in a HANA landscape.

SAP S/4HANA Cloud

The SAP S/4HANA Cloud is a SaaS solution that consists of a range of industry-specific offerings. These include manufacturing, professional services, and financial services. SAP S/4HANA is a full-blown, heavy-duty enterprise class ERP solution and business suite. It can run On-Premises and in variety of private and hybrid Cloud architectures at massive scale. S/4HANA Cloud is a more limited service that is best suited to small-to-medium businesses (SMBs).

SAP S/4HANA Cloud does not need a lot of customization, nor can it offer much. It is SaaS, so it is quite cheaper than an On-Premises version. SAP performs maintenance and governance tasks like applying patches and upgrades. At the same time, SAP S/4HANA Cloud has limitations. It only supports Greenfield implementations, meaning there is no upgrade path that will get enterprises from your existing SAP landscape. You have to start from scratch. Nor does it support all countries and languages that the On-Premises version of S/4HANA does. Additionally, S/4HANA Cloud cannot run in a private Cloud or hybrid environment. It does not support third-party software or custom code either.[1]

The SAP HANA Enterprise Cloud (HEC)

SAP HEC is a scalable and secure private Cloud. SAP runs HEC, hosting it for enterprises out of their own Data Centre facilities. HEC consists of the two upper tiers of the S/4HANA service. The S/4HANA Cloud Private

Option, the lower of these tiers, is a standardized SAP private Cloud. They can be hosted in whatever language, country, or region. They have the whole range of HANA functionality, and share responsibility for governance with software buyers just like in a standard S/4HANA landscape. The Private Option does have a few limits, though.

- It lacks the ability to do a "brownfield migration"
- Tenants must build a new landscape from scratch
- Modifications of the software, such as custom code, are also not allowed

The top tier, the Custom HEC removes all these limitations. Enterprises gain the ability to migrate their existing landscapes (the brownfield approach) and modify their S/4HANA solution in whatever way they see fit. The drawback of this tier is the price. As a SAP-managed, fully customizable solution, it's generally only going to be an option for companies with roughly $1 billion annual revenue or more.

SAP on the Public Cloud

SAP initially did not offer public Cloud hosting for providers like AWS and Microsoft Azure claiming various reasons such as public Cloud was not known for strong performance. However, almost all public Cloud providers, such as AWS and Azure, now offer full SAP services on Cloud. These include choices for high-performing, dedicated hardware along with well-tuned instances of SAP software hosted in the public Cloud on demand. Inline to the SAP public Cloud journey, SAP introduce the SAP embrace initiative.

SAP Embrace Initiative

SAP embrace is an initiative by SAP that helps enterprises to move from On-Premises toward public Clouds. In October 2019, SAP and Microsoft announced Project Embrace—"a go-to-market partnership to help customers adopt S/4HANA and SAP Cloud platform on Microsoft Azure."

SAP Embrace is formed around the following key pillars:

- Market Approved Journey—this initiative is to demonstrate that SAP on Cloud has been successful for several enterprises; therefore, other enterprises can safely move their SAP workloads to Cloud.

- Reference Architecture—means that there is a proven Cloud hosting architecture which enterprises can leverage after moving to public Clouds. These architectures were jointly prepared by SAP and public Cloud providers such as Microsoft.
- Digital Business Services—as part of the embrace initiative SAP provides profession services support for enterprises that desire to move to public Cloud providers, be it AWS or Azure or Google Cloud.

SAP embrace initiative works with all the three Cloud providers (AWS, Azure, and Google) but the preferred partner for SAP at the moment is Microsoft Azure.

Point of View (POV) on Different Cloud Providers

May enterprises have still not finalized their public Cloud partner of choice for their SAP workloads and almost all Cloud providers such as AWS, Google Cloud, and Microsoft Azure have been trying to capture market share with several offers. In terms of sheer market share what I had noticed is that AWS has maintained a large share of more than 40% followed by Azure and Google. In terms of technical ability to support the SAP workloads, all three now are equal. However, AWS has been first in many aspects, as an example:

- It was the first public Cloud platform, which was certified for HANA.
- AWS was the first to bring the concept of regions and Availability Zones, which is very important when it comes to hosting actually disaster recovery architectures for SAP workloads. Amazon Cloud computing resources are hosted in multiple locations worldwide. These locations are composed of AWS Regions, Availability Zones, and Local Zones. Each AWS Region is a separate geographic area. Each AWS Region has multiple, isolated locations known as Availability Zones.

In terms of some technical differences over the past few years, my experience is that storage solutions are more expensive when it comes to Azure, as compared to AWS, and storage is cheapest on Google when it comes to SAP landscapes.

From Google Cloud perspective they are the third entrants to support SAP on Cloud. However, they have come out with some very strong Cloud acceleration programs, especially for SAP workloads to attract customer. As an example one Google proposition says that if enterprises are ready to spend a minimum of USD 3 million over a 3-year period, then Google will invest back at least a third of the amount which further can be used to fund the migration programs for the enterprise. Further, Google also promises that hosting price will be discounted till the point of the production go live for the first 12 months. So, if you go live in the first 12 months you will have free hosting for these 12 months.

SAP Cloud Migration Strategy

Moving SAP solutions to the Cloud is a complicated and crucial process implying the transition of data, applications, and technologies from the company's local infrastructure to a remotely managed platform. Cloud migration for SAP becomes quite complex if right treatment is not applied on the applications. Below are some of the key treatment mechanisms that can be applied for SAP landscape.

Homogeneous System Copy

One point that comes up every time during SAP migration is about whether a homogeneous system copy is allowed in the case of a database or operating system upgrade.

Homogeneous Export/Import also called as Homogeneous System copy is performed when source and target platforms are the same (although perhaps on different releases or versions). If you are upgrading your operating system, for instance, from Windows Server 2003 to Windows Server 2012 R2, you are not changing your operating system platform. Therefore, this remains a homogeneous system copy. If you are upgrading your database platform, for instance, from SQL Server 2005 to SQL Server 2012, you are not changing your database platform, and so, again, this is a homogeneous system copy. With homogenous system copy, upgrades are possible during the migration process.

Refer to Figure 7.1 and it is evident that with Homogeneous Export/ Import efforts, complexity, and risks are quite low, and therefore is considered the best Cloud migration strategy during Cloud migrations.

	Migration Effort	Downtime	Cost	Migration Complexity	Risk to Business
1 Homogeneous System Copy	Low	Low	Low	Low	Low
2 Heterogeneous System Copy	Medium	Medium	Low	Medium	Low
3 Heterogeneous Migrate to SAP HANA	High	Low	High	High	Medium
4 Near Zero Down Time (NZDT)	High	Low	High	High	Medium
5 Conversion for S/4HANA	High	Medium	High	High	Medium

Figure 7.1 SAP migration approaches and their complexities

Heterogeneous System Copy

Heterogeneous system copy is performed when source and target platforms are different. Enterprises perform a heterogeneous system copy if they are changing operating system, database platform, or both i.e., from Unix to Windows or Oracle to SQL Server or migrating to HANA. Another example is when enterprises are on legacy operating systems for example, a Unix platform. Unix platform cannot run on Cloud, and therefore Heterogeneous system copy is the solution.

Heterogeneous Migrate to SAP HANA

Heterogeneous migrate to SAP HANA is performed when enterprises move from ECC version of SAP to SAP HANA. The source and target platforms are different, and therefore it is called as Heterogeneous Migration.

SAP Near Zero Downtime (NZDT)

Minimizing the business downtime is an important part of planning and executing SAP ERP upgrade projects. With NZDT approach the downtime for software upgrade to SAP S/4HANA and migration to Cloud can be minimized. SAP's Software Update Manager (SUM) SP4 is a tool that is equipped with downtime minimizing features that enables minimize the business downtime which occurs while applying Support Packages, installing an Enhancement Package or during upgradations of a SAP system. However, NZDT is quite an expensive option and need to be implemented on a case-by-case basis.

System Conversion for S/4HANA

There are several approaches to Cloud migration, and system conversion is by far the most common within the industry and becoming more popular as the tooling support matures. This methodology is applied when enterprises do not have any major process changes (re-engineering) to make to their SAP system. A system conversion transforms application layer, along with the DB and OS layers. The process may involve extensive changes to the way current SAP landscape is run and managed. The new and upgraded system will likely have greater automation, and may require different competencies than On-Premises legacy system. Brownfield migration is the most common path for a SAP Cloud migration from ECC to S/4HANA.

S/4HANA conversion journey divides into pre-conversion, conversion, and post-conversion phases. In pre-conversion phase, enterprises perform all pre-steps which are required to start conversion. This will help to find any issue in early phase of project. During conversion, systems are converted to new world of SAP S/4HANA. The actual conversion can be performed with SAP's SUM tool. SUM performs execution part including Database migration (DMO) and SAP S/4HANA conversion.

And final phase is post-conversion, where follow-up activities are performed to make sure enterprises can get maximum use of SAP S/4HANA. As an example, enterprises need to look at which Business Processes can be optimized on SAP HANA database to provide maximum performance.

Now these are some typical migration approaches which enterprises always leveraged when it comes to moving SAP to public Clouds.

Figure 7.1 provides a view on the efforts and migration complexity of each of the migration's strategies described above. In majority of my experience Approach 1, Approach 2, and Approach 3 were most widely used for SAP migration to Cloud.

There are several tools existing in the market for successful implementations and migrations of SAP. There are tools that help to reduce manual tasks by more than 60%. As an example, AWS and Azure have their own set of tools for Cloud migration and management.

Key Considerations for SAP Migration to the Public Cloud

2020 has been the hallmark year and there is a sharp increase in the number of customers moving on "SAP running on Cloud platform." SAP migration to Cloud is not a simple exercise and should be carefully planned. The nine key areas where 70% of the enterprises overlook during their SAP migration planning are depicted in Figure 7.2.

Operating system (OS) and Database strategy needs to be formalized—there are several enterprises that think they want to leverage existing OS and Database licenses. However, it is very important to know that using existing licenses on Cloud can many times increase the cost as compared to in the past. As an example running Oracle on public Cloud is an expensive proposition as far as SAP is concerned, purely because the license count typically doubles for Oracle licenses. In such cases it is beneficial for enterprises to adopt something like a Sybase or a HANA database, which is far cheaper as compared to Oracle.

Without clearly outlining the DB and the OS strategy, it is impossible to reap the benefits by moving to public Cloud platform.

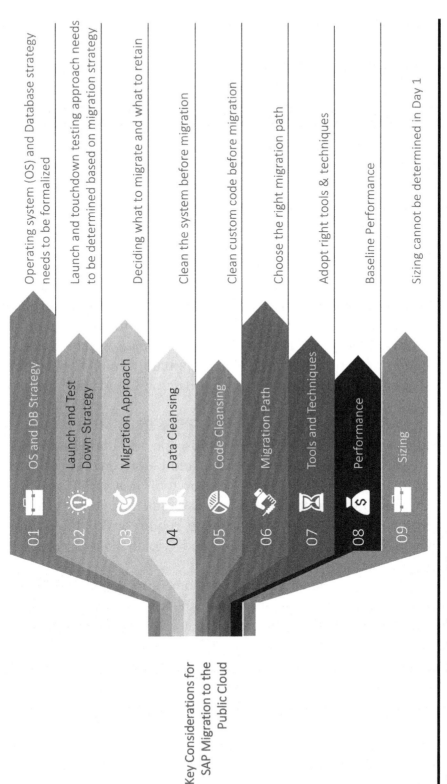

Figure 7.2 SAP migration key considerations

Key Considerations for SAP Migration to the Public Cloud

01 OS and DB Strategy — Operating system (OS) and Database strategy needs to be formalized

02 Launch and Test Down Strategy — Launch and touchdown testing approach needs to be determined based on migration strategy

03 Migration Approach — Deciding what to migrate and what to retain

04 Data Cleansing — Clean the system before migration

05 Code Cleansing — Clean custom code before migration

06 Migration Path — Choose the right migration path

07 Tools and Techniques — Adopt right tools & techniques

08 Performance — Baseline Performance

09 Sizing — Sizing cannot be determined in Day 1

Launch and touchdown testing approach needs to be determined based on migration strategy—Many SAP solutions are running on legacy operating system and database combinations that are unavailable on public Cloud. In other words, there is no opportunity to "lift and shift" all such applications. Instead, enterprises must change the operating system and/or database of the SAP solution, which impacts how it runs and requires additional testing. This can contribute significantly to the migration timeline and costs of the overall effort.

Deciding what to migrate and what to retain—SAP workloads are not easier to migrate as there are several SAP legacy flavors. Not all versions of SAP can directly be moved to Cloud, and a thorough analysis needs to be performed on workloads that can move to Cloud.

It is important to clean the data before migration—Many enterprises have accrued massive amounts of SAP data, some of which they seldom use. Inconsistent source data, corrupted or missing data, and unreadable data formats can introduce lot of complexities during SAP migration to the public Cloud, if not planned properly. It is important to cleanse, archive, and purge data to reduce data anomalies and, more importantly, minimize the time and labor costs to move, maintain, and support data on Cloud after migration that does not add value.

Cleaning custom code before migration is essential—Enterprises will find custom code in almost every SAP landscape and during every migration such custom codes need to be eliminated before enterprises can move their SAP workload to Cloud. There are tools that can be used (prior to the conversion) to perform a technical assessment to identify, analyze, and categorize the custom code adjustments required. Few tools automatically correct majority of key custom code violations to accelerate the conversion project.

Choosing the right migration strategy—Some applications can be homogeneously migrated while some applications need to undergo Heterogeneous system copy. Choosing the right migration path is very critical. In many cases, business users cannot provider downtime for more than 24 hours and since each migration strategy has its own requirements on downtime, choosing the right migration strategy is very essential.

Adopting right tools and techniques—In many cases you may find that enterprises have not used proper tools for their existing SAP landscape. As an example, in one of the case studies I have dealt with SAP Solution Manager tool, which is key for any SAP landscape, has not been configured properly. In another case study, an enterprise was not using a proper batch management tool. All these are very essential to analyze before moving to Cloud so that a proper tools strategy is defined that can enable enterprises to manage their SAP applications on Cloud better going forward.

Performance baselines—Performance issues are most likely to occur in SAP landscape after moving to Cloud, and therefore it is very important to ensure that clear baseline of the as-is state is taken before migration, and validation is performed against these baselines after migration.

Right Sizing cannot be determined on Day 1—Once SAP workloads move to Cloud, it typically takes few weeks or even months to understand which applications are peaking in infrastructure usage and which are the ones that are underutilizing the allocated hardware. SAP early watch reports are used to understanding how SAP applications behave with respect to the underlying infrastructure usage. These reports can be generated on weekly basis to keep an eye on the whole Production System status based on which appropriate adjustments and optimizations can be made on the infrastructure.

One specific SAP migration case study we will discuss is with ABC Gas where we were moving from ECC to a SAP HANA system. Source database was Oracle which was on a private Data Centre hosted by Service provider A which needs to be migrated to Sybase database hosted on AWS Cloud. There were several challenges with this migration few which are listed below and ABC Gas has given us a business downtime window of 19 hours during the weekends:

- AS-IS applications (source systems) were using Oracle databases which was more than 15 terabytes in size. We tried to compress the database; however, it was not possible due to technical limitations.
- The other key challenge during this migration was that their SAP systems were hosted in third party Data Centre and we did not have full access to the source systems.
- The third challenges was that the customer was unable to provision additional network bandwidth and the current bandwidth did not allow for bulk data migration that could complete within the 19 hours window.

All of these challenges actually complicated the whole migration strategy. What we did was, we split the entire migration into two parts. We were supposed to move from a Data Centre to AWS Cloud, but because we did not have a proper bandwidth from source system to the target system, we first did a full export of the AS-IS Oracle database during business uptime hours. We put this export within the existing Data Centre and then during non-business hours we push this export into pre-production (staging) systems into AWS. Now at this point, the database remained Oracle on source and in the AWS staging environment as well. Once we imported all the required files to AWS environment, then we started the final step, which was Heterogeneous Migration. We migrated from Oracle on AWS to Sybase on AWS which was performed in a seamless manner utilizing AWS specific toolkits. The complete migration took more than 8 months starting from assessing the SAP landscape of ABC Gas until moving to AWS public Cloud. Though the migration looks simple in the way it has been described, this was one of the most complex SAP migrations I have come across in my entire career.

Note

1. Venkatesh Upadrista. (1 Sept. 2008). Managing Offshore Development Projects: An Agile Approach Paperback.

Chapter 8

Application Programming Interface (API)

Digital transformation continues to dominate enterprise strategy, and almost all enterprises are in the race to digitally transform themselves. Enterprises do however need to realize that legacy applications form the backbone of many enterprises and there is no way they can be eradicated; the main challenge is that they are holding organizations back from leveraging new digital technologies such as Cloud, Internet of Things, Artificial Intelligence, and mobile. These are all required to create modern experiences for customers and partners and for enterprises to compete in the market.

One of the reasons why digital transformation is difficult is due to legacy systems, as they can be cumbersome, unruly, and challenging to update. A legacy system is a computer system, software solution, or similar technology that is outdated and difficult to manage, yet vital to workflow processes within an organization. Almost all of the time, these cannot be replaced.

Common examples of legacy systems include:

- Operating systems
- Old Enterprise resource planning software
- Old Customer relationship management software

Legacy will be part of life for many organizations, and enterprises need to find a way to both rapidly connect legacy systems to modern applications and do so whilst minimizing disruption to these systems. In this chapter, we are going to discuss about enabling such seamless integration between legacy and modern applications.

Figure 8.1 depicts the four quadrants of Formula 4.0 methodology which has been discussed in Chapter 2. We also discussed how different applications within an enterprise will be classified into one of the four quadrants of Formula 4.0 methodology.

A brief summary can also be found below:

■ The **Hot Zone** has systems which are part of the existing client facing Business Processes that differentiate the enterprise in the market are placed.
■ The **Warm Zone** is a zone where systems that are part of future Business Processes and new business models are placed.

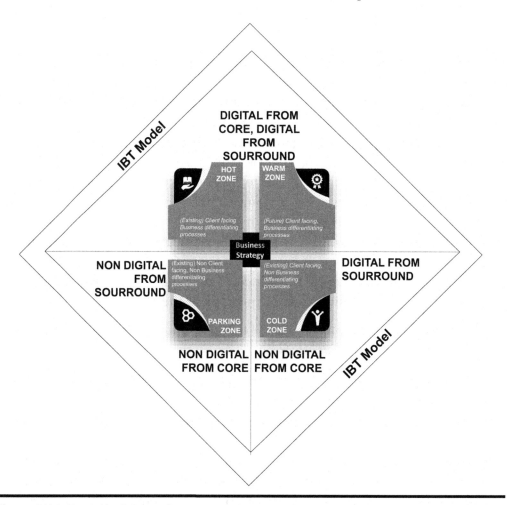

Figure 8.1 Formula 4.0 quadrant

- The **Cold Zone** is a zone where systems that are part of existing client facing Business Processes which are Non Business differentiating are placed.
- Systems which are Non Client facing and Non Business differentiating processes Business Processes are placed in the **Parking Zone.**

Digitally transformed from surround means that the core functionality of the system is retained as it is and new functionalities, capabilities, or technologies are added to the surroundings of the system that can make the system benefit from the modern technologies.

The key to success of any enterprise in their digital transformation journey lays in the way systems within these four zones interact with each other. It is mandatory that they need to be integrated seamlessly, irrespective of the treatment given to each of these applications. Application programming interfaces (APIs) are the solution to addressing this issue.

The most common description of an API is a set of functions and procedures that allow applications to access the features or data of an operating system, application, or other service to extend its capability or even create an entirely new feature. APIs are an essential component of merging the old and the new IT platforms, capturing vast amounts of data and ultimately achieving the enterprise's digital transformation strategy.

The potential of APIs to deliver business advantage cannot be underestimated; APIs are igniting a cultural shift within many organizations, enabling the integration of diverse IT systems, building more collaborative IT environments, and deriving revenues from existing IT assets.

Gartner claims that APIs can minimize the friction often caused by organizations implementing a "bimodal" IT strategy[1]—where legacy applications run alongside more innovative digital solutions. It is believed that APIs are the layer through which "Mode 1" and "Mode 2" can connect, bridging the gap between core data and functionality, and a more experimental, innovative application.

DEFINITIONS

Mode 1 *are areas that are more predictable and well-understood. It focuses on exploiting what is known, while renovating the legacy environment into a state that is fit for the digital world.*

Mode 2 are areas that are exploratory and experimental in solving new problems and focusing on areas of uncertainty. These initiatives often begin with a hypothesis which is tested and adapted during a process involving short iterations, potentially adopting a minimum viable product (MVP) approach.

Both modes are essential in creating substantial value and drive significant organizational change. Marrying a more predictable evolution of products and technologies (Mode 1) with the new and innovative (Mode 2) is the essence of an enterprise bimodal capability. Both play an essential role in digital transformation.

Service-oriented architecture is a style of software design where services are provided to the other components by application components, through a communication protocol over a network.

APIs have and continue to be the de facto standard for building and connecting applications. In the simplest terms, APIs let systems talk to other systems.

Although enterprises have used APIs for years, there has been a shift in the way these interfaces are viewed within organizations. An enterprise service bus (ESB) was used in the traditional world which now has been replaced by APIs since APIs are lightweight in nature. An ESB implements a communication system between mutually interacting software applications in a service-oriented architecture.

As you can guess from the above discussions, ESBs and APIs share capabilities and functionality. Despite their similarities however, APIs and ESBs are two entirely different things.

Here are the main differences between APIs and an ESB:

- APIs often have a much more robust, feature-rich set of capabilities, such as security and authentication policies, load balancing and routing features, monitoring, and analytics capabilities.
- APIs are more flexible and optimized for newer tech developments such as microservices, whereas ESBs are not. A consumption-based model is a service provision and payment scheme in which the customer pays according to the resources used. API solutions are typically consumption-based, while ESBs do not have such models.

Many competitive, forward-looking businesses now think about APIs not just as an integration technology to connect applications and data but as software products that empower developers to unlock new digital business models and opportunities. The adoption, design, and management of APIs are increasingly driven not by IT requirements but by strategic business goals. What this means is that two separate teams can develop products on their own without any dependency on each other, and using APIs these two products can be enabled to talk to each other. This is known as parallel development.

APIs have played a very significant role in the success of mobile applications development. As APIs began to prove their benefits, mobile computing emerged in a big way, and businesses everywhere focused on the need to create a new type of application (mobile applications), that could deliver data and services to customers wherever they are. Mobile applications required, and continue to require, a different set of security and developer workflows than those used in traditional enterprise architectures, and these needed to be supported with new operational models to stimulate new types of mobile services. While mobile applications do not have a clear analog to traditional enterprise architectures, they *do* have something in common, namely that APIs are the mechanism used to share data and services.

All of these trends have meant that many successful companies have shifted to smaller, faster-moving teams that leverage APIs to work in parallel without slowing one another down. Compared to legacy paradigms, the API-first approach is often seen as being more adept at keeping pace with rapidly shifting market dynamics and continually evolving customer preferences.

API Gateway

APIs are important for any digital enterprise and managing those API centrally is of vital significance. An API gateway is system that sits between a client and a collection of backend services and manages their interactions via APIs. It acts as a reverse proxy to accept all API calls, aggregate the various services required to fulfill them, and return the appropriate result.

Any enterprise embarking on their journey toward digital transformation needs to have a robust API strategy in the center of their approach and needs to ensure that systems communicate with each other via APIs. They also need to ensure that APIs are managed centrally via an API gateway to enable unified communication between all systems within an enterprise.

Importance of API Gateway

At its most basic, an API service accepts a remote request and returns a response. Large-scale API deployments are however quite complex. Figure 8.2 depicts the key considerations during API deployment:

- APIs need to be protected from overuse and abuse. To achieve this, authentication service and rate limiting should be used. Rate limiting is used to control the amount of incoming and outgoing traffic to or from a network; for example, if you are using a particular service's API that is configured to allow 50 requests/minute. If the number of requests you make exceeds that limit, then an error will be triggered.
- Enterprises need to know how APIs are being used, and therefore monitoring is important.
- Monetized APIs are required to connect to a billing system. API monetization is the process by which businesses create revenue from their APIs.

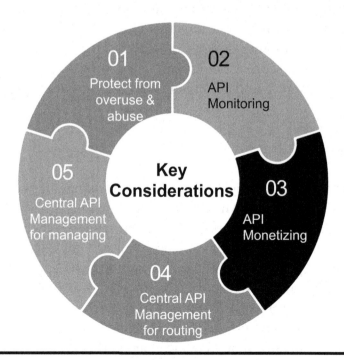

Figure 8.2   API management key considerations

■ Enterprises may have adopted a microservices architecture, in which case a single request could require calls to dozens of distinct applications, and API gateway plays a major role to centrally manage it.

■ New API services are added and create a need to retire older APIs; however, clients will still want to find all services in the same place. API gateways play a central role in managing such changes on a real time basis.

There is a clear need to offer enterprises a simple and dependable experience in the face of all the above complexities. An API gateway is a way to decouple the client interface from backend implementation. When a client makes a request, the API gateway breaks it into multiple requests, routes them to the right place, producing a response, and keeping track of everything.

An API gateway is a part of an API management system as depicted in Figure 8.3.

The API gateway intercepts all incoming requests and sends them through the API management system, which handles a variety of necessary functions to complete the request. In Figure 8.3, API management system takes requests from several external or internal applications which are depicted to the left and routes these requests to back end services on the

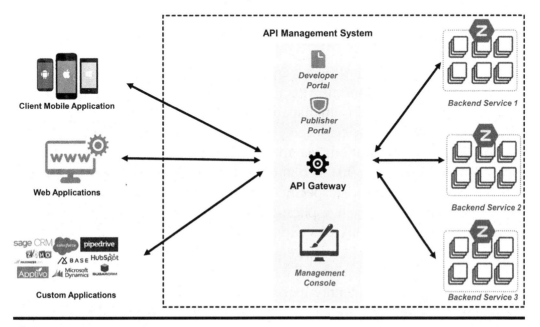

Figure 8.3 API management system

right via the API gateway. The developer portal is utilized to develop an API, published portal is utilized to publish the API, and management console is used to manage all APIs. Utilizing API management system enterprises will have a single place where they can control all their APIs.

There are several API management tools that are popular and widely in use:

Dell Boomi API Management—Boomi API Management supports the full life cycle of APIs in a hybrid environment. It can configure APIs and expose real-time integrations effortlessly and can centrally test and deploy APIs and enforce contracts and policies with an API gateway. Boomi API Management monitors the health of APIs with usage dashboards and engages API developers using the catalog and developer portal.

Azure API Management—Azure API Management is a fully managed service that enables enterprises to publish, secure, transform, maintain, and monitor APIs. With a few clicks in the Azure portal, enterprises can create an API facade that acts as a "front door" through which external and internal applications can access data or business logic implemented by custom-built backend services, running on Azure.

Apigee is another API gateway management tool offered by Google to exchange data across Cloud services and applications.

The API Implementation Journey: Creating an API Platform

We have discussed APIs, API gateways, and API management tools. API gateways bringing together all APIs to one central location, and an API management tool is used to manage these APIs.

The most important aspect for any enterprise is to enable all application to application communications via an API management system. To enable such communication, the first step after an API management tool is identified is to create an enterprise specific API custom platform (also known as an API platform) after which applications can be brought on the API management system. To simplify this explanation, we will consider that Dell Boomi is chosen as the API management system.

Creating an API platform means integrating Dell Boomi with enterprise specific tools in area of identity management, role-based access control management, monitoring and alerting systems, development and operations (DevOps) pipeline, and so on.

DEFINITIONS

Identity management, also known as identity and access management, is a framework of policies and technologies for ensuring that the proper people in an enterprise have the appropriate access to technology resources. This is enabled via identity management tools such as Oracle Identity Cloud Services.

Role-based access control (RBAC) is a method of restricting network access based on the roles of individual users within an enterprise.

Solar Winds Access Rights Manager (ARM) is a lightweight role-based access control software.

Once the API platform is created, all applications need to be onboard to the platform. An application could be a software, an ERP system, or a java application.

In addition, an enterprise which has initiated its API journey will already have several APIs developed. All such APIs need to be brought to the chosen API platform. Secondly, there would be several applications that would have been exchanging data and communicating with each other via different mechanisms such as direct application to application calls. All such interactions should be identified, and communication should be streamlined via API platform. Finally, for enterprises which currently use an ESB for communication, there may be a need to migrate all current communication from ESB to an API platform.

The end goal is to ensure that all application interactions within an enterprise are enabled via an API platform. This is known as API onboarding or creating an API platform specific to the enterprise.

As another example, if you consider Apigee as an API gateway, you could use an Apigee SAS platform, which is hosted on the Cloud or you can use Apigee Edge, which is On-Premises. Irrespective of what platform is chosen, the focus is to make it integrate into your applications and IT landscape in the most efficient way. This means that Apigee needs to talk to your enterprise identity management tools and role-based access control tools and should also be integrated with monitoring and alerting systems, DevOps pipeline, and so on. All of this integration needs to happen after which Apigee API platform is considered to be ready for use within the enterprise.

Once the platform is built, there is a need to onboard APIs on the Apigee platform. Many enterprises may already have several APIs that are built, so it is important that all these APIs are brought on to the Apigee API platform so that they can be made available to the consumers. A consumer could be an internal application requesting specific data or an external application that wants to connect to an enterprise database. Once built, all communications would take place via the API platform.

New APIs need to be built for existing applications which are not traditionally built to communicate via APIs. As an example, if an enterprise has SAP applications running in their IT organization, these SAP applications will be exposing a lot of backend services and it is essential that none of the other applications or consumers talk to these SAP services directly, and that they route all their requests via an API gateway. To enable this, wrappers need to be created around the SAP applications that can interact with these APIs for sending and receiving information.

API Enablement Team

An API enablement team needs to be formed by an enterprise aspiring to move into an API lead enterprise. An API enablement team constitutes solution architects, tools experts, API platform leads, and API developers. The API tools expert is the one who helps to identify the API management tool based on the enterprise IT landscape and the future enterprise needs. API solution architects, API platform leads, and API developers work with the business and IT groups to create an API platform specific to the enterprise and subsequently create new APIs or migrate existing APIs to this new platform. Doing this is not a simple exercise and a detailed analysis needs to be performed to define the API strategy. In parallel to creating the API platform and onboarding APIs to it, there is a need to write wrappers around existing applications to enable application to application interaction via an API platform.

I have had many experiences where enterprises are not sure which API management tool to choose, how to onboard enterprise capabilities on to the API management tool to create an API platform, and finally how to onboard APIs on the platform.

All these require specialized skills, and an API enablement team needs to be formed to ensure that the API journey for an enterprise is successful.

T-Mobile Case Study

One of the case studies which I will discuss for T-Mobile. Many of you may be aware that T-Mobile revolutionized the whole telecom industry with its unique un-carrier proposition. Un-carrier means a cellphone, smartphone, or a mobile connection is sold without a carrier agreement.

At one point of time, telecommunications consumers were reportedly the most frustrated and disappointed consumers. In 2013, T-Mobile entered the market and took advantage of all this frustration, using the "un-carrier" brand positioning. What looked like an impossible strategy by competitors gave T-Mobile maximum mileage in terms of revenue growth and new customer acquisitions. When T-Mobile's CEO at the time stated: "I'm all about customers and employees" that did not seem too different to what any other CEO would say to the market or to its customers. However, T-Mobile's CEO proved his statement with his actions when they introduced the un-carrier move to no contracts. This is a classic disruptor strategy which made the main competitors (AT&T and Verizon) look disconnected from what consumers want.

This is a company that challenged the complete mobile industry. From a business standpoint this was quite a radical and unique strategy to compete in the market. However, to make this a reality, the underlying IT system needed to be able to support such new business models in a very agile way.

T-Mobile used to announce new products and business models to the market every 4–6 months and the IT team had just 2 or 3 months to implement this business model.

A few of the new product launches announced by the CEO are listed below:

■ Launch of no contracts
■ "Jump" allowed customers to upgrade their phone up to two times per year, by trading in their phone to purchase a new one at the same price as a new customer
■ Enabled free international roaming
■ Launched the "Get Out of Jail Free Card" offer where T-Mobile agreed to pay customer early termination fees from the competitors

In the second phase, the company announced additional offers as listed below:

■ Gave consumers a chance to try out a new phone for a week
■ "Music Freedom" with data used on certain streaming music services would no longer count to users' data limits
■ Partnered with Gogo inflight internet for free texting on all flights using Gogo

- "Data Stash" let users carry over unused high-speed data usage for up to 1 year
- Business program allows every line unlimited talk and text, with 1 GB of data
- "Binge-on" allowed users to watch streaming services without counting toward their data
- Tuesday free stuff, including Domino's Pizza, Lyft Credits, and Wendy's
- Unlimited talk, text and wireless service and access fees (in an effort to make the pricing more transparent)

Such new business propositions and products were supposed to be launched every 6 months and IT systems needed to be prepared for quick product launches. Due to these innovative and customer centric products, there was a massive increase in new customers, with customers frequently queuing for hours on end outside stores in anticipation of new product releases. If you have read the news, you will see that they have gone from 33 million customers to almost 80 or 90 million customers in just 2 years after they first launched these products. All of their customer satisfaction ratings have also been extremely encouraging.

T-Mobile was using several legacy systems initially and the enterprise was unable to cope up with the demand after new products were launched. T-Mobile main challenge was how to make all IT systems work in an integral way to enable this vision of being an un-carrier and being able to launch new products every few months. The systems that were in place were legacy and were not fully integrated with each other. As an example, if you went to the store and bought a phone, your data would go to a one backend system and if you went online and purchased the same product, it would go to different one.

T-Mobile IT was completely transformed with a combination of microservices and an API based platform. Several applications were rewritten using microservices based architecture and several others were transformed with digital surround capabilities. The complete IT landscape was transformed in such a way that all application interactions were enabled via an API platform.

In a matter of 6–8 months the T-Mobile was able to:

- Achieve new activation in less than 5 minutes for hundreds of customers at the same time
- Achieve more than 30% operational cost savings
- Process more than 6 billion transactions per day

The success of this transformation was again proven somewhere in 2017–2018 when Apple released the iPhone 10. There was a huge rush of customers trying to buy this phone, and of all the vendors in the United States except for T-Mobile were unable to withstand the traffic and their IT crashed in one way or another. The only reason T-Mobile was able to withstand this spurt of traffic is because their entire end-to-end architecture was refactored to an extent that all systems were built for 99.9999% reliability and availability. Even if one system went down, it did not have an impact on the other systems since the complete IT was built using API and microservices based architecture.

Note

1. https://www.gartner.com/smarterwithgartner/apis-are-at-the-heart-of-digital-business/

PEOPLE, PROCESSES, AND TOOLS

People are core to the success of any transformation, and therefore having the right individuals for a given tasks is extremely important. In this section, we will discuss the need for enterprises to transition to a product-based organization along with a methodology on how to enable such transitions. Moving to a product-based organization requires a change to the human resource function of an enterprise. We will discuss how individuals need to be identified for the product teams that will make a Product Organization successful. We will also discuss agile methodology for product development and DevSecOps, which is a set of practices that combines software development and IT operations with security.

Chapter 9

Product Organization

Digital transformation can mean different things to different enterprises. For some enterprises, digital transformation is adopting technologies such as AI, RPA, or Big Data. For other organizations, digital transformation is the use of new-age technologies over traditional ones to build a scalable IT environment. One final interpretation is that digital transformation means achieving the desired speed at which an organization can bring new features to the market.

All the definitions above are correct in the respective context; however, digital transformation is all about achieving speed, agility, reliability, and cost effectiveness in whole rather than in parts to achieve a business outcome. This is achieved by defining the business goals and then enabling the enterprise to adapt best of breed processes, tools, and technologies to achieve the goal. In this Chapter we are going to discuss about the importance of transformation from a project-based organization to a Product Organization which addresses the process part of digital transformation using Formula 4.0.

What Is a Project Or a Project Organization?

In simple terms, a project is a container for all the activities that is laid out in sequence. We plan and then we analyze, we design, we implement, and then we test everything. And at the end, we ship everything that works well. A project has three main interdependent constraints namely time, cost, and scope. This is also known as Project Management Triangle as depicted in Figure 9.1.

This means to deliver a project; fixed scope is required after which fixed cost and time is decided. As a good project manager, you deliver your project on time, scope, and budget.

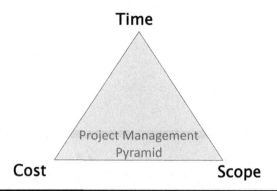

Figure 9.1 Project management pyramid

A typical project runs between 6 months and few years. A project-based approach works well if the market around us does not change during the course of project execution. Today we are in a market which is transforming at a very fast pace. This is one of the reasons why organizations following a project model are failing even though they are delivering on cost, time, and scope.

A quote of the former CEO of a large phone manufacturer named ABC Mobile who lost their business to their competitor (Apple) comes to my mind during this discussion. He said that he did not do anything wrong but somehow, he lost. The projects his company was performing were all running fine, they embraced agile methodology, and they had an awesome track record of really building phone after phone. But while ABC Mobile was building phones in a project approach, the market changed, and people were not buying the kind of phones which this company was selling and they lost their complete user base to another company (Apple).

This is the biggest challenge with project-based organization. A project manager comes up with the plan for the scope, schedule, and the budget which gets approved by a steering board and then a couple of weeks later this project is initiated and then it is executed with the only goal to deliver the project based on the scope, ignoring the market and by the time the project is delivered the market changes.

The above is one perspective on ABC Mobile. In contrast to the earlier discussion, another interesting perspective about ABC Mobile is that they realized a year before that something is going to change fundamentally with phones. They knew that there was going to be phones with large glass screens and Apple was going to make something called as iPhone. With that ABC Mobile realized that customer experience with the mobile phone was going to be basically driven by software (with widgets and apps stores), and it will no longer going to be physical buttons.

A lot of people think that ABC Mobile missed the revolution by not realizing that they needed big glass screens. However, the reality is that they know a year before that the industry will move toward software driven phones. Once they realized it, they brought in some of the best consultants, they hired more developers, they realized that they needed to become software innovators and develop in a more iterative manner—and they did this all. They embraced agile methodology to develop phone. In 2009, I remember ABC Mobile was the poster child to adopt agile methodology, their employees were trained in agile and everyone started developing using agile methodology. The main focus for ABC Mobile during that time was on agile trainings and embracing agile methodology and this is what ABC Mobile called as transformation. Within the company developers were trained on agile, they were using agile tools, using agile methods, and building the phones but nothing was moving faster. The CEO was measuring the transformation through these metrics whether people were trained on agile and whether they were using the agile toolkits and with these metrics it appeared to the executive that the whole transformation was on track.

But then this way of working was actually not solving their core problem. Their core problem ABC Mobile had was with their software architecture. The operating system they had did not allow them to fit the big screens effectively or could support an app store. By the time they realize this gap, iPhone was released, and ABC Mobile went out of market. ABC Mobile adopted a project-based structure, though they adopted agile, which was the main reason for this failure. They operated in a project-based structure with fixed scope, time, and cost (using agile) and this turned out to be quite disconnected in terms of how they were measuring their agility and how value is actually flowing in the organization.

From the above discussion it's very clear that technology or processes cannot solve business problem. Understanding the market and adapting to market changes are the mantras for any business to be successful and these cannot be achieved in a project-based structure.

Product Organization

A Product Organization is all about delivery business outcomes or business value in shorter intervals keeping in mind the market changes and adapting immediately to the market changes. Forrester defines an outcome as an achieved end state that can be verified through measurable results.[1] An outcome could be additional revenues, higher customer satisfaction, new customer acquisition, and so on.

An example of outcome is listed below:

By July 2022, we aim to increase sales of clothing by 25% by making the checkout process faster and more transparent for shoppers who are frustrated with the time it takes to purchase our product.

Once we define an outcome we want to achieve, it probably may be too much to do in a short timeframe, so we have to really ask what is the highest possible value and what is the minimum viable product that can be shipped in shortest possible time so that it can be released to the market to validate the acceptance of the feature or product.

An example of highest possible value and minimum viable product outcome is listed below:

In next 3 months we aim to increase sales of kids clothing by 60% by adding quick checkout option available to shoppers.

Many enterprises are still operating in project mode. Transforming from project to product (outcome based) thinking organization is the need for any enterprise to be successful.

It is very easy to talk about business outcomes and transforming from project to Product Organization. But the ground realities are very different, especially for many enterprises that are in business from last several decades.

When we talk about making the change from project to product, there are four impediments that every enterprise is challenged with:

- **IT is disconnected from business and vision**—this means that having IT to work with business is the biggest hurdle with almost all enterprises
- **Executives are tracking activities and not business results**—this is clearly driven by the fact that success of an IT manager in an enterprise is determined by how many tasks are completed as against the plan
- **Project funding is broken**—this is one of the major issues especially with large enterprises. Projects are still funded on an annual funding cycle which usually are for a 12–18-month cycle
- **Business feels IT is solving its own problems**—this is because of the fact that IT is generally focused on making developers more productivity, reducing defects, ensuring business continuity is maintained, and so on, none of which delivers business outcomes

Most of the enterprises these days want to switch from linear-based projects to more products and product developments. When I speak about Product Organization, I remember a CIO asking me on how unicorns such as Google, Amazon, and Microsoft do long-term planning despite being so big. The answer is that these companies never do long-term planning, and their budget cycles are 3–6 months. What this means is that the board comes together every 3–6 months to allocate budgets based on the market needs and they operate with a product centric mindset.

It is really hard to respond to any changing market needs with a lengthy budgeting cycle such as 12 months or 18 months. And if anyone has to do and achieve success with such a lengthy cycle, they need to have an absolute forecasting ability to determine what they need to do for next 18 months and this is an ability no one possesses. Therefore, enterprises are bound to be disappointed with the results.

With a Product Organization, there is hypothesis that enterprises fund, the hypothesis is converted to a prototype, it is tested in the market and once the market responds positively further enhancements are done and functionalities are released to market in very short intervals. This concept is called "Hypothesis to Cash." We are going to discuss about Hypothesis to Cash in the subsequent sections. To make concept of Hypothesis to Cash a reality, business and IT teams need to work together and should share a common goal of business outcomes. IT needs to start conversations with business about business outcomes and align technology solutions to those business outcomes. Enterprises need to move away from a contractual relationship between business and IT to a one-team model. A one-team model is where IT and business have the same targets—this is what Product Organization is all about.

Such a transformation cannot be achieved in 1 or 2 weeks or 1–2 months; it takes time and there should be acceptance from both IT and business teams on the model. Business takes the lead in a Product Organization model, and IT works with business to realize the business outcomes. From the technology side, IT brings in methodologies to delivery faster such as agile and development and operations (DevOps).

A Product Organization always has a measurable outcome, offers quicker business results, improves customer experiences, reduces friction within the organization, and offers more flexibility. All of these result in increased trust across the business since a product has its own measurable business benefit. A product-centric setup allows for better engagement and full ownership between IT and business units since product owners from the business side are part of the team delivering the product end to end. The measurable outcome in a product-based organization for every enhancement or new business functionality is based on how fast the new functionality is released to the market, how many new customers a new feature is able to attract, and if the customer satisfaction has improved after adding a new feature to the overall product. This measurement contrasts with traditional metrics in a project organization where for every new business functionality development, teams are measured on the number of defects in production, quality of the resources, and so on. Traditional metrics in Product Organizations do not vanish but are treated as secondary measures to the product success.

Product Life Cycle

A product life cycle constitutes of five phases: introduction, growth, maturity, decline, and abandonment. This is depicted in Figure 9.2.

■ The first phase of the product life cycle is the introduction phase. During this phase the product is officially launched into the market with minimal features. The marketing team does everything it can to encourage customers to buy the product.
■ After a few months of development, the product gains popularity, enters the growth phase, and new features are added. Sales start booming for the product. During the growth phase, users are delighted with more enriched business functionalities that make the product more and more attractive and increase sales. Sales tend to gradually increase every year.
■ In the maturity phase, the business has already established itself. The management can effectively predict sales figures because they know their clients. In this phase, sales and demand remain fairly constant.
■ After a while, customers grow tired of the product and move on to something else. The result is a decline in demand and overall sales. During the decline phase there is a complete freeze on enriching the product with new features. The organization ensures that the product is up and running in its current state without any disruption.

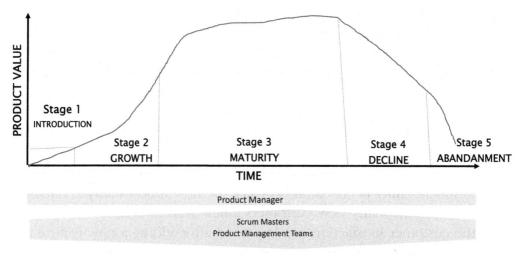

Figure 9.2 Product life cycle

■ The final stage is abandonment where the product no longer brings value and the company stops investing in it. The complete product team is dismantled.

Hypothesis to Cash

Introduction, growth, and maturity are the three phases where most product development and product enhance happens and this is where Hypothesis to Cash model is applied for each new feature that is added to a product.

The Hypothesis to Cash model has four phases as depicted in Figure 9.3. It is mandatory that business and IT teams work together in all phases of product development.

Hypothesis—this is a phase in which a new idea of a product or an enhancement is brainstormed. A hypothesis in Product Organization is an idea that is proposed so that it can be tested to validate if it has a potential to generate more revenue for the product or enterprise.

Funding—this is a phase in which funding is approved based on the acceptance of hypothesis.

Develop and test—once funding is approved; the idea is converted into a prototype. A prototype is an early sample, model, or release of a product built to test the hypothesis.

Release to the market (and generate cash)—once developed, the prototype is released to the market to validate acceptance of the idea from end users. Based on the market acceptance the hypothesis to cash is applied to enhance the feature with full functionality.

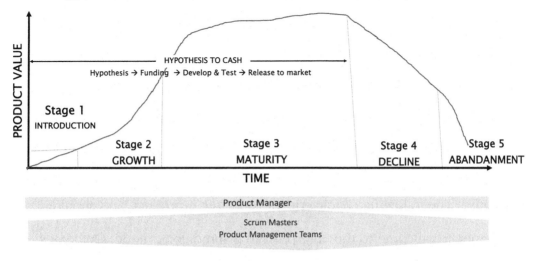

Figure 9.3   Hypothesis to cash

As you can see a product has its own life cycle and, in a product-based organization, business is broken down into multiple products or features. A cumulation of all these products forms the organization business.

What Does Transforming to a Product Organization Mean?

Transforming to a Product Organization means that:

- Business and IT work together in developing products i.e., business and IT together take lead in developing products
- Changes are embraced based on market needs at any point of time—so no lengthy or long budgeting and development cycles
- Technology is utilized to develop and release products to market faster
- Each member of the team needs to know why and what he is building i.e., everyone in the team understands the business context
- Move away from traditional IT metrics into business outcome-based metrics. We are going to discuss about product metrics in subsequent sections
- Creating self-sufficient project teams that can deliver and maintain product end to end, known as the product engineering team

DEFINITIONS

*In product terms, **build** is the term used to develop a software or a product.*

***Run (operations)** is the term used to support the software after the build phase—the type of work the run team does is resolving bugs, any performance issues, etc. Many times, minor enhancements to the product are part of the run team.*

In a Product Organization, each product delivers an outcome or business value. A summation of all products within an organization defines the core business of the enterprise. Each product within the enterprise is broken down into epics which are further split into user stories. Each product, epic, or user story should have an outcome attached to it—what this means is that a product, epic, or user story should provide a benefit and measurable value to an enterprise. The following characteristics constitute a product, and should:

- generate outcome to the enterprise in a standalone mode. Outcomes could be revenue generation, customer satisfaction improvement, or new customer acquisitions

- have a life cycle of its own starting from product introduction to product abandonment
- follow the hypothesis to cash model
- be measured via business metrics instead of IT metrics. We are going to discuss Formula 4.0 product metrics in subsequent sections
- be independent of other products in the organization

As depicted in Figure 9.4, expectation from a product-led organization is that the product teams should be self-sufficient to manage the end-to-end life cycle of the product both from horizontal scaling as well as a vertical scaling perspective.

The product team should be formed with a goal that a stable team will continue to exist working on the same product, starting from the introduction phase until the product is abandoned—this is known as vertical scaling. The second expectation from the product team is that this should be a self-sufficient DevOps team. This means a product team is formed and led by a product manager with a cross-functional team who can code, test, manage infrastructure, and security for the build and run phases. This is known as horizontal scaling. A combination of horizontal and vertical scaling teams makes up the product engineering team in Formula 4.0 terms.

To achieve the above aspiration of a product engineering team, there are two major changes which enterprises need to bring into the DNA of their operating model:

Team Characteristics—it is misconception that a developer, tester, or operational engineer can be cross trained to become a security engineer or an infrastructure engineer. Motivated individuals can only learn the concepts and apply some basic knowledge to perform a task that is outside their scope of core expertise.

Core skills are those which the job or task cannot be carried out without having. On the other hand, secondary skills enhance performance, but the job or task can be accomplished without them. There is a third skill called a supporting skill, which is a variant of a core skill. Supporting skill means that an individual will need to have this as mandatory skill; however, they can be a beginner level in this skill and this skill can be acquired with training or on the job learning. As an example, in context of a Java developer, core skills are Java and J2ee. Supporting skills can be experience in C++ programming language, knowledge in a specific security tool, expertise on an operating system on Cloud infrastructure, installing a tool

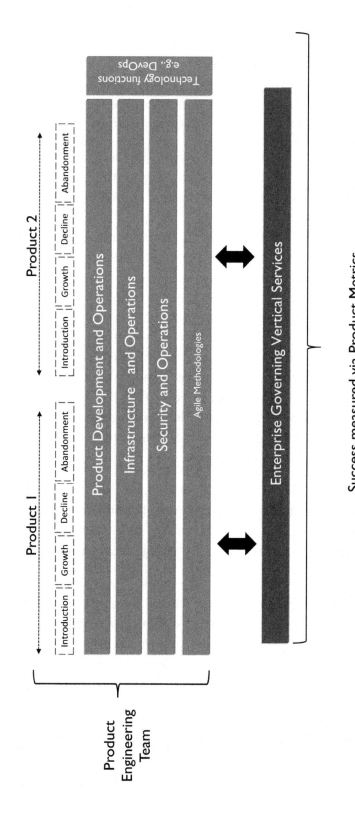

Success measured via Product Metrics

1. DORA Metrics : Lead Time, Cycle Time and Deployment Frequency, Change Fail, Availability, Time to Restore
2. Product Metrics : Product Gross Margins, new Customer Acquisition Index and Customer Satisfaction Index

Figure 9.4 Product organization and team structure

on Cloud infrastructure, monitoring infrastructure, and so on. Every product team should define core skills and supporting skills specific to the product requirement, and only individuals who possess these skills should be inducted into the product engineering team.

All Feature Automation—all feature automation is the term used when DevOps including infrastructure and security management is automated to the fullest.

As discussed above, individuals will bring a lot of expertise in their core skills, and enterprises should ensure that technology is utilized to the fullest which will enable the product engineering team to be a self-sustained team. What this means is that DevOps should be automated to such an extent that all manual activities which were not previously carried out by the DevOps team can now be easily completed by the product engineering team, with support from tools, automation, and minimal training. As an example, with minimum knowledge any individual from the product engineering team should:

- As a developer—identify any security breaches or security vulnerabilities without being a security expert. This can be achieved if a security tool is installed in the DevOps pipeline.
- As a developer—move code from one environment to the other automatically without being an infrastructure expert. This can be achieved by implementing a continuous deployment tool. Continuous deployment is the process of moving software that has been built and tested successfully from one environment to the other automatically. The environment can be a development, test, or production environment.
- As a developer—review code, without being a quality assurance analyst. This can be achieved by deploying a static or dynamic code quality tool.
- As a developer—test code from a performance perspective without being a performance test expert. Deploying performance test tools in the DevOps pipeline can achieve this.
- As a developer—create a development environment without being an infrastructure expert i.e., create an instance and deploy all required tools and software and start development. This can be achieved by using Cloud self-service features.
- As a scrum master—release an unused infrastructure (e.g., development environment) without being an infrastructure expert. This can be achieved by using Cloud self-service features.

DEFINITIONS

Development environment *is the infrastructure provided to the team to develop and unit test their code.*

Test environment *is the infrastructure provided to teams to test the functionality after multiple developers integrate their code and create a working functionality.*

Pre-production environment *(also referred to as a pre-production sandbox) is a system testing area or simply a staging area. Its purpose is to provide an environment that simulates the actual production environment as closely as possible so an application can be tested in conjunction with other applications.*

Production environment *is a term used to describe an environment where software and other products are put into operation for their intended uses by end users.*

Regression testing *is re-running functional and non-functional tests to ensure that previously developed and tested software still performs after a change. A combination of all regression test cases is known as the regression test suite.*

Static code analysis *is the analysis of computer software that is performed without executing programs, in contrast with **dynamic analysis**, which is analysis performed on programs whilst they are executing.*

At first glance, creating a Product Organization with all feature automation may look like a difficult task. However, with several technologies and tools available in the market, enterprises can achieve all feature automation in just a few months. Between 2015 and 2019, I set-up Product Organization for eight enterprises and more importantly achieved all feature automation in all these cases. This can be explained with a short case study for QWR Financials where all feature automation was implemented. QWR Financials was matured in agile processes and were in the process of implementing DevOps within their organization. The approach we took for this customer to achieve all feature automation was to deploy the following tools in their DevOps pipeline:

■ A security assessment tool that will scan code from a vulnerability perspective which is downloaded from other projects, the Internet or open sources, etc

- Tools to perform static code analysis and dynamic code analysis
- A test automation tool with a full set of regression test suites built in the DevOps pipeline for each environment (e.g., development, testing, pre-production, and production). Automation was enabled to an extent, where a code deployed in one environment is automatically tested using regression packs and if tests are successful code is automatically moved to the next environment until it reaches pre-production. We went to an extent where a tool was deployed in DevOps pipeline which can convert a requirement written in a human read language to manual and automation test scripts and execute these cases automatically
- Cloud management tools which can manage and monitor infrastructure from a single place. Using these tools, product engineering teams were able to:
  - Automatize provision environments with the click of a button
  - Automatically stop environments when not in use i.e., during weekends and non-peak hours
  - Monitor and manage all infrastructure and services via a Cloud console
  - Utilize disaster recovery features from a Cloud provider
  - Utilize security features of the Cloud provider

QWR Financials was able to achieve all feature automation in 3 months and moved to a Product Organization in less than 6 months.

Breaking Product into Epics and User Stories

A product will be split into work items called epics and these epics will be further split into user stories as depicted in Figure 9.5. Products should be independent and have a business value of their own.

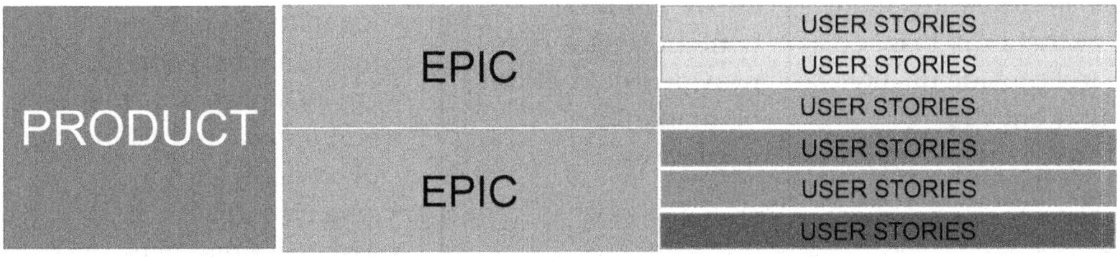

Figure 9.5   Products, EPICS and user stories

DEFINITIONS

Epics *are large bodies of work that can be broken down into a number of smaller tasks (called stories).*

Stories, also called "user stories," are short requirements or requests written from the perspective of an end user.

A *Product* *is a combination of multiple epics.*

Some examples of epics and stories are listed in the following Table. For each product there will be a product owner.

Epic	User Story	Acceptance Criteria
As an Acquisition User, I need to access the acquisition ordering platform behind a secure login so that I can purchase products.	As an Acquisition User, I need to select an auction product in the acquisition ordering platform so that I can bid on it.	Ensure the Acquisition User is able to: • log in to acquisition gateway. • navigate to the auction page. • select the product(s) to bid on.
	As an Acquisition User, I need to review my previous bids in the acquisition ordering platform so that I can remove expired bids.	Ensure the Acquisition User is able to: • log in to acquisition gateway. • navigate to a page to review items previously bid upon. • select one or multiple expired bids. • remove expired bids.
As a Marketing Lead, I want to have a content management system so that I can manage and provide quality content and experience to my readers.	As a Content Owner, I want to be able to create product content so that I can provide information on market to customers.	Ensure the Content Owner is able to: • log in to the content management system. • create a page of content. • edit/update an existing page of content. • save changes. • assign content page to Editor for review.

Epic	User Story	Acceptance Criteria
As a Marketing Lead, I want to have a content management system so that I can manage and provide quality content and experience to my readers.	As an Editor, I want to review content before it is published so that I can assure it is optimized with correct grammar and tone.	Ensure the Editor is able to: • log in to the content management system. • view existing content page. • edit/update page of content. • add mark-up comments—save changes. • save changes. • reassign to Content Owner to make updates. • schedule content publishing.
As an HR Manager, I want a virtual job openings board so that I can view job status and manage company personnel needs.	As an HR Manager, I need to view a candidate's status so that I can manage their application process throughout the recruiting phases.	Ensure the HR Manager is able to: • log in to the virtual job openings board system. • view/edit/add the status for job candidates. • update for each phase (e.g., phone screening completed, in-person interview scheduled, background check in-progress, and so on. • send email communication to staff regarding candidates.
As a Marketing Data Analyst, I want to create forecast and trend reports so that I can support the sales efforts of region 9 Marketing Representatives.	As a Marketing Data Analyst, I need to run the Salesforce & Google analytics reports so that I can build the monthly media campaign plans.	Ensure the Marketing Data Analyst is able to: • access the Salesforce & Google analytics reports. • create the monthly media campaign plan for a specified region (e.g., region 9). • access a contacts list. • email the prepared monthly media campaign to one or more selected contacts.

Formula 4.0 Product Metrics

Metric is a standard of measurement. It measures the degree of the properties a system has. Metrics are probably the most important aspect in any product development process due to several reasons:

- To plan work items
- To measure performance
- To measure productivity, and a lot more

Metrics aim to improve the quality of the product. This is primarily done by determining the quality of the existing product:

- Metrics can increase return on investment
- Metrics can manage workloads
- Metrics minimizes overtime and reduces costs
- Metrics can identify the areas which need improvement

In addition, metrics are also very important for planning, organization, control, and improvement.

In IT development, there are several traditional metrics largely in use, some of which are listed below:

Planned Value—Planned Value, sometimes also called Budgeted Cost of Work Scheduled (BCWS), is a measure of the estimated cost of planned activities at any given time.

Earned Value—While Planned Value provides the scheduled value of the project, Earned Value gives the actual value. It is based on the work you have already done, not the work you should have done.

Actual Cost—Actual Cost is the third of the baseline metrics alongside Planned Value and Earned Value. This is a measure of the actual expenses incurred in completing all of the work done to date.

Schedule Variance and Cost Variance—These two related metrics tell you how far the project has strayed from its estimated budget and schedule.

The metrics discussed so far provide a good view on the progress of the development mostly in a waterfall model. Product Organization embraces an agile methodology, and Formula 4.0 mandates adapting a two-factor measurement technique to measure success of a product, which is depicted in Figure 9.6.

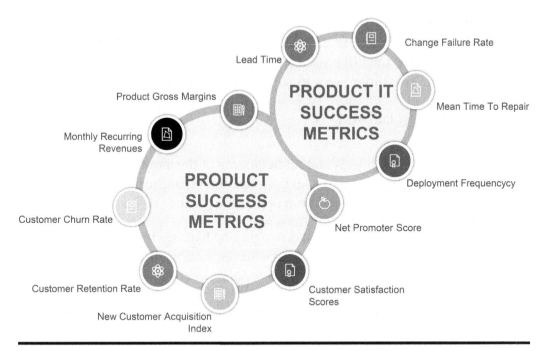

Figure 9.6   Formula 4.0 product metrics

The first area is known as product business metrics which is the primary metrics to measure success of a product thinking organization, and the second area is known as product IT success metrics which measures success of product DevOps.

Product Business Metrics

Product business metrics measure how profitable a product is for the enterprise, including the customer satisfaction index on the product and its features. Key metrics under which product success is measured are:

Product Gross Margins—one of the most important measures for enterprises to gauge the success of the product is by calculating the gross margins of the product at any given point of time.

The formula to calculate gross margin as a percentage is:

$$\text{Gross Margin} = (\text{total revenue} - \text{cost of product development and maintenance so far}) / \text{total revenue} \times 100.$$

Monthly Recurring Revenue (MRR) —this measures the total amount of predictable revenue that a company expects on a monthly basis. MRR is used for tracking monthly revenue figures and to understand the month-to-month differences in subscription service.

The formula to calculate MRR as:

$$= \begin{matrix} (\text{Monthly revenue at beginning of the month} \\ + \text{monthly revenue from new customers for the month} \\ + \text{monthly revenue gained from upgrading features by customers}) \\ - \\ (\text{monthly revenue lost from downgrading features by customers} \\ + \text{monthly revenue lost due to customer exiting the product}) \end{matrix}$$

A product may have multiple features. Upgrading means adding new features and downgrading means opting out of existing features.

Customer Churn Rate—a measure to determine customer satisfaction index. In terms of product success, customer churn is as important as revenue churn. Customer churn rate metrics provide a view on customer satisfaction.

Customer client churn rate can be measured in one of the following ways:

- Total number of customers lost during a specific period
- Percentage of customers lost during a specific period

Customer Retention Rate (CRR)—CRR is the percentage of customers who stayed with the product after a certain time period.

The formula to calculate CRR is:

$$\text{CRR} = \text{customers at the end of the calculated period} - \text{new customers} / \text{customers at the start of the calculated period} \times 100$$

Based on customer retention rate, product strategies can be altered as enterprises can understand if and for how long existing customers are using the product. In case CRR drops, the product team needs to look for new features or changes existing features to achieve higher CRR.

New Customer Acquisition Index—the second metrics to capture is the number of new customers acquired over a specified period of time. A good product will keep on increasing their customer base upward of 10% every quarter. Once the new customer acquisition index stops increasing or starts dropping, it gives an indication that the product is no longer appealing to the client.

The formula for calculating new customer acquisition index is:

$$= \left[\frac{(\textbf{Total new customers} + \textbf{Existing customer}) - \textbf{Existing Customers}}{\textbf{Existing customers}} \right] \times \textbf{100}$$

Customer Satisfaction Score—while customer churns rate provides metrics on how many customers are lost in a given period of time, customer satisfaction scores provide a measure to validate quality of product as perceived by the customer. Based on the customer satisfaction scores, actions can be taken to improve the quality or features of the product. Usually asked on a scale of 1–10, customer satisfaction scores can be calculated by adding up the sum of all scores and dividing the sum by the number of respondents.

Net Promoters Score—one of the key metrics to measure the number of loyal customers who are likely to recommend a product (promoters), and those customers who hate it (detractors) is known as net promoter score (NPS). NPS is one of the most important metrics to determine which phase a product is in i.e., in the growth phase, maturity phase, or decline phase. Low NPS in the long-term means that the product is entering the decline phase. Either the product features need to be enhanced to bring the NPS to an acceptable level or enterprises need to stop investing in the product and be ready for a gradual abandonment of said product.

Product IT Success Metrics

Product IT success metrics determine how successful the product is being developed and managed from IT perspective. Enterprises can use these metrics to create strategies and increase the life span and profitability of the product. For Product Organizations under Formula 4.0, the product IT metrics are lead time, change failure rate, mean time to repair, and deployment frequency. These metrics aid planning and inform decisions about the process of improving product development.

Lead Time—how long it takes a product team to go from idea generation on a new epic or product feature to delivered or working software. A product team is expected to have a lead time of less than 3 weeks for every new product feature released to the market. I have come across several examples where matured enterprises have their lead times in days rather than weeks.

Change Failure Rate—a measure of how often deployment failures occur in production that requires immediate remedy (particularity, rollbacks). A matured Product Organization has a change failure rate between 0% and 15%.

The formula to calculate change failure rate is:

$$Change\ Failure\ Rate = \frac{Total\ number\ of\ failures}{Total\ number\ of\ Deployments}$$

Mean Time to Repair—a measure of how long it takes to get a product or subsystem up and running after a failure.

Mean time to repair is generally defined through the following formula:

$$Mean\ Time\ to\ Repair = \frac{Total\ Maintenance\ Time}{Number\ of\ Incidents}$$

Deployment Frequency—also known as throughput, deployment frequency is a measure of how frequently product teams deploy code. This metric is often represented as a percentage and is calculated based on the formula below. It also answers the question: how often do product teams deploy to a production or pre-production environment?

A matured Product Organization have a deployment frequency of multiple times per day to pre-production, calculated by the following formula:

$$Deployment\ Frequency = \frac{Number\ of\ Deployments\ Per\ Day}{Total\ Numbr\ of\ Opportunities\ Available\ to\ Deploy}$$

Product IT success metrics are part of the DORA metrics. DORA (DevOps Research and Assessment)[2] is a digital transformation research firm and is known for its research into the DevOps space and reports on business technology transformation.

Many enterprises today have started adopting a combination of Product business metrics and product IT success metrics to determine their product and team's performance.

Agile Software Development Methodology in Formula 4.0 Product Development

Project management has existed for decades. Many different software development life cycle models have also evolved over the past several years. Over time, people developed what have become today's standards, which are treated as the guiding principles in the IT industry. In the modern world, technical challenges and customer requirements have revolutionized the need for better life cycle models to keep pace with changing demands. Modern practices and principles differ from those of the past.

Traditional software methodologies have lost their appeal almost a decade back due to limitations in their ability to accommodate changing needs and to control large, complex projects. Reliably delivering expected project results is dependent on the difficult skills of estimating and managing software development. It must be recognized that these methodologies were developed years ago and drew heavily on the engineering principles of the construction industry, which were then transformed and adopted by the Information Technology (IT) industry. As a result, they stressed accuracy (which required that every last detail be planned before the project starts), predictability, and linear development cycles (requirements transforming to design, leading to development). Along with accuracy and predictability, stability was expected—which included stable analysis, stable requirements, and stable design, which are rarely possible in IT projects.

Anyone who has been in the industry for a while and worked on a large development project has probably experienced the "big design up front" (BDUF) approach to software development, which is highly risky because it does not support change. Most people are unable to describe exactly how the entire system should behave up front. More often than not, the business thinks they have got it right at first, but begin to change their minds as more analysis is performed and they get closer to the details. While traditional methodologies have worked for some organizations in the past, and may still work in some circumstances, for many organizations they only add to the frustration caused by unmanageable changing requirements; ultimately leading to unpredictable project outcomes.

The current and rapidly changing environment imposes constraints on quality, time, and costs, as well as legal, cultural, and logical parameters.

In addition, several principles are being modernized to keep pace with the industry. Agile is one such methodology which has moved from so-called "emerging methodology" to mainstream "development methodologies." This is providing value to the customer by providing better project transparency, better requirements trade-offs, faster time to market, reduced defects, and enabling the building of a mature, quality product.

Agile is a software development methodology in which systems are built in increments; where requirements and solutions evolve through collaboration between cross-functional teams and over a period of time. Agile methods generally promote a light-weight project management process that includes frequent monitoring and adapting to changes quickly that encourages teamwork, self-organizing, and self-accountability. In addition, there is a set of good practices that allows for rapid delivery of high-quality software, as well as a business approach that aligns development with business needs and the organization's goals. Scrum is one such Agile methodology where software is built in smaller increments called sprints. A sprint is a short, time-boxed period when a scrum team works to complete a set amount of work. Sprints are at the very heart of scrum and Agile methodologies. A combination of multiple sprints is called a release.

Although agile has been around for quite some time, many have misunderstood the concepts and have assumed and promoted the model as being successful only in a collocated environment. Several experiences have proven that agile can be used very successfully in any environment including distributed development. There are several organizations that have reaped the benefits and are successfully operating with agile using combined outsourcing and offshoring strategies.

DEFINITION

Collocated Agile *is a model in which projects execute the agile methodology with teams located in a single room. The methodology requires that the complete team be in close proximity to each other to improve coordination between the members. Collocated Agile teams have proven that the real power of project success lies not in administration, but in acumen, chemistry, loyalty, and dedication between the collocated teams.*

I have personally seen many statistics and conducted research within my own teams that has demonstrated the right collocated team see at least a 10% productivity improvement by sitting together.

I can strongly recall the words of one of my teachers: the reasons why people get along are:

- They work for the same boss and share common impressions
- They have a common goal and share common interests
- They share similar views
- They feel they are at the same level of intelligence
- The chance that one talks to the other is inversely proportional to the distance between their seats. That is, if the distance between the individuals is doubled, communication drops by a factor of two. If it is doubled again, communication drops by a factor of four
- The best collocated teams will take advantage of all of these factors

Although the above considerations about a collocated team are accurate, as a manager, you should have the capacity to personally manage points one, two, and five. The other two factors are strengths and weaknesses within each individual. If the individuals on the team do not get along, the whole point of collocation is defeated and if not managed properly, you may end up with a productivity loss rather than a gain.

I have heard many stories about conflicts within a collocated team that have led to a drastic drop in team motivation and productivity, thereby leading to project failures.

Distributed development is a fact of life for many organizations. In today's environment, where everyone is focused on controlling costs, distributed development has played a very crucial role in meeting these demands. As software development has trended toward global distribution, many organizations have shown an interest in blending agile with distributed development strategies, but they are skeptical about the challenges that would be faced in terms of communication, culture, and team collaboration.

Distributed Agile, as the name implies, is a model in which projects execute an agile methodology with teams that are distributed across multiple geographies.

Although Collocated Agile approaches in the past have successfully guided project execution, they have moved the industry backward, defeating the overall advantage of the cost controls gained by offshoring. There has been a perception in the industry that Distributed Agile cannot be carried out successfully, this was mainly due to the fact that success stories in Distributed Agile were not publicized. There is also very little literature in the industry about applying the principles of distribution to a successful agile implementation.

Many of my customers were skeptical about the success of Distributed Agile because they did not understand how to execute agile projects in a distributed environment. I had the opportunity to interact with several of these customers and demonstrate, with multiple case studies, that Distributed Agile has been successful provided the right methodology is in place to address all the challenges of distributed development.

Although there is still skepticism in the minds of some, the concept of Distributed Agile has gained in popularity. In addition to being viewed as an efficient software development methodology, it is also starting to be considered a successful trend for meeting current day requirements and challenges.

I personally acknowledge the fact that there are overheads and risks involved in a Distributed Agile approach when compared to Collocated Agile, but putting the right model in place to overcome these challenges can produce a successful implementation. There are several methodologies available in the market such as the design for a Hybrid Agile Adoption framework, which provides a clear guidance on how to execute agile programs in a distributed environment.

A well-defined Distributed Agile methodology can provide numerous advantages to an organization for both the short and long term some which are depicted in Figure 9.7. One such advantage is a reduction in costs by utilizing the strategy of distributed development in agile projects. This is one of the major reasons why today, many organizations are moving toward Distributed Agile implementation. There are also several benefits an

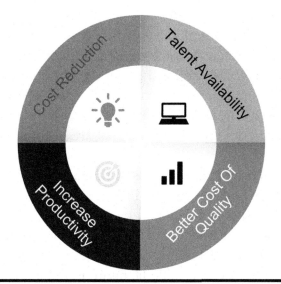

Figure 9.7   Benefits of distributed agile

organization may gain by having access to a broad talent pool and on-time resource availability which is depicted in Figure 9.7 and listed below.

Reduced Cost

Many successful organizations have benefited from operating in a distributed environment in which costs can be optimized by having the majority of the team work at low cost centers. A traditional Distributed Waterfall methodology, for example using an onsite-offshore model, can expect attractive and realistic savings of 40–50% in the long term, taking into account the reduced productivity of distributed teams and additional cost overheads. In the Distributed Agile world, one can expect a similar cost saving when compared to Collocated Agile methodologies. In addition, the other benefits of agile are achieved too, such as: increased productivity of the teams, high visibility to stakeholders on project progress, adaptability to changing requirements, reduced defects, faster time to market, and reduced risk.

Global Talent Pool

Leaders looking beyond the cost savings that may be gained by the distributed team model are also motivated by the quick availability of local talent to fulfill their project needs. Hence, the concept of Distributed Agile development has gained momentum because the model provides the overall benefits of agile, plus it enables them to access a broad base of skilled talent. This flexible staffing model for acquiring the right talent at the right time allows the organization to meet demands to quickly ramp-up and ramp-down resources, thereby providing timely and cost-effective solutions.

Although many have not seen the benefits of distributed development and agile together due to a lack of proper guidance on how to apply both these models together, the concept is of interest to many organizations today, because these two strategies together create the best software development process.

Increased Productivity

Although there are certain downsides to Distributed Agile, such as a dip in productivity during the first few days when compared to a collocated approach, the benefits reaped due to distribution far outweigh these weaknesses. Industry experiences have demonstrated that there can be as much as a 20% loss of productivity when a team is distributed. In my experience, over time, as the team matures and uses the same processes with the same

customer, several case studies have shown that the productivity of collocated and distributed teams equalize. In many other cases, with a proper
Distributed Agile methodology in place, I have observed that teams working
for the same customer in a distributed environment have higher productivity
than collocated teams, in the long term.

Based on research and my experience using the different models, I was
able to draw an illustration, Figure 9.8, comparing the three approaches of
Distributed Waterfall, Collocated Agile, and Distributed Agile for the different
parameters of cost, talent pool, productivity, and the cost of quality.

I started the analysis by collecting data from eight different projects
where cost, talent pool, productivity, and cost of quality were measured.
Each of these projects was broken into three phases where each phase was
8–10 weeks in duration. Each of these eight projects were executed in a
Distributed Waterfall approach in the first phase where the first measurement
was carried out. In the second phase, the projects adapt the Collocated Agile
model and the second measurement was performed on cost of the project,
talent pool availability, productivity of the teams, and the cost of quality.
Finally, after executing for a few more weeks using the Collocated Agile
model, the projects matured to use the Distributed Agile method in the third
phase where the third measurement was performed. The illustration shows
that overall Distributed Agile provides greater benefits than any other models.

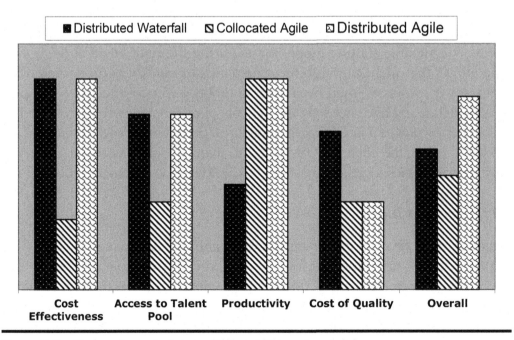

Figure 9.8 Comparisons between different life cycle models

Cost of Quality

Several projects following the waterfall approach have tried to attain high quality results. I have observed several such projects but these rarely succeed. This is because of the sequential development approach due, in which defects get postponed to later phases and need to be corrected resulting in a higher cost of quality.

I personally have experienced that by following agile there is a vast benefit achieved in cost of quality and several projects have demonstrated superior results. Unfortunately, none of the agile methodologies today concern tracking or measuring cost of quality. Irrespective of whether the teams are collocated or distributed, following agile and measuring cost of quality, one can expect superior results in cost of quality.

Agile—A De Facto Formula 4.0 Methodology

Digital transformation is all about developing software for future in the nimblest fashion that can revolutionize the way business is conducted, and future-proofing your enterprises for the continuously changing internal factors, external competitors, industry trends, and new technologies and finally reducing costs.

With this in mind, an agile approach to rolling out new products for an enterprise has become mandatory for any product development organization.

Figure 9.9 depicts benefits of agile methodology, thereby implying that agile is the best way to go for any digitally transformed enterprise.

Flexibility

At the heart of agile is the flexibility it offers in developing software in iterations and deploying to production or production like infrastructure. Similarly, at the heart of digital transformation is the Atomic architecture that has the ability to develop software independently and in isolation. A combination of these two features provides enormous benefits to enterprises in their digital transformation journey.

Traditionally, new business initiatives are carved out with detailed requirements and little room for change, particularly as the project kicks off. The agile process accepts change, and even expects it. If the team discovers that a different solution provides better results for their specific challenges, then they have the flexibility to switch. Likewise, if the businesses priorities change halfway, changes can be adapted much faster with agile.

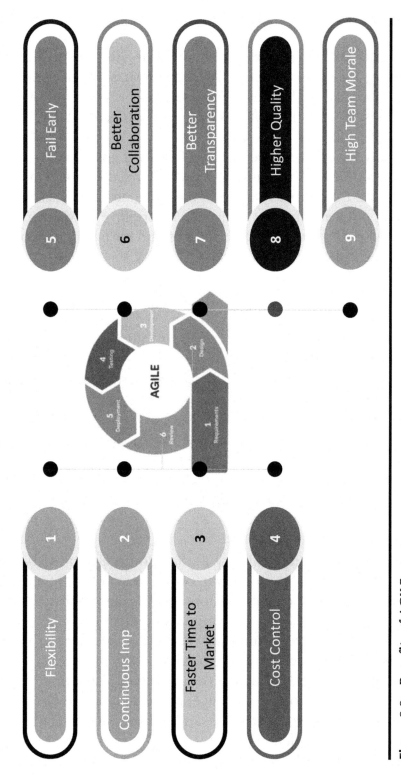

Figure 9.9   Benefits of AGILE

Continuous Learning and Developments

Agile teams are always learning, collaborating, and adjusting throughout regular iterations, reviewing what is working well and what can be improved. It means everyone has the time to not only expand their own knowledge, but all learnings can be identified, shared, and applied to the product development at each stage before moving forward.

Frequent Value Delivered

Working in short, productive sprints mean that epic or user stories are delivered incrementally as the product evolves. It is not surprising to hear digital transformation projects expected to last up to 1 or 2 years, if not more. In fact, digital transformation is a process that should never end. Working in an agile manner ensures that an enterprise's digital transformation journey happens in parallel to the product development and learnings are applied at frequent intervals. At the same time, continuously valuable products are delivered, more frequently, applying the latest learning and best practices.

> **DEFINITION**
>
> A ***sprint*** *is a short, time-boxed period when a product team works to complete a set amount of work.*

Cost Control

Keeping sprint lengths the same throughout product development allows the team to know exactly how much work can be accomplished, and therefore the cost for each sprint. It also allows for budget refinements on a regular basis and changes to be made, often without exorbitant costs as a result.

Failing Early or No Failure

An agile approach to digital transformation projects practically eliminates the chance of failing late in the process, which means there are no failures to a program as whole. Daily updates, constant communication, regular testing, and collaborative feedback along with working software at the end of each sprint ensure nothing is missed and every issue is captured and dealt with early.

Higher Collaboration, Communications, and Engagement

Digital transformation will never be achieved with just one team. To be successful the business and IT units need to work in unison with a clear vision of the organizational challenges that need to be solved. Agile in a product enterprise encourages regular communication, constant collaboration, feedback sessions, and continuous stakeholder management, which is critical to the success of any product team.

Full Transparency

With regular collaboration, communication, and updates between multiple agile teams yield higher visibility across the business. With working software being delivered in shorter intervals this transparency and visibility on progress of product development becomes much more apparent. Agile ensures every team member up to the key stakeholders has the opportunity to know how product development is going. Daily updates and progress charts offer concrete, tangible ways to track progress and manage expectations at every level.

High Quality

Quality of work improves within an agile environment because testing and optimization starts from the very beginning. It naturally allows for the early sight of any issues and relevant adjustments to be made quickly. Agile within digital transformation also encourages teams to embrace innovation and technological excellence.

Higher Team Morale

There is no change or innovation without people. To create a highly motivated and high performing product engineering team requires a level of self-management, the encouragement of creativity, time to reflect, regular knowledge sharing, and continuous learning—all of which are advantages of the agile process. Teams that are constantly working overtime to meet unrealistic deadlines will inevitably lack the inclination, or time, to think about anything else other than the task in hand, stifling the creation of any new and innovative ideas.

Notes

1. https://go.forrester.com/blogs/10-04-26-how_would_you_define_customer_outcome/
2. https://www.devops-research.com/dora-joins-google-Cloud.html

Chapter 10

Human Resource Management

As digital technologies dramatically reshape industry after industry, many companies are pursuing large-scale change efforts to capture the benefits of these trends or simply to keep up with competitors. In a McKinsey global survey on digital transformations, more than eight in ten respondents stated that their organizations have undertaken such efforts in the past 5 years.[1] Yet success in these transformations is proving to be elusive. While McKinsey said that earlier research has found that fewer than one-third of organizational transformations succeed at improving a company's performance and sustaining those gains, the latest results find the success rate of digital transformations to be even lower.

Enterprises that have achieved success in their digital transformation journey have first defined their business drivers for the transformation and then have focused on the following four characteristics: leadership, capability building, empowering workers, and upgrading of processes, tools, and technologies. These categories suggest where and how companies can start to improve their chances of successfully making digital changes to their business.

As per the McKinsey survey, the results from successful transformations show that these organizations have deployed more technologies than less successful ones do. Combined with technology, the most important aspect is to have the right set of people and culture within an organization, which provides a definite path to success for any organization in their digital transformation journey.

Formula 4.0 People Identification

A high-performing team delivers exceptional results time and time again, irrespective of the challenges they encounter. While continuously delivery these high results may seem unrealistic, lots of efforts go into building such a team, both by the members themselves and their leaders.

Formula 4.0 supports the creation of high-performing teams with a framework that attracts individuals who are of the right caliber to support an enterprise in their digital transformation journey.

Traditionally, enterprises follow a triangle pyramid as depicted in Figure 10.1 where juniors are placed at the bottom of the pyramid and seniors at the top. This is how traditional enterprises have operated and it was indeed the right model since technology was stable with little unknowns. Project execution was quite methodical in nature with little to medium level of automation in project life cycles.

Referring to Figure 10.1, section C consists of resources with fewer than 3 years of experience and typically also includes a percentage of recent college graduates. This is called the *bottom* of the pyramid. These are typically junior developers and testers.

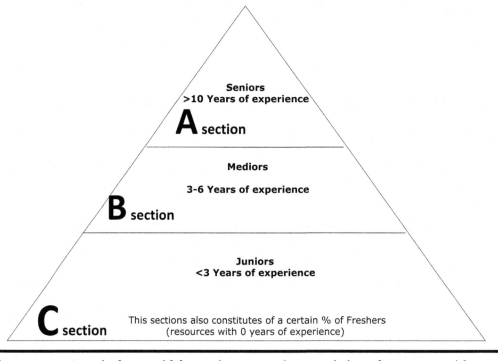

Figure 10.1   A typical pyramid for project execution consisting of resources with different experience levels

Section B consists of resources with mid-level experience (3–6 years), also known as mediors. These are typically developers and testers along with some junior designers, senior developers, and senior testers. This is also referred to as the *bottom +1* of the pyramid.

Section A consists of highly experienced technical resources, including architects, senior designers, and senior developers and testers. This section is typically referred to as the *top −1* of the pyramid. Section A also consists of a Scrum Master and Product Manager including enterprise and business architects, referred to as the *top* of the pyramid.

Over time this pyramid structure has rooted into the competency of resources within an enterprise. As depicted in Figure 10.2, this means that a small portion of high-performing individuals exist within a team and these are the ones depicted at the top of the pyramid.

Section D consists of elite performers who are core for the success of any enterprise or engagement. These are individuals who are good at what they do and can go the extra mile to learn and adapt to any new changes within the industry or enterprise, be it from a technological or business side. They have a high appetite to learn and contribute to the overall product and enterprise success.

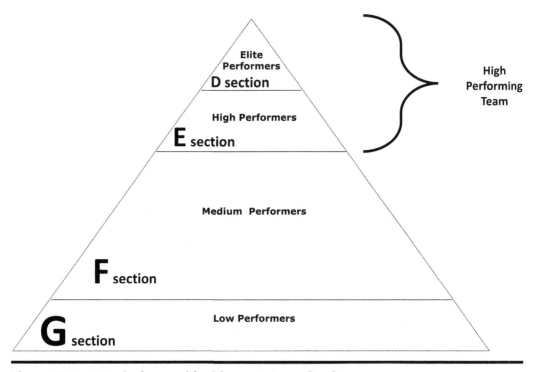

Figure 10.2   A typical pyramid with competency levels

Section E consists of resources who are high performers and are important to the product team. These are individuals who are good at what they do and support the enterprise in their area of expertise and contribute to the overall product success.

Section F consists of resources with medium competency. These are individuals who are good at what they do but do not necessarily go the extra mile to support the program or project, not because they are not willing to, but because they do not have the technical competency to do so.

Section G consists of resources who are low performers and many organizations during their annual appraisal or performance review cycle fire these from the organization.

Several enterprises are still operating in the traditional pyramid structure described earlier, and at the same time are aspiring to transform their whole organization to digital. The traditional pyramid is not the right for model for a digitally transformed organization.

Enterprises need to mandatorily change their structures to ensure success in their digital transformation journey. Formula 4.0 mandates that a Product Organization needs to move to a diamond structure in contrast to the traditional pyramid. It also moves away from measuring competency of resources based on their experience level. The only measure in a diamond-based Formula 4.0 structure is the competency of individuals, which are categorized into one of the three quadrants as depicted in Figure 10.3. There is no place for low performers in a diamond structure.

Section A consists of elite performers; Section B consists of competent resources; and Section C has resources with medium competency.

Across the diamond structure in all the three sections, individuals with all variety of roles can be found such as agile coaches, a Scrum Master, Product Managers, enterprise and business architects, and product engineering teams.

The Cost Implications of a Traditional Pyramid

In a traditional triangle pyramid, juniors fall at the bottom which constitute 50–60% of the team, mediors fall in the middle quadrant which constitute of 30–40% of the team respectively, and rest are seniors which constitute of roughly 10% of the team.

This model has existed for decades and typically organizations start at a low-cost baseline since it is considered as a highly optimized pyramid. Due to the large number of juniors in this mix, the initial level productivity

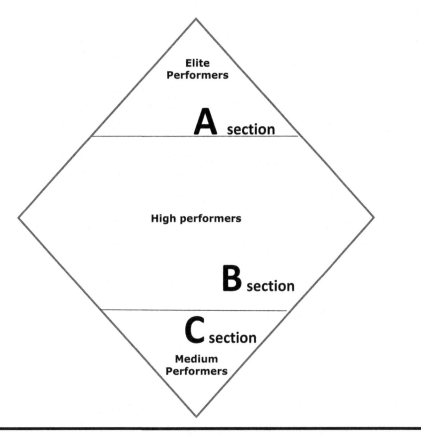

Figure 10.3 Diamond structure with competency levels

during the first few months is always low since the learning curve tends to be high. In addition, during my 20+ years of experience, I have encountered that a minimum of roughly 20–30% of the team gets replaced in the first 6 months due to a mismatch of individual competencies against project demands or capabilities. Due to this, I personally have found that it takes somewhere between 3 and 5 months for a team of 20–30 resources to stabilize and deliver a reasonable level of productivity.

Figure 10.4 provides a view on how productivity levels increase and stabilize over a period of time within a traditional pyramid structure. It is clear from Figure 10.4 that the initial productivity levels are quite low and mature gradually to a stable state. This implies that the cost of the product team is higher during the initial stages when compared to the value or productivity they deliver.

In contrast to a traditional pyramid, the Formula 4.0 diamond structure depicted in Figure 10.5 provides guaranteed higher productivity results from the first month as compared to a traditional pyramid. This is due to the fact

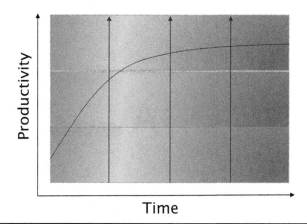

Figure 10.4 Productivity levels for a traditional pyramid

that only competent resources that fit the job are introduced into the product team from the start.

In summary, the cost of the diamond structure will not be higher than a traditional triangle pyramid once enterprises start measuring the productivity of the team over time.

My personal experience with more than six enterprises that have transitioned from a traditional pyramid to a diamond structure has demonstrated that product teams using the diamond pyramid are over 30% cheaper than a traditional pyramid. This data was measured for a 12-month period in these case studies.

Utilizing the Formula 4.0 diamond structure, enterprises have reaped better results in terms of cost of the average resource compared to a

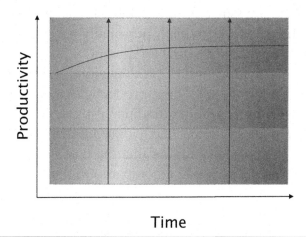

Figure 10.5 Productivity levels of a diamond structure

traditional pyramid. Results do however need to be measured for a minimum of 12 months period in the following areas:

- Ramp-up costs—any new resource inducted into the product team will incur ramp-up costs such as increased wages compared to existing resources, cost of transition from old resource to new resource, time taken to understand the new product, and so on.
- Productivity of individuals within the team.

The diamond structure is mandatory for enterprises to succeed in their digital transformation journey using Formula 4.0. It is essential that a motivated and competent product engineering team is identified that will develop the best product for an enterprise in the most agile and cost-effective manner. The Hackfest model assists in identifying the right product engineering teams, which will be discussed in more detail below.

Formula 4.0 Hackfest Model

Hackfest is a Formula 4.0 model which provides an approach on how product engineering teams need to be identified. Hackfest follows a step-by-step approach starting from shortlisting individuals for the Product Organization to identification of competent resources until the time they are trained and deployed into individual product development teams.

The Hackfest model evaluation and selection process moves away from subjective-based evaluation to being fully objective-based. Therefore, the chances of recruiting a motivated and skilled resource doubles compared to traditional hiring processes.

The four phases in the Formula 4.0 Hackfest model are depicted in Figure 10.6.

Each enterprise needs to tailor the Hackfest model based on their organizational landscape. Formula 4.0 provides a guideline below on how this can be enabled for each of the four steps.

Shortlisting

The first phase is the shortlisting phase, where all potential individuals of the product engineering team are evaluated comprehensively on their core skills. Enterprises need to be prepared with a technical assessment kit that can support the shortlisting of individuals for the next phase.

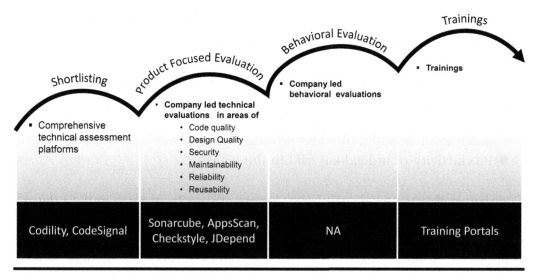

Figure 10.6   Four-phase Hackfest model

Alternatively, there are lot of industry leading platforms such as Codility, Codesignal, and Hackerrank that can help enterprises in the shortlisting of resources through online coding tests.

Product Focused Evaluation

The second phase is product focused evaluation where individuals are evaluated on their technical skills by asking them to develop EPICS or User Story that are specific to the actual product. During the shortlisting phase, individuals are assessed on their core skills based on industry standards; however, during product focused evaluation individuals are assessed on how they will perform during real-time situations, specific to the product. Enterprises need to ensure that a development platform is made available with all tools and technologies that replicate the actual live environment of the product development team. Such a platform is known as a product focused evaluation (PFE) platform.

For one of the enterprises I worked with named ABC Corporation, we developed a PFE platform with a replica of the actual development environment. ABC Corporation was developing a retail banking product using java language and microservice architecture. A development and operations (DevOps) pipeline was created with version control tool Github, Maven for build automation, CA DevTest tool for unit testing automation, and uDeploy Ansible tool for deployment automation.

Formula 4.0 recommends creating a PFE platform replicating the actual development environment which the product team will be working in. Such a platform will aid in evaluating how well individuals will deliver productivity once they are deployed into the product engineering team. Individuals need to perform development for the EPICS or user Stories utilizing the complete PPE platform. Once development is completed by individuals, evaluation is performed on:

- Code quality
- Design quality
- Level of security considered in the code
- How well code has been written from maintainability perspective
- How well code has been written from reliability perspective, and so on

There are several tools available in the market which can perform the above validation. In the above case study for ABC Corporation, tools such as SonarCube was used for static code quality analysis, jDepend was used to validate design quality with respect to maintainability, performance and reliability, and AppScan was used for code security.

Behavior Evaluation

All applicants who successfully complete a product focused evaluation are further assessed on their behavioral skills. Behavioral evaluation is a process to discover how interviewees act in specific employment-related situations. The logic on how one behaved in the past will likely predict how that individual will behave in the future i.e., past performance predicts future performance. There are several tools available in the market such as Chally assessment which assesses individuals on their behavioral skills that can be utilized, or specific inhouse evaluation mechanisms can be created by enterprises themselves.

Trainings

In Chapter 9, we discussed team characteristics and the definition of core secondary and supporting skills.

Once an individual successfully completes behavioral evaluation the next step in the Hackfest model is to prepare individuals for deployment to the product team. To ensure that there is the right level of productivity achieved from day 1, individuals need to be supported with training on their supporting skills, if required. Individuals should be trained to a level that they will be able to utilize the supporting skill with minimal supervision required from their superiors and peers.

The Hackfest model may look like a lengthy four-stage interview process, but if you understood the nuances of this model, there is just one round of comprehensive evaluation in each area. With such an evaluation, a 360-degree assessment can be performed on each individual. As an example, with product focused evaluations an individual is assessed on their development skills from several angles such as code quality, security, reliability, and maintainability. This clearly articulates the coding style of an individual and provide a view on their strengths and weaknesses, based on which decisions can be made. This implies that projects will be far more successful if the right resources can be introduced in the product development teams.

With the Hackfest model enterprises can assess hundreds of resources in one go, providing necessary infrastructure such as a PFE platform is available at scale. My own personal experience have demonstrated that a well-planned Hackfest can be completed in 2 days for around 200 applicants, which is quite an attractive prospect for large scale resource requirements with tight deadlines to meet.

Note

1. The online survey was in the field from January 16, 2018, to January 26, 2018, and garnered responses from 1,793 participants representing the full range of regions, industries, company sizes, functional specialties, and tenures. Of them, 1,521 have been part of at least one digital transformation in the past 5 years at either their current or previous organizations. To adjust for differences in response rates, the data are weighted by the contribution of each respondent's nation to global GDP.

Chapter 11

Importance of DevSecOps in a Product-Based Organization

In Chapter 9, we discussed the importance of agile methodology in a Product Organization. Agile is an iterative approach which focuses on collaboration, customer feedback, and small, rapid releases. Agile methodology has delivered superior results to many organizations that have transitioned from a project-based organization to a product-based organization. Followed by agile is a term most widely used in the information technology (IT) industry, which is development and operations (DevOps). DevOps is an approach to software development that accelerates the build life cycle (formerly known as release engineering) using automation. DevOps focuses on continuous integration (CI) and continuous delivery (CD) of software by leveraging on-demand IT resources (infrastructure as code) and by automating integration, test, and deployment of code. This merging of software development (Dev) and IT operations (Ops) reduces time to deployment, decreases time to market, minimizes defects, and shortens the time required to resolve issues.

Using DevOps, leading companies have been able to reduce their software release cycle time from months to (literally) days. This has enabled them to grow and lead in fast-paced, emerging markets. Companies like Google, Amazon, and many others now release software many times per day. By improving the quality and cycle time of code releases, DevOps has gained in popularity and been a great success for a number of enterprises. Traditionally, what happens in the legacy world is that developers create their code, pass it to quality assurance or testing teams, who then test the code, identify any bugs, and pass its back to developers. Developers will then fix the code and return it for more testing, before it is handed over to the operations team for support and maintenance of the product. This is a common practice which is followed in a waterfall development methodology. An agile software development process also partly follows this model with an exception that developers and testers within development cycle work in tandem without any handoffs, although handoffs are still passed to operations team after testing for deployment. This clearly shows a lack of collaboration between development, testing, and deployment teams which ultimately leads to a slow development and deployment cycle. DevOps eliminates this challenge completely since there is only one team for development and operations, and therefore there are no handoffs.

A DevOps life cycle spans across several stacks such as version control, CI, and CD and deployment. All these stacks are monitored continuously as part of the DevOps principles.

Figure 11.1 is a logical representation on how code moves from one phase to another in a DevOps environment.

Any new functionality that is built or differs from the existing functionality follows the same DevOps cycle. Imagine a new code is developed. The first step is that the code is committed into a version control system by the team of developers. Next, it goes through the build phase after which testers test the code and provides a defect report which moves the code back to the build phase again. Once the code is defect free, it is moved to deployment for integration and retesting. Once all integration defects are resolved, it is moved to production and then into the operations cycle. Any code changes by the operations team follow the same procedure of version control, build, test, and deployment.

In a DevOps model, the above process is fully automated from the time the development team starts to develop and commit the code to the time

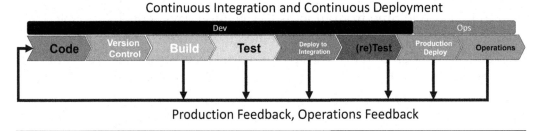

Figure 11.1   DevOps life cycle

code is deployed into production. This is known as the DevOps pipeline. The pipeline is automated via different tools available in the market. As an example, Jenkins is an open source automation server, which enables developers to reliably build, test, and deploy their software. CVS (version control system) is used for version control, Git repository is used for the development team to commit the code, and so on.

According to the 2015 State of DevOps Report:[1] "high-performing IT organizations deploy 30× more frequently with 200× shorter lead times; they have 60× fewer failures and recover 168× faster."

Figure 11.2 depicts the importance of DevOps. DevOps improves collaboration between all stakeholders from planning through delivery and automation of the delivery process, in order to:

- Improve the frequency of deployment and shorten lead time between fixes—high-performing organizations deploy code 30× more frequently than their peers who do not follow DevOps.
- Achieve faster time to market—the time required for changes to go from "code committed" to successfully running code in production is 200× faster for these high-performing DevOps teams when compared to their peers.
- Lower failure rate of new releases—matured DevOps organizations have 60× fewer failures in the first place.
- Improve mean time to recovery—matured DevOps organizations have 60× fewer failures in the first place and recover 168× faster when an incident does occur.

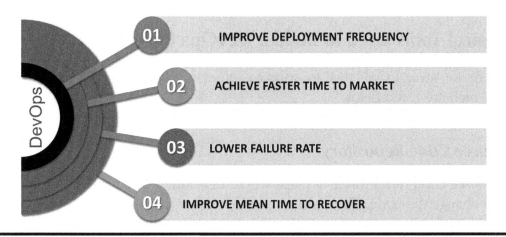

Figure 11.2   DevOps advantages

Continuous Integration (CI) and Continuous Delivery (CD) in DevOps

CI and CD are two of the best practices for DevOps teams to implement. CI and CD embody a culture, set of operating principles, and collection of practices that enable application development teams to deliver code changes more frequently and reliably. The implementation is also known as the CI/CD pipeline.

CI is a coding philosophy and set of practices that drive development teams to implement small changes and check in code to version control repositories frequently. The technical goal of CI is to establish a consistent and automated way to build, package, and test applications. With consistency in the integration process in place, teams are more likely to commit code changes more frequently, which lead to better collaboration and software quality.

CD picks up where CI ends. It automates the delivery of applications to selected infrastructure environments. Most teams work with multiple environments other than the production, such as development and testing environments, and CD ensures there is an automated way to push code changes to these environments. CI and CD tools help store the environment-specific parameters that must be packaged with each delivery.

CI and CD require continuous testing because the objective is to deliver quality applications and code to users. Continuous testing is often implemented as a set of automated regressions, performances, and other tests that are executed in the CI/CD pipeline.

Typical Tools Used to Build a DevOps Pipeline

There are several tools that are used to automate the DevOps pipeline, some of which are listed below.

Source Code Repository

A source code repository is a place where developers check in, check out, and change the code. The source code repository manages the various versions of code that are checked in, so developers do not write over each other's work. Popular source code repository tools include Git, Subversion, Cloudforce, Bitbucket, and TFS.

Build Server

The build server is an automation tool that compiles the code in the source code repository into an executable code base. One of the popular build server tools is Jenkins.

Configuration Management

Configuration management is a practice of managing and automating all the configurations of the software applications. Popular configuration management tools are Puppet and Chef.

Test Automation Tools

DevOps testing focuses on automated testing within the build pipeline to ensure that by the time you have a deployable build, you are confident it is ready to be deployed. Popular tools are Selenium and Cucumber.

CI/CD Tools or Pipeline Orchestration

A CI/CD pipeline is like a manufacturing assembly line that begins from the time a developer develops the code to the time the code gets deployed to the production environment. A CI/CD tool such as CircleCI, AWS CodeBuild, Azure DevOps, Atlassian Bamboo, or Travis CI is used to automate the steps and provide reporting for a CI/CD pipeline. A typical CD pipeline has build, test, and deploy stages.

Infrastructure

Cloud infrastructures such as Amazon Web Services and Microsoft Azure are examples of virtual infrastructures. A DevOps pipeline can be completely built using features of the Cloud in a few minutes. There are also private Clouds such as vCloud from VMware. Private virtual infrastructures enable you to run a Cloud on top of the hardware in your data center.

DevSecOps

With business demand for DevOps, agile and Cloud services, traditional security processes have become a major roadblock targeted for elimination, and it is lot easier to bypass all of them together. Traditional security operates from the position that once a system has been designed and built, its security defects can then be determined by security staff and corrected by business operators before the system is released. A process designed this way only works where the pace of business activities is a waterfall approach and is agreed by all parties. Unfortunately, the belief that security must operate in a waterfall manner is flawed with the introduction of agile methodologies and has since created inherent risks within the system because business decisions need to be addressed at the speed at which the business wants.

One big issue that is seen in an agile DevOps environment is that application developers do not understand security and the infrastructure network, security teams do not understand applications, and this skill gap has created a large hole in the organizations strategy from a cybersecurity standpoint. Most attacks these days are being seen on applications rather than the network and this is because security is thought of too late in the process. This is the key reason why DevSecOps becomes so important. With the introduction of DevSecOps, traditional security is no longer an option because traditional security comes too late in the cycle and the pace at which product releases are required in the digital world clubbed with automation using DevOps makes tradition security practices obsolete.

DevSecOps introduction eases this challenge. The purpose and intent of DevSecOps is to build on the mindset that "everyone is responsible for security" with the goal of safely distributing security checks and balances at speed and scale to everyone within an enterprise via the DevOps pipeline. DevSecOps means introducing security features within the DevOps or CI/CD pipeline as depicted in Figure 11.3. This is known as shift left security.

DevSecOps aims to embed security in every part of the development and operations process. It is about trying to automate core security tasks by embedding security controls and processes in the DevOps workflow rather than being bolted on at the end when code is pushed to the production stage.

An ideal DevSecOps should begin when a developer starts to write a code or download the code from any external sources. This means that security should be embedded right at the code creation stage before it is committed in the DevOps cycle. This includes checking libraries, third party components, and so on.

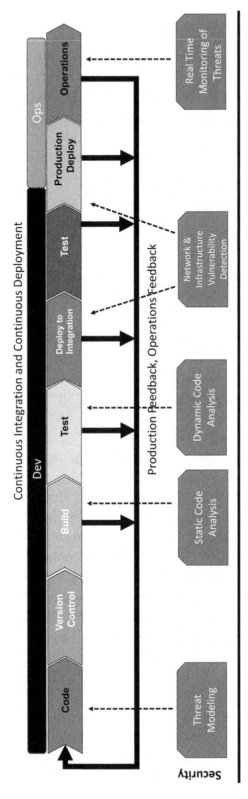

Figure 11.3   DevSecOps pipeline

Once the code is moved to build and test, there is a need to do a full-fledged static and dynamic code analysis. As the code gets ready to move to production in the DevOps pipeline, infrastructure and network infrastructure scanning and assurance capabilities need to be introduced to ensure there are no vulnerabilities. Finally, once the code is in production, operations should be enabled with real-time monitoring and resolving of threats.

Some of the key security features to be included in the DevOps pipeline to enable a highly secure DevSecOps pipeline are described below.

Application Security Threat Modeling

The Software Engineering Institute estimates that 90% of reported security incidents result from exploits against defects in the design or code of software. Ensuring software integrity is key to protecting the infrastructure from threats and vulnerabilities and reducing the overall risk of cyber-attacks.[2]

Security in application development is often an afterthought and seen as an impediment to developers. This had traditionally led to more critical vulnerabilities in production and an increased risk to the business. The remediation costs are greater than those of implementing security by design in the early stages of the software development life cycle (SDLC). Threat modeling is a solution that implements security in the design phase of the SDLC, before any code ever gets written.

Threat modeling is the practice of identifying and prioritizing potential threats and security mitigations to protect something of value, such as confidential data or intellectual property. By continuously threat modeling applications, enterprises can better protect applications while educating the development team and building a culture of security throughout the enterprise.

Threat modeling delivers more value if it is executed consistently and repeatedly. Often, when threat modeling is conducted on a consistent basis throughout an enterprise application portfolio, secure design patterns begin to emerge that can be documented, leveraged, and reused by application development teams. This contributes to the establishment of a proactive DevSecOps culture.

Design patterns also serve as the basis for standard, repeatable application security requirements for the enterprise. For example, all data in transit should be encrypted, and all internal applications should leverage single sign-on (SSO) for authentication. Standard design patterns and requirements developed from threat modeling can go a long way toward reducing risk to the organization and remove a lot of the variety and complexity in security architectures that often lead to breaches.

The Microsoft Threat Modeling tool is an example that makes threat modeling easier for all developers through a standard notation for visualizing system components, data flows, and security boundaries. It also helps threat modelers identify classes of threats they should consider based on the structure of their software design.

Static Application Security Testing (SAST)

SAST is a set of technologies designed to analyze application source code for coding and design conditions that are indicative of security vulnerabilities. SAST solutions analyze an application from the "inside out" in a nonrunning state.

SAST is frequently used to identify flaws prior to deployment. SAST provides vulnerability information and remediation suggestions for development teams to resolve. There is relation and overlap between SAST tools and static code analysis software, but SAST is more focused on security testing. Static code analysis products, on the other hand, combine a number of analytical practices, test management, and team collaboration features.

Coverity static analysis by Synopsys is one such SAST tool that integrates seamlessly into the DevOps pipeline and helps development and security teams to find and fix defects and security flaws in code as it is being written. Another such tool is HCL AppScan Standard which protects against web application attacks and expensive data breaches by automating application security vulnerability testing.

Dynamic Application Security Testing (DAST)

DAST is a security checking process that uses penetration tests on applications while they are running. The more applications exposed to the Internet, the more potential vulnerabilities to a cyber-attack. The difference between SAST and DAST is that SAST tools scan the code for vulnerabilities, whereas DAST tools scan the application once it is functional.

DAST in the traditional world used to occur once applications have gone into production; however, with the introduction of DevSecOps, DAST is performed during the development process itself. Runtime tests integrated into the DevOps pipeline help in catching cyber-attacks and threats that may only be obvious once an application has gone live.

DAST continually scans websites as they evolve and continues after execution, allowing for automatic detection and assessment of anomalous behavior and code alternations. Once vulnerability is discovered, the developer is provided with an alert for fixing. Together with SAST, DAST is vital for web application security program effectiveness, as some errors and vulnerabilities only appear once production has started.

There are many DAST tools and vulnerability scanners in the market which easily integrate with CI tools and other applications. Some of them have powerful interfaces and provide developers with an intuitive UI and with relevant information about the vulnerabilities that it finds (how to fix, evidence, description). As an example, if you are using CircleCI as your CI tool, Probely's Orb can be a good DAST tool. Probely allows you to scan web application for over 1,000 vulnerabilities.

Open Source Vulnerability Assessment

It is a well-known fact that the number of open source components in any codebase of proprietary applications keeps rising. With this, the risk of these applications being compromised by attackers leveraging vulnerabilities in them increases.

Compiled after examining the findings from the anonymized data of over 1,100 commercial codebases audited in 2017 by the Black Duck On-Demand audit services group,[3] a report revealed that:

1. 96% of the scanned applications contain open source components, with an average of 257 components per application.
2. The average percentage of open source in the codebases of the applications scanned grew from 36% last year to 57%, suggesting that a large number of applications now contain much more open source than proprietary code.

Today, open source is being used extensively irrespective of the size of the organization. The reasons are quite obvious, namely that open source lowers development costs, speeds time to market, and accelerates innovation and developer productivity.

Though open source codebase is widely used by many organizations, they pose a risk to enterprise security despite their many benefits. Vulnerabilities and exploits in open source software's and tools are regularly disclosed through a variety of online sources, such as the National Vulnerability Database, mailing lists and project home pages. With over 80% of all cyber-attacks occurring at the application level, fixing known vulnerabilities in both commercial and internal applications should be of extreme importance to enterprises. Fixing vulnerabilities while in development is an important step in the DevSecOps world.

While there were bugs such as Heartbleed, Shellshock, and the DROWN attack which made headlines that were too big to ignore, most bugs found in code often go unnoticed.

DEFINITIONS

The ***Heartbleed Bug*** *is a serious vulnerability in the popular OpenSSL software library. This weakness allows the stealing of protected information, under normal conditions, by the SSL/TLS encryption used to secure the Internet.*

Shellshock, *also known as Bashdoor, is a family of security bugs in the Unix Bash shell, the first of which was disclosed on 24 September 2014.*

DROWN *is an acronym for Decrypting RSA with Obsolete and Weakened Encryption. DROWN allows attackers to break weak encryption to read and/or steal data.*

There are several tools available in the market which carry out third party vulnerability scans and can be plugged into the DevOps pipeline. Veracode SCA, for example, scans open source dependencies for known vulnerabilities and makes recommendations on version updating. Veracode SCA integrates into the DevOps pipeline through a simple command-line scan agent and delivers results in seconds. Teams can even use the same agent directly in their integrated development environment (IDE) to get feedback earlier.

WhiteSource is another such tool which is compatible with over 200 programming languages, as well as a wide variety of build tools and development environments. It runs automatically and continuously in the background, tracking the security, licensing, and quality of open source components, and matching them against WhiteSource's comprehensive database of open source repositories to provide real-time alerts as well as guidance on prioritization and remediation.

Network Vulnerability Detection

Network vulnerability scanning, also commonly known as "vuln scan," is an automated process of proactively identifying network and security vulnerabilities. The scanning process includes detecting and classifying system weaknesses in networks, communications equipment, and computers.

The dynamic nature of today's Cloud, On-Premises, and hybrid network environments requires continuous network vulnerability scanning to defend against the evolving threat landscape. Constant application updates and changes to applications and system configurations can introduce vulnerabilities and leave enterprises susceptible to an attack, even if these enterprises are keeping security controls up to date.

Tools such as AlienVault Unified Security Management (USM) help detect and remediate vulnerabilities in the environment before attackers exploit them. AlienVault USM delivers vulnerability scanning software as part of a unified platform that also includes asset discovery, intrusion detection, behavioral monitoring, event correlation, and log management.

Real-Time Monitoring of Threats

Real-time monitoring of threats involves the continual monitoring of enterprise networks or endpoints which could become access areas for hackers. This is because businesses currently face risks from viruses, malware, identity theft, worms, and web-based attacks. This is one of the reasons why real-time threat monitoring has become so important.

Integrating real-time threat monitoring in operations can help enterprises identify threats which might otherwise go unnoticed and by capturing them immediately, this ensures that they never become a problem. A reliable threat monitoring process ensures that an enterprise:

- Has a view on who is using networks, why, and whether activity poses any risk
- Understands data regulations in accordance with current network usage
- Monitors sensitive data at all times in accordance with data compliance
- Finds vulnerabilities straight away and fixes them

Datadog is one such tool that automatically detects threats across Cloud environments. It enables full security visibility across applications, networks, and infrastructure and detects security threats in real time.

Notes

1. https://puppetlabs.com/2015-devops-report
2. https://www.us-cert.gov/sites/default/files/publications/infosheet_
   SoftwareAssurance.pdf
3. https://www.em360tech.com/wp-content/uploads/2018/09/Synopsys-Open-
   Source-Security-and-Risk-Analysis.pdf

DATA ANALYTICS, AUTOMATION, IT-OT INTEGRATION, AND ENTERPRISE GOVERNANCE

V

This section will discuss the importance of data and how organizations need to utilize data for making business decisions.

We will further discuss the importance of automation using robotic process automation and AI that enables cost savings, process improvements, efficiency gains, and customer satisfaction.

We will also discuss that with Formula 4.0, Internet of Things can become a reality for enterprises.

Finally, in this section, we will discuss the importance of moving away from a business unit siloed operating model to enterprise-level governance. Enterprise-level governance is a recipe of success for any enterprise embarking on their digital transformation journey.

Chapter 12

Big Data and Analytics

The early 1990s, we saw the rise of the information age. Network connected computers and digital communication meant businesses were able to collect and leverage customer data to help develop new business models. This led to more efficient customer engagements, and the rise of online services has opened up a whole new way of working in many industries. Over the last 20 years, data strategy has become the foundation, and digital transformation is now largely reliant on data.

A digital transformation is not only about digitizing a channel or simply doing more things digitally, it has much broader scope than that. Digital transformation is about improving customer experiences and understanding the customer and competitors much better and using technology to address the business demands. To achieve this goal, enterprises need insights which purely come from data. This is one of the core reasons why data has become so much more important, and hence why the "data first" philosophy has become so popular. Data first effectively means that for any enterprise, data is the first thing to look at when making any business decisions.

Getting better data is key to eliminating the unknowns of a digital transformation. At Sprint, as Chief Data Officer Rob Roy explains, leaders call for "a new company culture that put data first."[1]

Having a data first mentality is a crucial first step; however, enterprises do need to put in place the processes and capabilities to be able to collect and make the data available in a fashion which can be used in the most timely and efficient way. The data also needs to be available at a speed by which businesses can make the right decisions and benefit from the insights generated from the data.

With the evolution of technology, data has evolved dramatically in recent years, in type, volume, and velocity. Earlier we had landline phones, but now we have smartphones—they are making our lives smarter as well as our phones smarter. Earlier we were using floppies to store data and now we use Cloud to store terabytes of data. Earlier we used to talk over phone and now we send texts, pictures, and make video calls over WhatsApp. With technology advancement, we are generating tremendous amount of data and this is called as Big Data.

Big data is a term that describes the large volume of data ranging from structured, semi-structured, and unstructured data.

Structured data is data which is organized into a formatted repository that is typically a database. It concerns all data which can be stored in database in a table with rows and columns. They have relational keys and can easily be mapped into predesigned fields. *Example:* Relational data.

Semi-structured data is the information that does not reside in a relational database but that have some properties that make it easier to analyze. With some process, one can store them in the relation database. *Example:* XML data.

Unstructured data is a data which is not organized in a predefined manner or does not have a predefined data model. *Example:* Word, PDF, Text, Media logs.

With big data, the deal is this data is not in a format that traditional database systems can handle. And apart from that, even the volume of data is also huge which traditional database systems cannot handle. This has given rise to big data platforms which provide massive storage for any kind of data, enormous processing power, and the ability to handle virtually limitless concurrent tasks or jobs and any type of data (structure, semi-structure, and unstructured).

(BIG) Data First Reference Model

Before we discuss about the data first reference model, let me give a bit of perspective on data pipeline.

In earlier days people used to walk miles to fetch water from different natural resources like wells and rivers and it was a manual process in which people used to fetch the water only for basic needs, but as the human race evolved, our needs also increased with time. We wanted more water in a more automated way, we wanted it more frequently and for multiple purposes, and so on. With the increase of needs, we invented new technologies to automate water supply into our houses which are the water pipelines. Using modern water pipelines, we receive water from wells and rivers to our home which is cleansed and can be used for multiple purposes.

Data pipeline goes exactly with the same concept as water pipelines. It is a mechanism to transfer data from point A to point B, through some intermediary steps, like points C and D. Points C, D, and E are the points where processing and cleansing takes place. So, in this basic about description point A is called as data producer, point B is data consumer, and points C and D are actual data pipeline.

Figure 12.1 provides an overview on the four core pillars in a data first reference model.

The first block is the data source, where data from external and internal sources arrive at the enterprise. In the data world there are different places from where data arrives such as external streams, feeds, mainframe systems, or simple excel files.

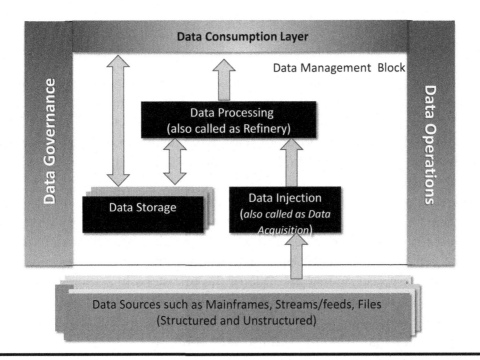

Figure 12.1   Data first reference architecture

The second block is the data management block (also called as data pipeline), where data is cleaned and refined to make it usable. This data is then made available for consumption in the appropriate format. Data management is a process that includes acquiring, validating, storing, and processing data to ensure the accessibility, reliability, and timeliness of the data for its users. Data acquisition, refinery, and data storage as depicted in Figure 12.1 form part of the data management layer.

The third block is data governance (DG), which is the process of managing the availability, usability, integrity, and security of the data in enterprise systems, based on internal data standards and policies that also control data usage.

The fourth block is called the consumption layer where data is consumed by different parties such as analytics platforms, reporting tools, or directly by data scientists or business users.

The fifth and final block is called the data operations layer. Data operations in context of Formula 4.0 is an automated, process-oriented methodology, to improve the quality of data, and reduce the cycle time of data analytics. Data operations applies to the entire data life cycle[2] starting from receiving data from data sources until managing and consuming the data.[3]

The Data Source

A data source is simply the point where data enters the organization. It can be structured data which comprises of clearly defined data types whose pattern makes them easily searchable, or unstructured data which is "everything else" and comprised of data that is usually not as easily searchable, including formats like audio, video, and social media postings or semi-structured data.

The data management block is where the data arrives at the enterprise from data sources and data management occurs. It includes everything from sales records, customer databases, feedback, social media channels, marketing lists, email archives, and any data gleaned from monitoring or measuring aspects of enterprise operations. One of the first steps in setting up a data strategy is assessing what enterprises have in the data source and measuring it against what they need. Enterprises might have everything they need already, or they may need to establish new sources.

The Data Storage Layer

The data storage layer is where enterprise data lives once it is gathered from different sources. It receives data from the various data sources and stores it in the most appropriate manner that is specific to the organization needs.

As depicted in Figure 12.1, the data storage layer sits at the bottom of the reference model. These are the technologies that store masses of raw data which comes from traditional sources such as online transaction processing (OLTP) databases, and less structured sources such as log files, sensors, web analytics, documents, and media archives.

Increasingly, storage is taking place in the Cloud or on virtualized local resources. Organizations are moving away from legacy storage toward commoditized hardware, and more recently to managed services offered by the likes of Amazon, such as Amazon S3.

As the volume of data generated and stored by companies has started to explode, sophisticated but accessible systems and tools are being developed.

There are several data storage systems, a few which are described below.

Hadoop HDFS—the classic big data file system. It became popular due to its robustness and limitless scale on commodity hardware.

Amazon S3—a service offered by Amazon Web Services that provides object storage through a web service interface, with 99.999999999% guaranteed durability. S3 is simple, secure, and provides a quick and cheap solution for storing limitless amounts of big data.

MongoDB—a mature open source document-based database, built to handle data at scale with proven performance. However, some have criticized its use as a first-class data storage system due to its limited analytical capabilities and lack of support for transactional data.

Data Injection Layer and Data Processing Layer

Data ingestion or data acquisition is the process for bringing in relevant data that has been created by a source outside the organization.

Data processing is the process of cleaning and refining the data for enterprise use. For any type of data, when it enters an organization (in most cases there are multiple data sources), it is most likely either not clean or not in the format that can be reported or analyzed directly by users inside or outside of the organization. Data processing is therefore needed first, which usually includes data cleansing, standardization, transformation, and aggregation.

Apache Spark, PostgreSQL, and Amazon Redshift are good examples of tools which can carry out this job.

Data Consumption Layer

This layer consumes the output provided by the data processing layer. Enterprises can run queries to answer questions the business is asking, slice and dice the data, build dashboards, and create visualizations, using one of many advanced tools.

In some cases, data in this layer is directly consumed by users within the organization and by entities external to the organization, such as customers, vendors, partners, and suppliers.

Using insights from this layer, enterprises can target customers for product offers. For example, with the business insight gained from data analysis, a company can use customer preference data and location awareness to deliver personalized offers to customers as they walk down the aisle or pass by the store.

These insights can also be used to detect fraud by intercepting transactions in real time and correlating them with the view that has been built using the data already stored in the enterprise. A customer can be notified of a possible fraud while the fraudulent transaction is happening, so corrective actions can be taken immediately.

There are several data consumption and analytic tools available in the market, some which are listed below.

> **Tableau**—a powerful BI and data visualization tool which connects to the data and allows you to drill down, perform complex analysis, and build charts and dashboards.
>
> **Chartio**—Cloud BI service that allows you to connect data sources, explore data, build SQL queries, and transform the data as needed. It allows for the creation of live auto-refreshing dashboards.
>
> **Looker**—Cloud-based BI platform that can query and analyze large data sets.

Data Operation

The term date operation or DataOps has taken its roots from the concept of development and operations (DevOps) and is more centered around software development. Data analytics can also achieve what software development attained with DevOps can, by bringing automation into development and testing of the data pipelines from source to consumption layers, and finally bringing automation into DataOps.

DEFINITION

Data Pipeline *is a broader term that encompasses steps in moving data from one system to another. In some cases, data may be moved from one system to another in raw format and in another case, it may be transformed by using the data injection and data processing layers. Referring back to Figure 11.1, data pipeline is the steps taken from data injection to the data processing layer including moving data back and forth to data storage.*

DataOps is the term used in the data world similar to DevOps being used in the software development world. DataOps can yield an order of magnitude improvement in quality and cycle time when data teams utilize new tools and methodologies in a model where data management and operations come together. The specific ways DataOps achieves these gains reflects the unique people, processes, and tools characteristic of data teams.

As depicted in Figure 12.2, the key to the success of DataOps is to bring different personnel together and enable a seamless integration and

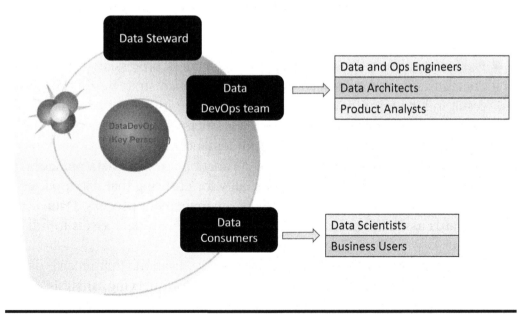

Figure 12.2   Personnel in DataOps

collaboration between them via set of practices, processes, and technologies. The key personnel in the DataOps world are listed below. These range from those who build the data pipelines to the ones who consume the data.

- Data Engineers and Operations Engineers—Data engineers core function is to create data pipelines i.e., ingestion, structuring and standardization, and processing of data. Operation engineers are individuals who support the management of the operations such as the setup of data infrastructure, helping to handle code deployment, the setup of data quality checks, and alerting & monitoring for the different flows. In the DataOps world data engineers and operation engineers are typically clubbed together.

- Data Scientists—Data scientist's roles can be quite varied and cover a wide range of skills. Depending on the specific position, they may end up in different parts of the enterprise. A data scientist turns raw data into valuable insights based on which enterprises create their business strategies. They interpret and analyze data from multiple sources to come up with solutions to existing problems or new ways to do business. They use industry knowledge, contextual understanding, and skepticism of existing assumptions to uncover solutions to business challenges.

- Data Architects—Data architects lead the overall architectural setup of projects involving data. They act as technical leaders with regards to what gets built, as well as choosing the appropriate technology stack for the data journey.

- Product Analysts—Product analysts are business professionals who help companies decide on which products and launch strategies are likely to result in long-term financial gain. They engage in market research, customer polling, and help choose new products or enhancements to the existing products that fill a need and demand in the market.

- Data Steward—Data stewardship is a functional role in data management and governance, with responsibility for ensuring that data policies and standards are followed in the data management process. Data stewards assist the enterprise in leveraging domain data assets to full capacity.

- Data Consumers—Individuals, groups, or applications that receive data in the form of a collection. The data is used for querying, analysis, and reporting. Examples of data consumers are data scientists or reporting tools such as Tableau.

Bringing all the above personnel together under one umbrella and integrating their work under an automation platform is called DataOps.

DataOps seeks to reduce the end-to-end cycle time of data analytics, from the origin of ideas to the literal creation of charts, graphs, and models that create value. The data life cycle relies upon people in addition to tools. For DataOps to be effective, it must manage collaboration and innovation between all these individuals. DataOps enforces agile development into data analytics so that data teams and users work together more efficiently and effectively.

In agile data development, the data team publishes new or updated analytics in short increments called sprints (a full explanation of sprints can be found in Chapter 9, if required). With innovation occurring in rapid intervals, the team can continuously reassess its priorities and more easily adapt to evolving analytics requirements. This type of responsiveness is impossible using a waterfall project management methodology, which locks a team into a long-development cycle with one "big-bang" deliverable at the end.

Agile development and DataOps add significant value to data analytics, but there is one more major component to DataOps. Whereas agile and DataOps relate to analytics development and deployment, data analytics also manages and orchestrates a data pipeline. Data continuously enters on one side of the pipeline, progresses through a series of steps and exits in the form of reports, models, and views. The data pipeline is the "operations" side of data analytics. It is helpful to conceptualize the data pipeline as a manufacturing line where quality, efficiency, constraints, and uptime must be managed. To fully embrace this manufacturing mindset, we call this pipeline the "data factory."

In DataOps, the flow of data through operations is an important area of focus. There are several software tools and frameworks in the market that support a DataOps approach to collaboration and increased agility. This includes date injection and data processing tools such as Alation, Talend, Stitch Data, Informatica, and Alteryx. There are also a number of log analyzer tools such as Loggly, Logz.io, and GoAccess. Finally, there are systems monitoring tools that support microservices architecture, as well as open source software that lets applications blend structured and unstructured data, which are also associated with the DataOps movement. Such software can include MapReduce, HDFS, Kafka, Hive, and Spark.

Data Governance

DG is the process of managing the availability, usability, integrity, and security of the data in enterprise systems, based on internal data standards and policies that also control data usage. Effective DG ensures that data is consistent and trustworthy and does not get misused. It is increasingly critical as organizations face new data privacy regulations and rely more and more on data analytics to help optimize operations and drive business decision-making.

A well-designed DG program typically includes a governance team, a steering committee that acts as the governing body and a group of data stewards. They work together to create the standards and policies for governing data, as well as implementation and enforcement procedures that are primarily carried out by the data stewards. In Chapter 15, we are going to discuss a mechanism where all key functions within the enterprise need to be governed at an enterprise level rather than in business unit silos. The DG team will be part of the enterprise governance team.

While DG is a core component of an overall data management strategy, organizations should focus on the desired business outcomes of a governance program instead of the data itself.

Without effective DG, data inconsistencies in different systems across an organization might not be resolved. For example, customer names may be listed differently in sales, logistics, and customer service systems. This could complicate data integration efforts and create data integrity issues that affect the accuracy of enterprise reporting and analytics applications. In addition, data errors might not be identified and fixed, further affecting analytics accuracy.

Poor DG can also hamper regulatory compliance initiatives, which could cause problems for companies that need to comply with new data privacy and protection laws, such as the European Union's General Data Protection Regulation (GDPR) and the California Consumer Privacy Act (CCPA). An enterprise DG program typically results in the development of common data definitions and standard data formats that are applied in all business systems, boosting data consistency for both business and compliance uses.

A key goal of DG is to break down data silos in an organization. Such silos commonly build up when individual business units deploy separate systems without centralized coordination or an enterprise data architecture. DG aims to harmonize the data in those systems through a collaborative process, with stakeholders from the various business units participating.

Another DG goal is to ensure that data is used properly, both to avoid introducing data errors into systems and to block potential misuse of personal data about customers as well as other sensitive information. This can be accomplished by creating uniformed policies on the use of data, along with procedures to monitor usage and enforce the policies on an ongoing basis. In addition, DG can help to strike a balance between data collection practices and privacy mandates.

Besides more accurate analytics and stronger regulatory compliance, the benefits that DG provides include improved data quality, lower data management costs, and increased access to needed data for data scientists, analysts, and business users.

Ultimately, DG can help improve business decision-making by giving executives better information. Ideally, that will lead to competitive advantages and increased revenue and profits for any enterprise.

Components of a Data Governance Framework

A DG framework consists of the policies, rules, processes, organizational structures, and technologies that are put in place as part of a governance program. It also spells out things such as a mission statement for the program, its goals, and how its success will be measured, as well as decision-making responsibilities and accountability for the various functions that will be part of the program. An enterprise DG framework should be documented and shared internally to show how the program will work, so that it is clear to everyone involved upfront.

DEFINITIONS

Metadata is *"data that provides information about other data."* In other words, it is *"data about data."* Many distinct types of metadata exist, including descriptive metadata, structural metadata, administrative metadata, reference metadata, and statistical metadata.

A *data catalog* is a collection of metadata, combined with data management and search tools, that helps data analysts and other data users to find the data that they need. It serves as an inventory of available data, and provides information to evaluate fitness data for intended uses.

A *data set* is a collection of data. In the case of tabular data, a data set corresponds to one or more database tables, where every column of a table represents a particular variable, and each row corresponds to a given record of the data set in question.

Data mapping is the process of creating data element mappings between two distinct data models.

Data Governance Implementation

The initial step in implementing a DG framework involves identifying the owners or custodians of the different data assets across an enterprise. The Chief Data Officer, executive sponsor, or dedicated DG manager then takes the lead in creating the program's structure, working to staff the DG team, identify data stewards, and formalize the governance committee.

It is mandatory that DG is managed at an enterprise level rather than within individual business units. Once the structure is finalized, the real work begins. The DG policies and data standards must be developed, along with rules that define how data can be used by authorized personnel. Moreover, a set of controls and audit procedures are needed to ensure ongoing compliance with internal policies and external regulations. This is to guarantee that data is used in a consistent way across applications. The governance team should also document where data comes from, where it is stored, and how it is protected from mishaps and security attacks.

Data Governance Tools

On the technology side, DG software can be used to automate aspects of managing a governance program. DG tools support program and workflow management, collaboration, development of governance policies, process documentation, the creation of data catalogs and other functions. There are several DG tools available from various vendors such as IBM, Informatica, Oracle, SAP, and SAS Institute, as well as data management specialists including Adaptive, ASG Technologies, Ataccama, Collibra, Erwin, Infogix, and Talend.

Data Security

Data security is a vital element in the DG framework and is the collective term for all the measures and tools used to guard both the data and analytics processes from attacks, theft, or other malicious activities that could harm or negatively affect them. In essence, data security is the process of guarding data and analytics processes, either on the Cloud or On-Premises.

What makes data big, fundamentally, is that enterprises have far more opportunities to collect it, from far more sources, than ever before. Enterprises use several data sources to collect data and many gather this data from millions of devices that are now Internet-capable such as smartphones and Internet of Things sensors. Data analytics emerges from this incredible escalation in the number of devices. It is really just the term for all the available data in a given area that a business collects with the goal of finding hidden patterns or trends within it.

Many of the tools associated with data analytics are however built with only limited features that can secure the data or protect enterprises against cyber-attacks. This is because data and analytics tools are not designed for security, but they are designed for analytics only. This poses a lot of security threats to enterprises which needs to be mitigated. Big data security risks include applications, users, devices, and more.

Data Security Tools

Formula 4.0 recommends that security is embedded in the data management process such that any vulnerable data does not move to production. Some of the security areas are listed below and for each of these areas there are specialized tools that can be deployed.

Encryption—encryption tools need to secure data in-transit and at-rest, and they need to do it across massive data volumes. Encryption needs to operate on many different types of data, both user and machine-generated. Encryption tools also need to work with different analytics toolsets and their output data, and on common storage formats including relational database management systems (RDBMS), non-relational databases like NoSQL, and specialized filesystems such as Hadoop Distributed File System (HDFS). Tools such as Eset Endpoint Encryption can be deployed into DataOps to do this job.

Centralized Key Management—centralized key management has been a best security practice for many years. It applies just as strongly in data environments, especially those with wide geographical distribution. Best practices include policy-driven automation, logging, on-demand key delivery, and abstracting key management from key usage. Amazon Web Services (AWS) Key Management Service (KMS) and Azure Key are two examples of effective key management programs.

User Access Control—user access control may be the most basic network security tool, but many companies practice minimal control because the management overhead can be very high. This is dangerous at the network level and can be disastrous in the data world. Strong user access control requires a policy-based approach that automates access based on user and role-based settings. Policy driven automation manages complex user control levels, such as multiple administrator settings that protect the big data platform against inside attacks.

Intrusion Detection and Prevention—intrusion detection and prevention systems are security workhorses. The nature of big data's distributed architecture lends itself to intrusion attempts. Intrusion prevention systems enable enterprises to protect the big data platform from intrusion. If at any point an intrusion happens, detection systems quarantine the intrusion before it can do any significant damage.

The above are just some of the areas where security plays an important role. In addition, data security must compliment other security measures such as endpoint security, network security, application security, and more to create an in-depth approach. By planning ahead and being prepared for the introduction of big data analytics, an enterprise will be able to help meet its objectives securely.

(BIG) Data First Strategy

The key to success for any organization is how well big data is being used in the organization to make business decisions. To make the right decisions, enterprises need to get the correct and relevant data at the right time to the business. This is one of the reasons why "data first" terminology has become so prominent. The strategy of data first is how we enable enterprises to move toward a data-driven organization where each and every major business decision is made from insights received from data. To make a data first strategy come true, data journeys need to be smartly managed.

The four key levers that make data first strategy succeed is depicted in Figure 12.3 and are detailed below.

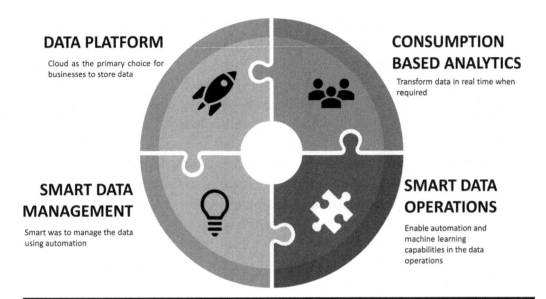

DATA PLATFORM

Cloud as the primary choice for businesses to store data

CONSUMPTION BASED ANALYTICS

Transform data in real time when required

SMART DATA MANAGEMENT

Smart was to manage the data using automation

SMART DATA OPERATIONS

Enable automation and machine learning capabilities in the data operations

Figure 12.3   Data first strategy key success levers

The First Lever: The Data Platform

Traditionally there had been a lot of platforms built On-Premises. However, over a period of time the characteristics of data have changed:

- Firstly, the volume of data has changed
- Secondly, the velocity of data has changed
- Thirdly, the variety of data has changed

Due to the constant change to these three elements, traditional systems are unable to adapt to the changes in the industry or meet business demands. Several organizations that embarked on their data journey a few years back are now starting to change their underlying data platform. Again new changes may emerge in future and changing data platform each time is not a solution. This is one of the reasons Cloud adoption for data has become essential, since Cloud makes the platform very adaptable and flexible to new changes. What this means is that enterprise can retire the old platforms or tools anytime they want and move to the latest ones in minutes without additional expenditure.

Cloud has become the primary location for businesses to store data; most have even moved their applications to Cloud platforms, and many of those businesses that have their data On-Premises today are soon planning to migrate to Cloud.

Enterprises are modernizing their data platforms to leverage new-age applications and advanced analytics, and at the same time they are moving their data and data platforms to Cloud.

Aside from the flexibility, Cloud provides to switch to the latest platforms based on an enterprise needs, there are several other reasons why enterprises want to move to Cloud, which are listed below.

Security and Data Protection—cybersecurity attacks are rising in sophistication[4] and because there is a shortage of security skills in the market this means that many companies are struggling to manage security in-house. Enterprises are therefore turning to third-party Cloud and managed security services, with Cloud providers delivering sophisticated cyber capabilities and solutions,[5] and Cloud helping to mitigate security incidents.[6]

Data Modernization—another reason for migrating to Cloud is because data modernization becomes much easier. Put simply, data modernization is the movement of data from legacy databases to modern databases. Enterprises today need timely and targeted analytics on existing data; many rely on a stream of insights based on data mining, exploration, and prediction.[7] Since much of that data is already on Cloud, it makes business sense for organizations to store their data in the same location.

Cost and Performance of IT Operations—this has long been a significant driver for Cloud adoption. However, cost has become less of a factor these days as there are so many benefits in moving to Cloud than outweigh expenditure.

The Second Lever: Smart Data Management

Once an enterprise receives the data, it needs to be managed correctly. What this means is that data arrives from different sources and all types of data are placed in a data storage layer such as Data Lake.

DEFINITION

*A **data lake** is a system or repository of data stored in its natural/raw format.*

Enterprises now need to decide which data needs to be brought into the enterprise to store it in the format it requires. Enterprises need to store the right data in the right format to carry out analytics and make the right deci-sions. For this a proper data management strategy should be in place, which means one needs to apply intelligence to the data instead of just cleansing data each and every time manually.

Now, how do we apply intelligence to clean the data?

This is called smart data management and is enabled with several AI lead tools that look at the past corrections that were made on the data. Based on the history of past corrections the system automatically takes a decision to correct data in real time. This means that enterprises do not need to wait for data quality analysts to come and manually correct the data, with smart data management accelerators and tools enterprises will be able to intel-ligently make a decision based on past actions. This is the essence of smart data management.

The Third Lever: Consumption-Based Analytics

Once we have the data lake set-up for an enterprise, it opens up access to a lot of individuals within the enterprise. Consumption-based analyt-ics means that data is transformed in real time whenever data is required for consumption. This means real-time transformation happens whenever any reports are to be generated or whenever a system needs data. With consumption-based analytics enterprises do not need to carry out data trans-formation offline and get the data stored into their data platform or send it to the downstream systems. This process is eliminated with the introduction of consumption-based analytics.

Combining consumption-based analytics with self-service analytics and embedded analytics makes the data analytics much more interesting. A lot of hard work goes into extracting and transforming data into a usable for-mat, but once this is done, data analytics should provide users with greater insights into their customers, business, and industry that can help them make the right decisions.

Self-Service Analytics—a form of business intelligence in which busi-ness professionals are enabled and encouraged to perform queries and generate reports on their own, with nominal IT support. Self-service analytics or ad hoc reporting gives users the ability to develop rapid reports, empowering them to analyze their data. End users can analyze their data by dynamically modifying, drilling through or adding calcula-tion functions to a report. This flexibility decreases IT resource drain freeing up valuable development resources. There are several tools such as Tableau or Qlik Sense that enable self-service analytics.

Embedded analytics—delivers real-time reporting, interactive data visualization, and/or advanced analytics, including machine learning, directly into an enterprise business application such as an HR or payroll system.[8] The data is managed by an analytics platform, and the visualizations and reports are placed directly within the application user interface.[8] In other words, embedded analytics is a digital workplace capability where data analysis occurs within a user's natural workflow, without the need to toggle to another application. Moreover, embedded analytics tend to be narrowly deployed around specific processes such as marketing campaign optimization, sales lead conversions, inventory demand planning, and financial budgeting. These analytics provide context-sensitive decision support within a user's normal workflow.

The Fourth Lever: Smart Data Operations

Smart data operations (also known as smart DataOps) means enabling automation and machine learning capabilities in data operations. Smart DataOps is also known as artificial intelligence operations or AIOps.

As we discussed, DataOps seeks to achieve a smooth, consistent, and rapid flow of data through enterprises. Many enterprises these days are processing petabytes and exabytes of information on a daily basis for their business needs. Such an uninhibited data flow is increasingly vital to enterprises seeking to make business decisions with data-driven insights. Automation powered by artificial intelligence and machine learning is therefore becoming far more essential.

Enterprises need to increasingly rely on AI technologies in data operations to help address rapid growth in data volumes and variety, and there is a need for teams to analyze this data and find ways to automate and predict issues before they occur.

AIOps is the application of artificial intelligence for data operations in IT. AIOps deals with combining algorithmic and human intelligence to provide full visibility into the state and performance of the IT systems that businesses rely on.

The "AI" in AIOps does not mean that human operators will be replaced by automated systems. Instead, humans and machines operate together, with algorithms augmenting human capabilities and enabling them to focus on what is meaningful.

AIOps works with existing data sources, including traditional IT monitoring, log events, application and network performance anomalies, and more. All data from these source systems are processed by a mathematical model that is able to identify significant events automatically, without requiring manual pre-filtering. A second layer of algorithms analyzes these events to identify clusters of related events that are all symptoms of the same underlying issue.

This algorithmic filtering massively reduces the noise level that IT operations teams would otherwise have to deal with, and also avoids the duplication of work that can occur when redundant tickets are routed to different teams. Instead, with smart DataOps virtual teams can be assembled on the fly, enabling different specialists to work around an issue that spans across technological or organizational boundaries. Existing ticketing and incident management systems can take advantage of AIOps capabilities, integrating directly into existing processes.

AIOps also improves automation, by enabling workflows to be triggered with or without human intervention.

As machine-learning systems become more and more accurate and reliable, it becomes possible for routine and well-understood actions to be triggered without human intervention, potentially resolving issues before users are impacted or even aware of any problem.

Almost all AIOps tools available in the market integrate with existing tools and processes, bringing together information, insights, and capabilities.

AIOps also improves and enables Information Technology Service Management (ITSM) by ensuring that only real actionable incidents are created, avoiding duplication. There is no need to discard the experience embedded in each organization's Information Technology Infrastructure Library (ITIL) based processes. Instead, AIOps addresses and removes many of the frustrations that users have with ITSM, due to the inherently sequential nature of ITIL.

DEFINITIONS

*ITSM is a set of practices, policies, and procedures that helps to manage the services delivered to end users, and **ITIL** is a framework that teaches the best practices to implement ITSM in an organization. To summarize, ITIL is a set of guidelines for effective ITSM.*

*A **runbook** is a manual containing an extensive set of instructions that helps IT specialists to maintain the daily routine and operations of a computer system or network.*

Finally, AIOps brings runbooks automation. IT organizations have typically developed large libraries of automated solutions over the years but need to ensure that they are triggered by only the correct conditions. AIOps ensures that this is the case, minimizing risk and maximizing value of existing investments in automation.

Self-healing is another capability that is infused with smart DataOps. Self-healing involves being able to identify and address system failures at speed, without human intervention. Much like the human body, self-healing systems will be able to return to their desired state after injury. AIOps platforms have emerged as a solution to many of these challenges and have proven to be a valuable tool that enterprises can rely on as they focus on digital transformation.

Smart DataOps can also augment IT functions such as event correlation and analysis, as well as anomaly detection.

DEFINITIONS

Event correlation *is a technique for making sense of a large number of events and pinpointing the few events that are really important in the mass of information. This is accomplished by looking for and analyzing relationships between events.*

Anomaly detection *is a step in data mining that identifies data points, events, and/or observations that deviate from a dataset's normal behavior. Anomalous data can indicate critical incidents, such as a technical glitch or potential opportunity, for instance a change in consumer behavior.*

There are several AIOps tools available in the market such as Moogsoft and Splunk. With Moogsoft managing the data volume, routine concerns are handled so that employees can focus on the unique problems that threaten enterprise business, leaving day-to-day operations to this tool. By integrating with monitoring tools, Moogsoft ingests event data and discards 90% plus of noisy and wrong alerts. It correlates important alerts and groups them into actionable, contextual situations. It also identifies probable root causes and prescribes solutions.

Smart DataOps is becoming popular with different enterprises, and in the next few years it will become a norm for every enterprise.

Big Data: Challenges and Mistakes

At times, enterprises fail to know even the basics: what big data actually is, what its benefits are, what infrastructure is needed, what tools and technologies are required, etc. Without this clear understanding many of the big data journeys that have started have unfortunately failed. There are several enterprises that have started their data journey with an agenda to benefit from data; however, they are now caught up in a situation that impedes the company's progress since the data strategy and implementation was not well thought out to begin with.

> ## DEFINITIONS
>
> ***Parallel computing*** *is a type of computation in which many calculations or the execution of processes are carried out simultaneously. Large problems can often be divided into smaller ones, which can then be solved at the same time.*
>
> ***Real-time analytics*** *is the analysis of data as soon as that data becomes available. In other words, users get insights or can draw conclusions immediately (or very rapidly after) the data enters their system. Real-time analytics allows businesses to react without delay.*

In the last few years many big data models, frameworks, and new technologies were created to provide more storage capacity, parallel processing, and real-time analysis of different heterogeneous sources. In addition, new solutions have been developed to ensure data privacy and security. Compared to traditional technologies, such solutions offer more flexibility, scalability, and performance. Furthermore, the costs of most hardware storage and processing solutions have now dropped considerably due to sustainable technological advances such as Cloud. The key challenge for many enterprises today that have already invested in big data is that there are several duplicate and obsolete tools, techniques, and technologies that exist within their enterprises. This is because many enterprises have been operating in business unit silos.

The big data analytics platforms enterprises have used previously or are using today are not guaranteed to be the ones they will want to use tomorrow. Whether we are dealing with Cloudera, Pivotal, IBM, Hortonworks, or any other platform, in the future enterprises may well have different requirements which may necessitate a different platform or tool. As the key providers start to specialize, many enterprises have deployed several platforms in business unit silos, to capitalize on different types of analytics capabilities and the expertise each tool provides. Because of this, these organizations have introduced a variety of big data technologies in their enterprise IT landscape.

To mitigate this challenge, enterprises should ensure that tools and technologies are governed at enterprise level rather than at business unit level. For organizations which have already deployed multiple tools and technologies, a tool consolidation exercise should commence and the key goal of this exercise should be to ensure that there is only one tool used for each job in the most efficient way, with zero duplication. Any new tool to be deployed to the data ecosystem should be governed at an enterprise level. Additionally, when consolidating infrastructure, organizations should ensure that they are able to switch between analytics platforms seamlessly.

Adapting to future data environments is something every organization needs to do, but the key to success will be to do it in the most optimal and centrally governed manner.

Formula 4.0 Data Maturity Levels

Today almost all enterprises have invested in several tools and process to manage data and insights. However, with multiple processes, tools and technologies that have evolved in the market and due to lack of governance at enterprise level, a lot of inconsistencies and inefficiencies have crept into enterprise data landscapes. Even though these organizations receive insights based on which decisions are being made, the speed at which insights are received and the quality of these insights may not be optimal enough for businesses to compete in their market space. This may lead enterprises to have increased costs, low business value, low efficiency, and maintainability in their data journey.

The Formula 4.0 data maturity framework is depicted in Table 12.1, which mandates enterprises to move away from a federated and unorganized way of working to a fully centralized, automated, and optimized organization that will give superior data insights in the most reliable, scalable, and cost-optimal manner.

DEFINITION

A ***data store*** *is a repository for persistently storing collections of data, such as a database or a file system.*

There are five maturity levels defined as part of the Formula 4.0 data maturity framework, as depicted in Table 12.1.

Table 12.1　Formula 4.0 Data Maturity Level

#	Capability Area	Maturity Level 0	Maturity Level 1	Maturity Level 2
1	Data Pipeline	Created in silos of individuals or business units	Data pipelines created for each data store or data source	Reusable pipelines at enterprise level
2	Data Governance and Security	Data governance framework exists but is not applicable for big data and is managed in business unit silos	Data governance managed at enterprise level, but framework is not applicable for big data	Well-defined data governance refreshed with big data considerations and defined at enterprise level
3	Data Operations	Development and operations as a separate team.	Development and operations working together	Smart DataOps powered by AI
4	Data Platform	On-Prem	On-Prem	Hybrid Cloud (choosing use case-based Cloud providers)
5	Tools	Tool adoption governance in business unit silos	Tool adoption governance at enterprise level but still a lot of duplicate tools in existence across the enterprise	Single toolset for a given job and governed at enterprise level

The First Capability Area: Data Pipeline

The first capability area is the data pipeline, where an unmatured enterprise creates pipelines in business unit silos. They also create these data pipelines without any reusability considerations. As an example, I have seen several enterprises that have created data pipelines for each data source separately—one pipeline to process data from social media data source, one pipeline to process transactional data, and so on. All such enterprises fall under maturity level 0 in the data pipeline maturity area.

Within an enterprise there may be multiple data storage and data sources, but for all these data stores and data sources, as per the Formula 4.0 data strategy, there should be only one data pipeline. This means that the most efficient data platforms are built only once and should be able to handle multiple data sources and multiple storages. This is the mandated for maturity level 2 of the Formula 4.0 data strategy.

The efficient flow of data from one location to another is one of the most critical requirements in today's data-driven enterprise i.e., from multiple data sources at the bottom of the reference architecture in Figure 12.1, to the consumption layer at the extreme top.

Useful analysis cannot begin until the data becomes available. Data flow can be erratic sometimes, because there are so many things that can go wrong during the transportation from one system to another. Data can become corrupted, it can hit bottlenecks (causing latency), or data sources may conflict and/or generate duplicates. As the complexity of the requirements grows and the number of data sources multiplies, these problems increase in scale and impact.

Utilizing industry leading tools and techniques to automate the steps in data pipeline creation is the most essential part to reach maturity level 2. Such data pipelines eliminate many manual steps from the process and enable a smooth, automated flow of data from one station to the next via the data injection and data processing layers. It starts by defining what, where, and how data is collected. It automates the processes involved in extracting, transforming, combining, validating, and loading data for further analysis and visualization using the data injection tools. It provides end-to-end velocity by automatically eliminating errors and combating bottlenecks or latency. It can process multiple data streams at once. In short, this is an absolute necessity for today's data-driven enterprise.

A data pipeline views all data as streaming data and it allows for flexible schemas. Regardless of whether it comes from static sources (like a flat-file database) or from real-time sources (such as online retail transactions), the level 2 data pipeline divides each data stream into smaller chunks and processes in parallel.

There are a number of different data pipeline solutions that have been created and each one is well-suited to different purposes. An effective data pipeline solution should not be mutually exclusive. As an example, an enterprise should create a data pipeline that is optimized to process for both Cloud and real time: The following list shows the most popular types of pipelines available.

Batch—this is most useful when you want to move large volumes of data at a regular interval, and you do not need to move data in real time.

Real-Time—this is useful when you are processing data from a streaming source, such as the data from financial markets or data from connected devices.

Cloud Native—these data pipelines are optimized to work with Cloud-based data, such as data from Azure buckets. These tools are hosted in the Cloud, allowing enterprises to save money on infrastructure and expert resources because they can rely on the infrastructure and expertise of the vendor hosting the pipeline.

Many organizations which have started their data journey 3–5 years back have systems which are still very old, with a mixture of multiple tools and technologies. During the early data days, pipelines used to be created for every use case but over a period of time reusable data pipelines have started to emerge.

The goal of an efficient data organization is to create a reusable data pipeline at enterprise level. Secondly, the data pipeline should be able to be reused for multiple data sources and multiple consumers with minimal configurations. This is maturity level 2 of Formula 4.0.

The Second Capability Area: Data Governance

The second capability area is DG. Governance efforts have little impact when they are walled off from technology, people, and processes. Cross-functional collaboration is the only way to create an effective framework and metrics and governance should be defined at an enterprise level.

In the traditional world of data warehouses or relational database management, it is likely that enterprises have well-understood rules regarding how data needs to be protected. For example, in the health world, it is critical to keep patient data private. Enterprises may be able to store and analyze data about patients as long as names, social security numbers, and other personal data are masked. Enterprises have to ensure that unauthorized individuals cannot access private or restricted data. This was all well managed until recently. In the big data world enterprises are flooded with data that come from a variety of sources such as commercial third-party vendors. It is likely that the big data sources may be insecure and unprotected and include a lot of personal data. During the initial processing of this data, enterprises will probably analyze lots of data that will not turn out to be relevant to the enterprise. Therefore, they do not want to invest resources to protect and govern data that they do not intend to retain. After enterprises decide that a subset of the data is going to be utilized within the enterprise, it is important to institute a process of carefully applying governance requirements to that data. If sensitive personal data passes across the network, enterprises may expose themselves to unanticipated compliance requirements. For data that is truly exploratory, with unknown contents, it might be safer to perform the initial analysis in a "walled" environment that is internal but segmented, or in the Cloud. This clearly implies that the rules and methodologies of governing big data are quite different from traditional data management.

Many enterprises today have embarked on their big data journey but have still not refreshed their DG rules and methodologies, and therefore are at Formula 4.0 maturity level 0 or maturity level 1.

Enterprises at maturity level 0 are those which have embarked on their big data journey but are still operating their DG in business unit silos. At the same time they have not modified the DG rules and methodologies based on big data requirements. Such enterprises carry a lot of legal risks since legacy DG practices are not fit for purpose for big data projects, and therefore lead to compliance and regulatory breaches.

Enterprises at maturity level 1 are those that have set up DG at an enterprise level but have not considered big data rules and methodologies in their DG. Similar to enterprises at maturity level 0, enterprises at level 1 carry lot of risks.

Formula 4.0 maturity level 2 demands organizations to have DG set up at enterprise level, with the ability to govern the big data environment with right big data rules and methodologies in place.

There are several DG tools such as IBM DG and OvalEdge that can support an enterprise in setting up a strong DG framework.

The Third Capability Area: Data Operations

An enterprise which functions with a separate DevOps team is earmarked at maturity level 0. Level 0 operates with a lot of inefficiencies and in many cases disparate tools and technologies are utilized in business unit silos.

DataOps is an automated, process-oriented methodology, used by analytic and data teams, to improve the quality and reduce the cycle time of data analytics. Operating in a DataOps model bring enterprises to maturity level 1.

Maturity level 2 is the Smart DataOps level where AI is brought into the DevOps framework that enables full automation capabilities. Maturity level 2 demands a fully automated system that will enable self-service, meaning business users should be able to perform queries and generate reports on their own, with nominal IT support.

The Fourth Capability Area: Data Platform

The fourth capability area for Formula 4.0 data maturity is the platform on which data and analytics resides. Utilizing Cloud for data is the demand from Formula 4.0 maturity level 2.

The Fifth Capability Area: Tools

The fifth and final capability area comes from the fact that most organizations so far have carried out their data journey in a highly fragmented way and in business unit silos resulting in a duplication of several tools and technologies, which remains ungoverned. Maturity level 2 demands that tools are consolidated, and a well-governed enterprise framework is deployed to avoid any future leakages of duplicate tools into the IT estate of an enterprise.

The Benefits of Moving to Maturity Level 2

Maturity level 2 is a mandate for any organization adopting the Formula 4.0 framework. All capabilities as defined in the Formula 4.0 maturity level 2 framework need to be adopted.

The benefits of moving to maturity level 2 are enormous. Maturity level 2 takes an organization from a typical triangle pyramid to a reversed triangle pyramid, also called the inverse pyramid.

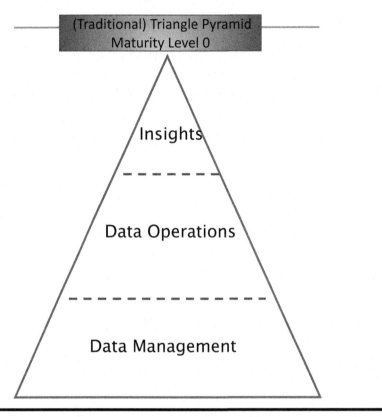

Figure 12.4   Traditional pyramid—maturity level 0 and maturity level 1

Maturity level 0 and maturity level 1 adopt to a tradition pyramid as depicted in Figure 12.4. What this means is that with a tradition pyramid most efforts are spent by enterprises in data operations and in creating data pipelines. This is because the enterprises have a lot of inefficiencies with minimal automation and minimal reusable components that leads them to spending more time in data management and data operations.

Maturity level 2 reverses the traditional pyramid in data space. What this means is that enterprises at maturity level 2 spend minimal effort on data operations and data management. Several solutions, tools, and technologies are brought into the data ecosystem that can enable faster, more reliable and automated data operations, and data management practices. This is achieved by creating a data ecosystem more distributed to serve multiple use cases and multiple lines of business across regions, making it more adaptive rather than having one monolithic data solution.

The end goal is to achieve a state where data quality becomes the responsibility of automation tools rather than data operations or the data

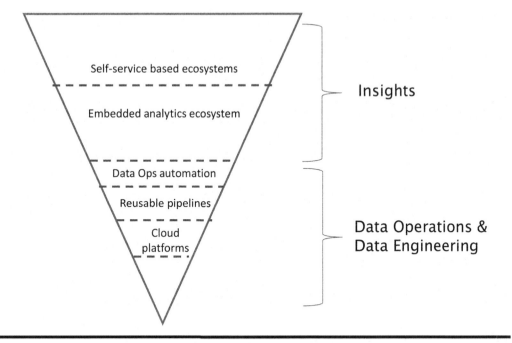

Figure 12.5 Inversed pyramid—maturity level 2

engineering team. This enables enterprises to spend less effort on data engineering and data operations since reusability and automation is infused into the model.

With automation and standards introduced in maturity level 2, the traditional pyramid is reversed as depicted in Figure 12.5. What this means is that their data operations and data management efforts reduce substantially enabling enterprises to divert money and efforts toward insights. With this, enterprises can centralize their efforts and generate better insights to improve their business and become more and more profitable.

Maturity Level 2 Case Studies

The first case study we are going to discuss is for a large real estate company named XYD Real Estates which had 22 subsidiaries across the United States. Each subsidiary had their data in their own IT infrastructure. XYD Real Estates receive data from all these 22 subsidiaries including multiple external sources. The challenge this enterprise had was that the quality of data was very poor. Due to this, XYD Real Estate had to spend lot of time and money on fixing data quality issues which was hindering their business growth since the speed at which they wanted to generate insights to act on a business problem was not uniformed.

The enterprise transformed from maturity level 0 to maturity level 2 in 6 months, with a focus on Smart DataOps capabilities that enabled XYZ to improve and eliminate data quality issues. Microsoft Azure was chosen as a platform where several toolkits such as Azure Data Factory and Azure Stream Analytics were utilized to improve data processing and data quality.

DEFINITIONS

The **Azure Data Factory (ADF)** *is a service designed to allow developers to integrate disparate data sources.*

Microsoft Azure Stream Analytics *is a serverless scalable complex event processing engine by Microsoft that enables users to develop and run real-time analytics on multiple streams of data from sources such as devices, sensors, web sites, social media, and other applications.*

XYD Real Estates started seeing a drop in data quality issues by month seven and by month twelve, the number of incidents arising from data quality issues was reduced by 50%. The end result for XYZ was 60% faster time to market since the insights were delivered 80% faster when compared to the past.

Another case study we will discuss is for a large retail giant in the food industry called ABC Co. ABC Co was competing against some of the biggest retail chains in the US market; however, the key differentiator for ABC Co is that it had a very competitive pricing strategy compared to the competition. ABC Co started their data journey in 2017 and the core reason why they embarked on this journey was to understand the competitor data on pricing front and create competitive promotions and a pricing strategy that would place them in the top quadrant as the most affordable and cheapest food retailer in the market. Once their promotions were live, they received feedback on how they performed compared to the past for the same product based on which success of a promotion is determined.

ABC Co used to spend lot of time on data management and DataOps which meant they had less time in data analysis to create better marketing strategies. As an example, for each promotion to be released for a product their cycle time was around 7–10 days, out of which 4–7 days was spent on data management. This would leave just over 48 hours to create a strategy and promotions based on insights.

Due to this lengthy cycle time, ABC Co used to lose business against some of their smaller competitors who were quite nimble and would release their promotion in just in 2–4 days after performing a thorough market analysis.

There were two main reasons why ABC Co had such a long cycle time:

■ ABC had five different business units and each unit created their own data analytics platforms utilizing their own tools and procedures. During 2007, after consolidation of these five business units into two, it left the organization with duplication and un-uniformed data management processes which were never optimized and consolidated.

■ The next issue ABC faced was to analyze data across multiple, disjointed sources across systems spread across different business units. Pieces of data were housed in different systems which led to incomplete or inaccurate analysis. As a mitigation step, data was being combined manually which was time-consuming and had data quality issues.

The key need for ABC Co was to generate insights from data with a very short lead time and in a near real-time basis, so that their promotional stunts could be released the next day.

ABC's data ecosystem was completely redesigned in just 18 weeks bringing the enterprise to maturity level 2. The key changes that were brought in for this enterprise are discussed in more detail below.

ABC redesigned their data platforms and consolidated their data ecosystem from regional to an enterprise level. DG and data operations were centralized along with tool consolidation. Over 66% of their tools were consolidated in all layers, starting from data source to consumption layer.

A comprehensive and centralized system was created where users have access to all types of information in one location. Not only did this free up time spent accessing multiple sources, it also relieved cross-comparisons issues and ensured that all data was complete. Data was moved to Amazon Web Services Cloud thereby improving its scalability.

Smart DataOps was implemented as the last step where complete data management and data operations were automated using Moogsoft AIOps.

With these changes, ABC Co was able to generate insights in less than 24 hours instead of 7–10 days, and promotions were delivered the very next day. In a span of 2 years, ABC was able to increase their revenues from 8% annual growth rate in 2017 to 22% annual growth in 2019.

Notes

1. https://www.mckinsey.com/business-functions/mckinsey-digital/our-insights/how-to-build-a-data-first-culture
2. "What is DataOps (data operations)?—Definition from WhatIs.com." SearchDataManagement. Retrieved 2017-04-05.
3. "From DevOps to DataOps, By Andy Palmer—Tamr Inc." Tamr Inc. 2015-05-07. Retrieved 2017-03-21.
4. Help Net Security, (May 23, 2019). "Cyber criminals continue to evolve the sophistication of their attack methods." View in article.
5. Mike Wyatt, David Mapgaonkar, and David Jarvis. (November 11, 2019). Rediscovering your identity, Deloitte Insights, Tech 21 Century, "The 5 best Cloud security solutions in 2019–2020." View in article.
6. Jeff Dennis. (June 25, 2018). "Three unbeatable security advantages of Cloud-based solutions for your business," Cloud Tech News, Gartner, "Cloud strategy leadership," 2017. View in article.
7. Philip Russom. (December 19, 2019). "Modernization projects will dominate data management through 2020," TDWI. View in article.
8. "Gartner Doc." www.gartner.com. Retrieved 2019-10-17.

Chapter 13

Automation with RPA and AI-ML

Automation is the application of machines to tasks once performed by human beings. Although the term mechanization is often used to refer to the simple replacement of human labor by machines, automation generally implies the integration of machines into a self-governing system. Automation has revolutionized those areas in which it has been introduced, and there is scarcely an aspect of modern life that has been unaffected by it.

Digital transformation and automation goes hand in hand. Digital transformation is the act of harmonizing Business Processes with current, automation-based technology to make entire breadth of cross-enterprise workflows convenient, optimized, and less erroneous. In other words, it shifts tasks from being siloed, department-specific and manually done to being streamlined, universally accessible, and strategically automated. It does this by introducing new software to the current systems. This software acts as an extension of those already in place, performing many of the repetitive and monotonous functions that would have previously fallen on multiple employees across multiple departments. Such was the main cause of business-process lag times and chokepoints as parts of that workflow stalled between departmental queues. However, with digital transformation technologies in place, employees need to spend less doing things "the old way." Bolstered by automated technology and streamlined, cross-department software, enterprises can now divert attention onto higher-level, high-order work resulting in a fine-tuned enterprise workflow process that minimizes waste and maximizes resource productivity.

The world is moving toward automation and there is no technical limitation on how much automation can be done in an enterprise. However, the benefits achieve from automation vis-à-vis the cost incurred on automation always need to be analyzed before making a decision. In simple terms, tasks which are highly repeatable need to be automated.

There are different tools and technologies that enable automation. Robotic process automation (RPA) is one such technology and is the term used for software tools that partially or fully automate human activities that are manual, rule-based, and repetitive. They work by replicating the actions of an actual human interacting with one or more software applications to perform tasks such as data entry, process standard transactions, or respond to simple customer service queries.

RPA tools are not replacements for the underlying business applications; rather, they simply automate the already manual tasks of human workers.

One of the key benefits of RPA is that the tools do not alter existing systems or infrastructure. Traditional automaton tools and technologies use to interact with systems using application programming interfaces (APIs), which mean writing code which can lead to concerns about quality assurance, maintaining that code, and responding to changes in the underlying applications.

With RPA scripting or programming needs to be performed for automating a repetitive task for which a subject matter expert (SME) is required who understands how the work is done manually. In addition, the data sources and destinations need to be highly structured and unchanging—RPA tools cannot apply intelligence to deal with errors or exceptions at all. But even with these considerations, there are tangible, concrete benefits from RPA. Studies by the London School of Economics suggest RPA can deliver a potential return on investment of between 30% and 200%—and that is just in the first year.[1] Savings on this scale will prove hard to resist. Last year Deloitte found while only 9% of surveyed companies had implemented RPA, almost 74% planned to investigate the technology in the next 12 months.

The limitation of RPA is that they mimic human behavior in a static way and they lack a human's ability or intelligence to adapt to change. Artificial intelligence (AI) is the next big technology that compliments RPA by making it possible for machines to mimic humans in functions such as learning and problem-solving. AI tools could learn from the past data and perform tasks in much more intelligent way as compared to RPA which can perform only repetitive tasks.

RPA and AI are coming together, and the cost savings and benefits are too compelling for companies to ignore. RPA, for example, can capture and interpret the actions of existing Business Process applications, such as claims processing or customer support. Once the "robot software" understands these tasks, it can take over running them and it does so more far more quickly, accurately, and tirelessly than any human. Complimenting RPA with AI algorithms can provide additional benefit that the robot can learn from data and from its mistakes so that it can improve its accuracy and performance over the period of time.

Applicability of RPA and AI combination can span in improving cost as well as Business Process improvement that can delight end users. A combination of RPA and AI can provide maximum automation capabilities for enterprises and is one of the most important elements to be considered during digital transformation.

Robotic Process Automation

As discussed, RPA is a technology that allows to configure computer software, or a "robot" to emulate and integrate the actions of a human interacting within digital systems to execute a Business Process. RPA utilizes the user interface to capture data and manipulates applications just like humans do. They interpret, trigger responses, and communicate with other systems in order to perform on a vast variety of repetitive tasks.

Many enterprises are turning to RPA to streamline enterprise operations and reduce costs. With RPA, businesses can automate mundane rules-based Business Processes, enabling business users to devote more time to serving customers or other higher-value work. RPA bots called as Virtual IT Support teams are replacing humans on repetitive mundane processes. Enterprises further are also supercharging their automation efforts by injecting RPA with cognitive technologies such as machine learning, speech recognition, and natural language processing, automating higher-order tasks that in the past required the perceptual and judgment capabilities of humans. This is called Artificial Intelligence.

The key difference that distinguishes RPA from enterprise automation tools like Business Process management (BPM) is that RPA uses software or cognitive robots to perform and optimize process operations rather than human operators. Unlike BPM, RPA is a quick and highly effective fix that does not require invasive integration or changes to underlying systems, allowing organizations to rapidly deliver efficiencies and cost-savings mainly by replacing humans with software "robots."

RPA is great for automation but there are limitations which need to be kept in mind. As an example, because RPA usually interacts with user interfaces, even minor changes to those interfaces may lead to a broken process.

Artificial Intelligence with Data Science

AI is the "science of making machines smart." Today, we can teach machines to be like humans. We can give them the ability to see, hear, speak, write, and move.

AI is a broad term that covers many subfields that aim to build machines that can do things which require intelligence when done by humans. These subfields are depicted in Figure 13.1 and are listed below.

Machine learning—Machine learning provides systems the ability to automatically learn and improve from experience without being explicitly programmed. Machine learning focuses on the development of computer programs that can access data and use it learn for themselves. Machine learning is the ability of computer systems to improve their performance by exposure to data without the need to follow explicitly programmed instructions. Machine learning is the process of automatically spotting patterns in large amounts of data that can then be used to make predictions.

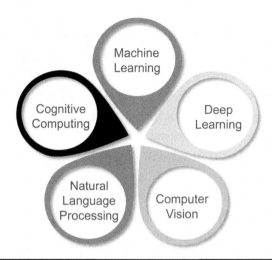

Figure 13.1 AI subfields

Deep learning—this is a relatively new and hugely powerful technique that involves a family of algorithms that processes information in deep "neural" networks where the output from one layer becomes the input for the next one. Neural networks are computing systems vaguely inspired by the biological neural networks that constitute animal brains. The data structures and functionality of neural nets are designed to simulate associative memory. Deep learning algorithms have proved hugely successful in, for example, detecting cancerous cells or forecasting disease but with one huge caveat: there is no way to identify which factors the deep learning program uses to reach its conclusion.

Computer vision—the ability of computers to identify objects, scenes, and activities in images using techniques to decompose the task of analyzing images into manageable pieces, detecting the edges, and textures of objects in an image and comparing images to known objects for classification.

Natural language/speech processing—the ability of computers to work with text and language the way humans do, for instance, extracting meaning from text/speech or even generating text that is readable, stylistically natural, and grammatically correct.

Cognitive computing—a relatively new term, favored by IBM, cognitive computing applies knowledge from cognitive science to build an architecture of multiple AI subsystems—including machine learning, natural language processing, vision, and human-computer interaction—to simulate human thought processes with the aim of making high level decisions in complex situations. According to IBM, the aim is to help humans make better decisions, rather than making the decisions for them.

Data Science

Data science is all about data. Almost all enterprises are out there collecting huge amounts of data to make business decisions based on this data. The more data enterprises have the more business insights they can generate. Using data science, enterprises uncover patterns in data that they did not even know it existed. For example, an enterprise was able to use data science to discover that few individuals from a United Kingdom based company who went for a holiday to Netherlands are most likely to take another luxury trip to Venice since the company they work for sponsors high performing sales executives with luxury trips to certain countries based on the sales they are making on a monthly basis.

Data science is being used extensively in such scenarios. Enterprises are using data science to build recommendation engines, and predicting user behavior, and much more. All of this is only possible when enterprises have enough amount of data so that various algorithms could be applied on that data to give more accurate results. This is AI using machine learning algorithms on huge datasets which is data science. Machine learning is used in data science to make predictions and also to discover patterns in the data and this is AI.

The Link between Artificial Intelligence and Data Science

The link between data science and AI is a one-to-one mapping as we discussed above. This means that data science helps AIs figure out solutions to problems by linking similar data for future use. Fundamentally, data science allows AIs to find appropriate and meaningful information from those huge pools of data faster and more efficiently. Without data science AI does not exist. AI is a collection of technologies that excel at extracting insights and patterns from large sets of data, then making predictions based on that information.

An example, Facebook's facial recognition system which, over time, gathers a lot of data about existing users and applies the same techniques for facial recognition with new users. Another example is Google's self-driving cars which gather data from its surroundings in real time and process this data to make intelligent decisions on the road.

A typical non-AI system relies on human inputs to work just like an accounting software. The system is hard coded with rules manually. Then, it follows those rules exactly to help do the taxes. The system only improves if human programmers improve it.

But machine learning tools can improve on their own. This improvement comes from a machine assessing its own performance and new data.

For instance, an AI tool exists that writes email subject lines for you. Humans train the tool's machine learning algorithms using samples of a company's data and then tool drafts its own email subject lines.

Importance of Quality Data

The key to AI success in digital world is having a high-quality data and data governance. AI can provide superior results only if it can learn from superior and high-quality data very specific to the use case enterprises are automating using AI. As an example, to solve a physics problem if you provide mathematics related data to AI system, then results would not be encouraging. Your systems will learn something, but efforts probably would not help the system answer your test questions correctly. Another example, if you train a computer vision system for autonomous vehicles with images of sidewalks mislabeled as streets, the results could be disastrous.

In order to develop accurate results using machine learning algorithms, you will need high-quality training data. To generate high-quality data, you will need skilled annotators to carefully label the information you plan to use with your algorithm.

If data is not good, then AI will fail in providing the desired results, because AI uses machine learning to learn from the data, and therefore enterprises need quality data. If data is not good, AI systems will not learn good, and therefore will not give good results. This means that organizations developing and using AI must devote huge amounts of resources to ensuring they have sufficient amounts of high-quality data so that their AI tools are giving desired results. This does not necessarily mean that enterprises need a fully matured big data platform to embark their journey on AI. AI can work on a subset of data specific to the use case, and enterprise can create a data store that can cater to the specific use case and use this data to train systems.

Today almost all products available in the market irrespective of what the tool specializes in, claims to have AI feature built in the tool which has caused a lot of confusion in the technology market on which tools to use for AI driven use cases. However, one needs to understand that almost all tools whose primary tool capability is not AI, or machine learning provides only generic AI capabilities and can perform very limited AI tasks. If one needs to apply AI as a capability at a broader level within their enterprises across a broad spectrum of use cases, then they need to procure AI specialized tools and train them with data for that specific use case. Some of the AI specialized tools are IBM Watson (SPSS) and Microsoft R.

Formula 4.0 Automation Methodology

RPA and AI combination make a very powerful automation journey for enterprises. This does not mean that traditional applications level automation scripting or utilities that enterprises used to be built need to be eradicated. In the digital world what it means is that more sophist tools and technologies have emerged that can reduce bespoke development save costs and be more efficient. Based on the need and level of automation required in an enterprise, decisions need to be made agnostic of tools and technologies.

Automation is not specific to a certain area and there is no limit to where it can be applied; however, each area that is planned for automation needs to be carefully analyzed on the benefits it can provide.

A Standard Operating Procedure (SOP) is a set of written instructions that document a routine or repetitive activity followed by an organization.

There are typically three levels of IT Support (Operations) for any enterprises:

L1 Support—this is a basic help desk resolution and service desk delivery team. L1 support includes interact with customers, understand their issue, and create tickets against it. In some cases, basic issues are even resolved by L1 Support team.

L2 Support—this is a team with in-depth technical support capabilities with deep knowledge of the product or service. They have more knowledge, more experience in solving related complex issues, and can guide/help L1 support folks in troubleshooting.

L3 Support—these are the technical experts who are expert in their domain and handle the most difficult problems. They do the code changes, research, and develop the solution for challenging new or unknown issues.

Priority 1 (P1) Ticket—in an IT operations world, a P1 ticket is raised when there is an emergency issue. This means that the system is not available, and productivity has been halted. The product is unusable in its current state.

Priority 2 (P2) Ticket—these are critical issues, which need to be resolved on priority; however, the product is still usable.

Priority 3 (P3) Ticket—these are tickets with **Normal** priority, which means that the system is having an occasional issue that has been identified as needing to be resolved, but the issue has not greatly affected productivity.

Some examples where automations add value are listed below:

Network monitoring—By correlating network events, RPA can generate alarms for multiple standardized (predefined) issues.

Remote troubleshooting and resolution—RPA can support issue tracking, data gathering, and ticket analysis. Incident-management systems that use RPA and AI can detect similar issues and resolve them, such as at a telco that uses RPA to improve its responses to network-equipment failures. The RPA bot executes steps according to a SOP, leaving human agents to resolve only those issues not yet fully documented as SOPs.

Self-help facilities—For routine L2 and L2 support requests, RPA can automate ticket logging, routing, and replies, which form the basis of self-help tools for customers. By minimizing the need for in-person call-center support, these solutions improve not only incident tracking, but also customer experience.

Business Process automation—With RPA, businesses can automate mundane rules-based Business Processes, enabling business users to devote more time to serving customers or other higher-value work.

Legacy systems automation—RPA is quite useful when the interactions are with older, legacy applications. These are applications that fall under WARM zone of Formula 4.0 Methodology. RPA are great tools for breathing new life into legacy systems and creating digital process flows, where before there was only spaghetti code and manual workarounds.

Formula 4.0 Automation Methodology recommends that automation strategy needs to be defined at an enterprise level and not in business unit silos. It is a good practice to do a pilot to understand the benefits of automation using RPA and AI, but even a pilot needs to be sponsored at enterprise level. Secondly to achieve superior benefits, automation should be defined at a theme level rather than trying to identify use cases in silos across the organization. A theme in Formula 4.0 terminology is a function within an enterprise that cuts across several departments but performs a specific end-to-end task which is measurable. Few examples of themes are listed below:

■ Infrastructure Operations—this includes managing software, network, storage, operating systems, database, and middleware either on the data center or the Cloud.

- Application Operation—this includes managing applications either on the data center or the Cloud.
- Business Process—this includes managing all Business Processes within an enterprise which is a cumulation of different departments such as finance, HR management, and so on.
- DevOps—this includes managing the development and operations pipelines across the enterprise.

Once a theme or set of themes are identified at an enterprise level, Formula 4.0 recommends identifying "cases" within the themes that can be automated using RPA or AI or a combination. A case in Formula 4.0 terminology is a unique function performed by human which is a candidate for automation. As an example, assigning an incident by a service desk agent to a support engineer could be a case under infrastructure operations theme.

Each case identified for automaton needs to be placed in one of the five quadrants of Formula 4.0 Case Assignation Tool, based on which complexity of automation can be determined. Formula 4.0 Case Assignation Tool is depicted in Figure 13.2. Based on the complexity, cost and efforts can be derived to create a bot for each of the case. A bot is a software application

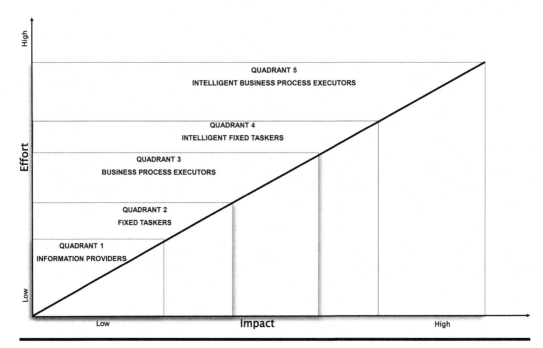

Figure 13.2   Formula 4.0 case assignation tool

that automates a specific case and runs automated tasks. Bots are built using RPA tools or AI tools and a combination.

A thumb rule based on several of my experience is that a very simple bot can be automated with an RPA tool in 4–6 weeks duration.

Information Providers—these are simple bots which provide information using predefined set of question and answers such as Help or providing a predefined answer to a question. Efforts to automate for these set of cases are quite simple.

Fixed Taskers—these are software bots that perform fixed set of steps based on a set of events or triggers and perform tasks across multiple systems if required. Typically, these are software robots that are used to automate L1 and L2 processes in application or infrastructure operations or perform a simple task for a business user.

Business Process Executors—these are software robots that automate the complete end-to-end Business Process such as a sales process or an invoicing process. In many cases Business Process executors and humans work together to complete a business transaction. As an example, Step 1 to 5 in a Business Process is performed by a bot, Step 6 and 7 is performed by human and again Step 8 to 10 is performed by a bot.

Intelligent Fixed Taskers—these are software robots that perform fixed set of steps or tasks based on a set of events or triggers with the ability to learn using data sets which enables them to improve over the period of time. These utilize capabilities of AI/machine learning to learn from data or from mistakes of the past.

Intelligent Business Process Executors—these are software robots that are involved in end-to-end Business Process automation and perform fixed set of steps or tasks initially based on a set of events or triggers with the ability to learn using data sets which enables them to improve over the period of time. These utilize capabilities of AI to learn from data or from mistakes of the past. Business Process is automated where humans and machines work together and learn together.

Categorizing cases under each of these five quadrants is the foremost step for an enterprise to initiate their automation journey. Over the period of time, enterprises can determine how much impact each quadrant (or bots within each quadrant) is having on their organization vis-à-vis the cost of these bots based on which they can make informed decision on the quadrant which they need to invest based on the business benefits they are achieving.

Full Stack Operations Automation

Full stack automation is one of the key areas where several enterprises have seen exceeding benefits not only from cost reduction perspective but also from efficiency improvement and business satisfaction. This is one of the reasons why full stack operation automation is being discussed here as a separate topic.

There are typically three major dimensions in a full stack operations automation value stream:

The first area of focus is called as tickets to resolve, where automation using RPA and AI plays a major role in trying to resolve tickets automatically, and only if it's unsuccessful they are routed for manual intervention.

The second is the DevOps pipeline automation where the complete DevOps pipeline is automated in a way that there is very minimal human intervention starting from code reviews to security related checks including code deployments to productions servers.

The third is the monitoring layer, where proactive identification and resolution of issues are enabled via automation. This is enabled with a combination of early detection, proactive intervention, predictive analysis, and automation.

Let me explain this with a case study for one of the large banks named Bank X. Bank X was aspiring to move from a traditional operating model into a fully automated operations, powered with RAP and AI. Bank X was having an average ticket count of more than 70,000 per month with a team of 500+ resources spread across L1, L2, and L3 support.

Key vision for Bank X with automation is to reduce cost of operations and ticket resolution time by more than 50%. An enterprise-wide operation automation transformation was undertaken with a combination of RPA and AI.

The first step in the process was to move support teams from business units' silos into a central enterprise level pool and create a one team across all business units. This means there is one team across the enterprise called L1, L2, and L3 support team in contrast to the earlier model where six business units use to have their own L1, L2, and L3 support teams.

The second initiative that was undertaken was adjacent skill training of resources, where each individual within the operations teams were trained on at least one new supporting skills in addition to his/her core skill. As an example, a windows support engineer was trained on Unix and Linux support.

The third step was to introduce RPA and AI into operations life cycle. Moogsoft was introduced as a tool for event correlation and Automation Anywhere tool was introduced in the RPA Layer to resolve repeatable tickets.

- Moogsoft AIOps is the AI platform for IT operations, powered by purpose-built machine learning algorithms. Moogsoft helps to improve the detection and remediation of incidents, ensuring continuous service delivery for business
- Automation Anywhere is an RPA tool that allows organizations to automate the processes which are performed by the humans
- Hardware and applications monitoring tools such as Dell Open Manage, CA Nimsoft, and SolarWinds were introduced for proactive monitoring of the systems
- Service Now IT Service management tool was used for capturing tickets

Dell Open Manage Enterprise is a new hardware management and monitoring console that provides a comprehensive view of the Dell EMC servers, chassis, network switches, and other third-party devices on the enterprise network.

Nimsoft products monitor and manage business services and specific systems within the IT infrastructure, including network components, servers, databases, applications, and virtualized environments.

SolarWinds® Network Performance Monitor (NPM) is a powerful network monitoring software that enables you to quickly detect, diagnose, and resolve network performance problems and outages. It enables Speeds troubleshooting, increases service levels, and reduces downtime.

As depicted in Figure 13.3, there are two approaches in which tickets are raised in ITSM tool. Every request that comes from a user is first routed to the AIOps platform where Moogsoft performs even correlation and raises a ticket in ITSM tool and then sends the request to RPA platform.

In the second approach Monitoring tools which sit on the IT landscape tries to proactively identify any issues that may arise in future and as soon as it detects an issue, it routes it to the AIOps platform which again raise a ticket in ITSM tool and assigns it to RPA tool for resolution. RPA tools then tries to solve the ticket else request is routed for human intervention to L1, L2, or L3 support.

Event correlation takes data from either application logs or host logs and then analyses the data to identify relationships. Tools that utilize event

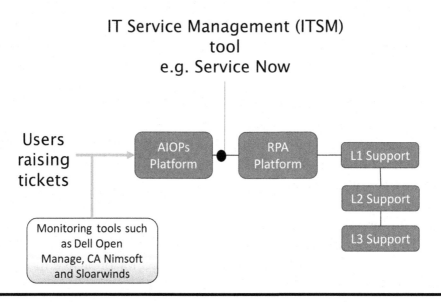

Figure 13.3   Operations automation using AIOps and RPA

correlation can then perform actions, such as sending alerts for hardware or application failures, based on user-defined rules. Correlation and root-cause analysis have been stalwarts of IT performance monitoring for some time. Both practices help IT departments to determine the underlying cause of a problem and resolve it quickly to minimize any business impacts and losses.

A SOP is a set of step-by-step instructions compiled by an organization to help employees or tools carry out complex routine operations.

There were 89 bots created using RPA tool to automate all possible scenarios and 130 SOPs were automated using RPA.

The end result after 15 months was that 70% of all tickets were being resolved automatically by the tools, either by AIOps platform or RPA. Moogsoft was further utilized for remediation of incidents and was working hand in hand with the RPA tool. Reminder 30% of tickets were solved manually by L1 and L2 team with only a 10% of tickets from these 30%, being resolved by L3 teams. L3 teams started focusing on large development projects and moved their focus out from solving tickets. Overall there was a net reduction of 60% in P1 and P2 tickets.

After this transformation to Full stack automation operations, Bank X achieved a 70% cost reduction, 44% efficiency improvement, and business satisfaction rose from 4/10 to 9/10 in 16 months.

How to Get Automation Programs Right

Automation is not for every enterprise and cannot yield the desired results if implemented in business unit silos. Automaton is an enterprise-wide initiative and should be governed at an enterprise level; else the results could be very destructive. As an example, department A of Company Y has installed several of RPA bots which has taken a lot longer and was more complex and costly than they have hoped. The platforms on which bots interact often changed, and the necessary flexibility wasn't always configured into the bot. Moreover, a new regulation requiring minor changes to an application form would throw off weeks of work in the back office on a bot that is nearing completion, or which was already complete.

Enterprises need to understand that the economic outcomes of automation implementations are far from assured. This means that while it may be possible to automate 40% of tasks in an enterprise, it does not translate into a 40% cost reduction.

Formula 4.0 guidelines for RPA implementation are listed below and depicted in Figure 13.4.

Build Automation Center of Excellence at Enterprise Level

Many automation and RPA initiatives have failed to yield the desired results because they are executed at department level rather than enterprise level. The most successful Automation implementations include a center of excellence defined at enterprise level staffed by people who are responsible for

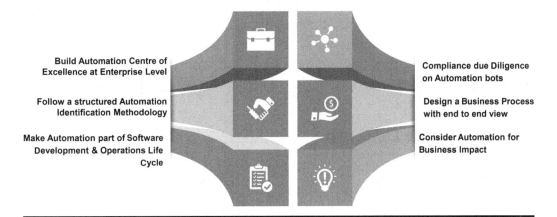

Figure 13.4   RPA implementation key guidelines

making automation programs a success within the organization. Not every enterprise, however, has the budget for this. The automation center of excellence develops business cases, calculating potential cost optimization and ROI, and measures progress against those goals. This group maintains full inventory of all automation initiatives, where they are deployed and how they are managed from security, compliance, and operations perspective. That group is typically small and nimble, and it scales with the technology staffs that are focused on the actual implementation of automation

Follow a Structured Formula 4.0 Automation Identification Methodology

It is very easy to get lost in the overall automation journey if a structured approach is not followed in identifying cases for automation at an enterprise level. Using Formula 4.0 Automation Methodology, enterprises need to identify the right themes, and cases for each theme to make automation journey successful.

Automation Should Eventually Be Part of the Software Development and Operations Life Cycle

Enterprises must automate the entire development life cycle that will ensure that changes to the code are syncing up with the already installed Bots, or they may kill their bots during a big launch. On the other hand, identification of automation use cases during development and operations is always an essential part of the process instead of a separate team flying in and identifying use cases for automation. New potential candidates for automation should be identified by the product engineering team which goes into a backlog that automation COE teams validate, perform a cost benefit analysis, and appropriate ones are chosen for implementation.

Compliance Due Diligence

One of the benefits of enterprise level automation governance via a center of excellence is to ensure that all aspects of bot development are considered including from compliance and legal angle. Whether deploying bots as part of a "managed service" or via an "in-house option" due diligence on compliances will be quite important.

Some issues which COE typically considers during bot development are:

- What data will the robots have access to and has data security/data protection been considered?
- For critical processes, is there business continuity in place if Bots are not able to operate (e.g., revert to manual processing)?
- What is the people impact of the use of RPA technology: is there a risk of redundancy/TUPE for those currently doing the work, do roles need to be re-profiled?
- Are the regulatory requirements applicable to that sector being complied (e.g., SYSC 8 in the financial services sector)? and
- will the enterprise be able to exit the bot or RPA or AI tool vendor, without disrupting ongoing operations?

For those familiar with outsourcing and long-term services arrangements, many considerations are not new or unique to automation. In deploying any new technology within an enterprise there will naturally be a greater anxiety, and a 360-degree analysis needs to be performed on the risks and benefits of the technology.

Design a Business Process with End-to-End View

Many implementations fail because design and change are poorly managed and done in parts. A well-defined automation project will ensure that Business Process is designed and implemented in whole rather than in parts, with bots plugged between the Business Process for performing specific tasks. It is very essential that communication exchanges, between the various bots and between bots and humans are designed accurately which will ensure end-to-end working of a Business Process. This means having a well-defined operating model design before implementation a Business Process using automation tool is important if a man and machine collaboration has to be successful.

Cost Is Important but Business Impact Is Much More Key

Many enterprises consider automation as an initiative to reduce cost; however, automation is a tool for business delight and improving efficiencies. There are many organizations that have improved customer satisfaction by employing automation bots in their Business Process since they automate many manual processes for example data entry, data validation, sending emails, or even updating multiple spreadsheets or systems. All the repetitive and mundane tasks which customers or business do not like to do, over and over again if automated increases customer satisfaction.

Note

1. Leslie Willcocks. (December 2016). Professor of technology, work, and globalization at the London School of Economics' department of management. Source: McKinsey.com

Chapter 14

IT-OT Integration

Industry 4.0 is the term most widely used to depict the current trend of automation and data including the industrial Internet of Things (IoT), Cloud computing, and cognitive computing. Whenever we talk about Industry 4.0, integrating IT systems with operational technologies always come first. In short this is called IoT or IT-OT integration.

Gartner, Inc. forecasts that the enterprise and automotive IoT market[1] will grow to 5.8 billion endpoints in 2020, a 21% increase from 2019. An endpoint, from an IoT perspective, is a physical computing device that performs a function or task as part of an Internet connected product or service. An endpoint, for example, could be a wearable fitness device, an industrial control system (ICS), automotive telematics unit, or even a personal drone unit.

Gartner reported that utilities will be the highest user of IoT endpoints, totaling 1.17 billion endpoints in 2019, and increasing 17% in 2020 to reach 1.37 billion endpoints. Electricity smart metering, both residential and commercial, will boost the adoption of IoT among utilities. Physical security, where building intruder detection and indoor surveillance use cases will drive volume, will be the second largest user of IoT endpoints in 2020.[2]

IoT (also called as IT-OT integration) is all about connecting devices over the Internet, allowing them to talk to each other and many different systems, applications, and so on. A classic example is the smart fridge. Using IoT, a fridge could tell us it was out of milk, text us if its internal camera saw there was no milk left, or that the carton was past its expiry date. All this is possible with IoT and this is one of the reasons why IoT is becoming so popular. When we talk about IoT it is a combination of both hardware and software talking to one another.

The hardware utilized in IoT systems includes devices for a remote dashboard, devices for control, servers, a routing device, and sensors. These devices manage key tasks and functions such as system activation, action specifications, security, communication, and detection to support-specific goals and actions.

The software used in IoT includes systems that collect data from the hardware devices. IoT software addresses key areas of networking and action through platforms, embedded systems, and middleware. These individual applications are responsible for data collection, device integration, real-time analytics and application and process extension within the IoT network. They exploit integration with critical business systems (e.g., ordering systems) in the execution of related tasks. These terms will be explained further below.

Data Collection—This is the process of retrieving data from all sensors. It uses certain protocols to aid sensors in connecting with real-time, machine-to-machine networks. It then collects data from multiple devices and distributes it in accordance with settings. It also works in reverse by distributing data over devices, and the system eventually transmits all collected data to a central server.

Device Integration—Device integration software brings all the devices together to create a consortium of the IoT systems. It ensures the necessary cooperation and stable networking between devices.

Real-time Analytics—These applications take data or input from various devices and convert it into viable actions or clear patterns for human analysis. They analyze information based on various settings and designs, after which certain actions are taken either manually or automatically.

Application and Process Extension—These applications extend the reach of existing systems and software to allow a wider, more effective system. They integrate predefined devices for specific purposes such as allowing certain mobile devices or engineering instruments access. It supports improved productivity and more accurate data collection.

From the above discussion it is clear that IT-OT integration is not just about devices. It is an integration between Information Technology (IT) and Operational Technology (OT).

DEFINITION

Shop floor *is the area of a factory, machine shop, etc. where people work on machines, or the space in a retail establishment where goods are sold to consumers.*

OT is about managing, monitoring, and controlling industrial operations with a focus on the physical devices and processes used in the shop floor where the production of goods takes place.

IT includes the use of computers, storage, networking devices, other physical devices, and infrastructure, as well as processes to create, process, store, secure, and exchange all forms of electronic data.

Operational Technology—A Preview

OT is about (heavy) machineries, safety of people, and so on. There is almost zero tolerance toward downtime, errors, or safety. This is one of the core reasons why OT has always operated in a highly risk averse manner. Another aspect of OT is that the machineries deployed at the factories cannot be upgraded or replaced at the same pace as IT systems, and these are the ones that will remain for years once purchased. This becomes a hurdle to deploy new innovative ideas on these machineries to make them more efficient. On the other hand, most of the machineries operate 24/7 and 365 days a year and stopping these machineries for any desired upgrades or modification is an almost impossible task.

In the consumer facing OT world in the last few years there has been tremendous advancements made. As an example, in the older days we were carrying analogue phones and now almost everybody uses a smartphone. We were also previously driving manual cars although many of us have now made the switch to electric or automatic.

The non-consumer facing OT world however has not changed at all— in the mining industry for example several decades ago hammers, chisels, pickaxes and shovels were being used, and still are to this day. Similarly, in the manufacturing industry years back they were using conveyor belts, painting robots, welding robots, and so on. Today they still have the same equipment. The three key reasons why changes have not occurred in these industries are because:

- **Safety**—Safety is to prevent or lessen the risk of workplace injury, illness, and death and therefore is of paramount importance in the OT world. Safety is keeping people away from physical harm and there is zero tolerance toward safety compromises.
- **Reliability**—Reliability is defined as the probability that a component (or an entire system) will perform its function for a specified period of time, when operating in its design environment.
- **Cost & Risk to Change or Upgrades**—The cost of change to machinery is quite high and with almost zero downtime expected on machineries, upgrades are also hard to manage. Secondly, an error from upgrading can lead to reliability issues. This is one of the reasons why in the OT world there is a tendency to avoid quick patches, software updates, etc., because they may result in safety or reliability concerns.

There are several challenges in making changes to the OT systems such as manufacturing or mining equipment's. However, with more and more benefits that enterprises are gaining because of IT-OT integration enterprises have the desire to change but an uncompromised requirement is safety and security. A poorly planned change (even as simple as an antivirus update) can introduce enough risk of disruption to an industrial network that OT experts are scared about as people's lives may be at risk because of a badly managed change.

In the long term, not making necessary changes such as upgrading, and not adapting to an IT-OT integration may lead to an increased risk of a deliberate disruption by a hacker. A well-known example of such a disruption was the Stuxnet attack in Iran. In January 2010, inspectors with the International Atomic Energy Agency visiting the Natanz uranium enrichment plant in Iran noticed that filters used to enrich uranium gas were failing at an unprecedented rate. The cause was a complete mystery and Iranian technicians replaced the filters. Five months later a seemingly unrelated event occurred. A computer security firm in Belarus was called in to troubleshoot a series of computers in Iran that were crashing and rebooting repeatedly. The researchers found a handful of malicious files on one of the systems and discovered Stuxnet virus. Another more recent event occurred last year in Germany, where hackers used malware to gain access to the control system of a steel mill, which they disrupted to such a degree that it could not be shut down. Thankfully, there was no damage to human life. These two examples highlight that OT systems are not fully secured and need to be upgraded at regular intervals. On the other side IT-OT integration is mandatory for all enterprises that wish to be relevant in the market.

The IT-OT Integration

Until today, OT had very limited integration with the IT. The reason behind this is that OT is all about machinery, safety of people, and the creation of products. Today, more and more organizations are embracing IoT technologies such as smart meters and self-monitoring transformers. We are also seeing production lines and farm equipment outfitted with sensors.

The rise of these new technologies has created a need for organizations to optimize how machines, applications, and infrastructure collect, transmit, and process data. Done right, IT-OT convergence gives businesses the ability to fix critical issues faster, make informed business decisions, and scale processes across both physical and virtual systems.

As depicted in Figure 14.1, the first two blocks are the IT layers where enterprise resource planning suites sit, such as customer relationship

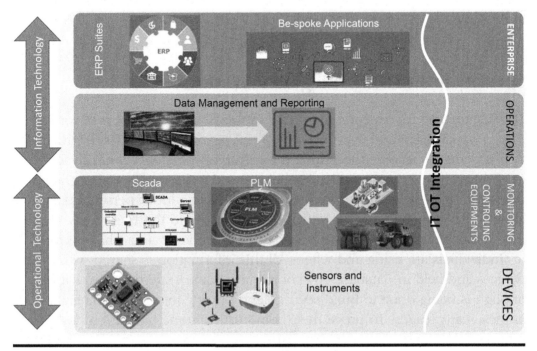

Figure 14.1   IT-OT integration reference diagram

management and sales applications. Data from these tools and software is routed to the data and reporting layer for reporting purposes. The bottom two layers are the OT layers. The monitoring and control equipment (MCE) layer is where the actual production of goods or processing takes place. This is where, as an example, cars are manufactured or mining occurs, and all these are controlled and monitored by supervisory control and data acquisition (SCADA) systems. SCADA is a system of software and hardware elements that allows industrial organizations to:

■ Control industrial processes locally or at remote locations
■ Monitor, gather, and process real-time data
■ Directly interact with devices such as sensors, valves, pumps, motors, and more through human-machine interface (HMI) software
■ Record events into a log file

Along with SCADA, product life cycle management (PLM) tools form part of the MCE layer. PLM refers to the management of data and processes used in the design, engineering, manufacturing, sales, and service of a product across its entire life cycle and across the supply chain.

As part of the IT-OT integration, all four layers integrate with each other thereby enabling a seamless data and information exchange between IT and OT.

Security in an IT-OT Integrated World

IT-OT integration is an emerging trend in the IT industry and is becoming more popular each and every day. Over the next few years IT-OT integration is going to become the standard for everyone. Security and privacy are however the biggest challenges being faced today as IT-OT integration deals with a lot of devices and sensors that collect a lot of personal data about people and enterprises which is then passed to the IT systems. As an example, a smart meter knows when a person is home and what electronics individuals are using and when. All this information is shared with other devices and held in databases by companies. Some experts argue that not enough is being done to build security and privacy into IT-OT integration at these early stages. To prove their point further some have even hacked a host of devices, from connected baby monitors to automated lighting and smart fridges, as well as city wide systems such as traffic signals.

Research shows that 55% of IT professionals list security in an IT-OT integration world as their top priority. This is according to a survey conducted by 451 Research.[3] From corporate servers to Cloud storage, cybercriminals are finding ways to exploit information at many points within an IT-OT ecosystem.

DEFINITION

Critical infrastructure *is the body of systems, networks, and assets that are so essential that their continued operation is required to ensure the security of a given enterprise, its economy, and employee's health and/or safety.*

Hackers have not spent much time or effort so far in hacking OT devices since there are not many enterprises or people who have integrated IT and OT fully, and hence it is not worth the effort. This is however going to be a new area of focus for cybercriminals as enterprises start utilizing IoT in their day-to-day business.

OT systems in an enterprise are the cash registers—whether it is a power generation unit, car manufacturing unit, oil refining, or chemical development, OT systems generate money for enterprises. All focus has therefore traditionally been placed on making sure that the OT systems that produce the products have been designed in a way that they are very safe, highly efficient, and productive with "long lived missions." Long lived mission means that an OT system of critical infrastructure is expected to run 24/7 and 365 days a year for several decades. Due to such a need, major patching or upgrading cycles do not happen for years, and therefore the types of vulnerabilities that exist live a very long time in those systems.

The current level of security awareness in the industry toward IT-OT integration is quite diverse. In the OT world, nearly 40% of enterprises believe that being isolated from external threats is a solution to being secure, and therefore they tend to be disconnected from the outside world. These enterprises consider isolation as a strategy to protecting themselves against cyber risks, and therefore have never been able to take advantage of the technology existing in the market. These are the ones who are at risk of losing business since there are better and cheaper ways to conduct it, which their competitors have likely already adopted.

On the other end of the spectrum there are fewer enterprises, say 10% of them, that are aware and are diligent on the advancements in the

IT industry and have increased their cybersecurity posture year after year to stay ahead of emerging threats. There are other organizations that are in the middle of both these categories, these are the ones that are in the regulated industries and have a compliance aspect in their mandate. They enhance their cybersecurity posture to simply meet their compliance requirements. Since these enterprises have not thought of cybersecurity beyond compliance, they are at a high risk of falling prey to cyber-attacks.

There are matured cybersecurity practices in the IT world, but these practices are not maturing in the OT world. Due to this, none of the cybersecurity practices in existence today is able to address the complex issues of protecting critical infrastructure and data in the IT-OT integrated world.

IT-OT integration is the reality of the future. For enterprises to reach the next level of maturity, achieve higher productivity and to delivery better and faster outcomes and be cheaper, becoming connected with IT-OT integration is their only option. Many enterprises have already realized this fact; however, being connected in a world where OT has never been thought of from a cybersecurity perspective poses the highest degree of risk to enterprises. Often, I have come across two types of enterprises—ones that are striving for this productivity outcome by compromising security and others that do not want to move toward IT-OT integration. Neither of these are right option. The only option is to address cybersecurity and take actions to secure both IT and OT, which should be mandatory for every enterprise.

In the IT era we have now come across several security incidents. Each and every time there is a new bug the manufacturer pushes a patch to address it. It is a reactive approach as with every new attack, enterprises respond with forensic investigations that ultimately lead to patching and ongoing monitoring to stop the problem from reappearing. However, such an approach is not possible in the OT world. A small incident can not only cause the plant to shut down losing millions of dollars, but there is also the chance of human losses and accidents due to cyber-attacks. On the other hand, there are trade secrets such as recipes that are often loaded on the OT control systems that need to be protected. This is one of the reasons why OT security is at the very top of security concerns. Unlike the IT world, OT systems have:

- Not learnt from cyber-attacks
- Not undergone upgrades like IT systems
- More aged infrastructure that have less controls since OT systems were never built to be exposed to the outside world
- Tools and systems that have not been developed to solve cyber-attacks

This is the biggest divide between the IT and OT worlds. It is clear that after IT-OT integration cyber-attackers will try to enter OT world via the IT systems. This is the biggest challenge in the IT-OT integration industry today.

We have seen in the past a rushed approach for IT-OT integration. One example is the smart metering payday of 2008 to 2011. This was the time when there was a lot of investment in the industry for new kinds of technology on the operational side of the house. Wireless systems were making it possible to gather information, to reduce operational costs thereby achieving operational efficiency. During this time, security in OT systems took a backseat and after some time the industry saw cyber-attacks on smart meters. As an example, some smart meter settings were changed by individuals so that meter readings did not go up, by placing large sized magnets on the meters. This was the evolution of the IT-OT integration where cybersecurity was thought as a secondary requirement, and because of this some utility providers lost millions and millions of dollars.

You can either think about cybersecurity at the start while embarking in an IT-OT integration journey or you can do it later. The effect of doing it later could unfortunately lead to dire situations such as shutting down the business entirely, as there are undoubtedly a number of unforeseen consequences that could ultimately lead to disasters.

In most cases with OT systems it is a trial and error process to hack the system. Hackers are just looking to see what they can access remotely, and trying to find ways to get into an operational system. I have also seen the opposite—in some case studies there have been situations where attacks have been launched against the OT side of the system and these systems were then used to gain access to the IT systems. This is what I call a pivotal attack, and these types of attacks are on the rise.

As we have discussed so far, security cannot be centered around IT and OT in silos in an IT-OT integrated world. They need to be operating together to prevent cyber-attacks, which take us into the next question: what does it mean to secure the IT-OT integrated systems? There are three main components, as depicted in Figure 14.2, that are necessary in order to effectively secure critical infrastructure of an OT ecosystem.

Industrial Mindset—The industrial mindset comes first in an IT-OT integration. This means enterprises on an IT-OT integration journey need to take into account things such as the missions of the OT systems, which are often focused around zero downtime safety as a practice. It is also concerned with the engineering discipline and the quality focus

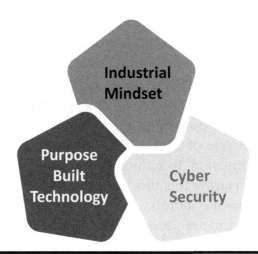

Figure 14.2   Components to secure OT infrastructure

that typically goes into designing these industrial systems and recognizing that these systems are the cash register of the business.

Cybersecurity—The second key aspect is to have cybersecurity expertise when enterprises deal with OT systems. Cybersecurity personnel need to understand the similarities and differences between IT and OT and should be experts in this particular field. The types of technologies that are used in some layers of OT or critical infrastructure are very similar to IT. There are workstations, standard software stacks, or standard applications, but as we reach deeper into the OT system there are different kinds of technology stacks, embedded equipment such as real-time operating systems and industrial proprietary protocols that are used to connect these systems together. Cybersecurity experts need to understand the differences in the technology and the differences in the vulnerabilities that OT systems have since these are legacy products with long lived missions. The consequences of a compromise can mean a danger to life.

Purpose Built Technology—The third area that needs focus is purpose-built technology. This means that enterprises need to look at technologies that are built to provide deep visibility and protection specifically for industrial connected systems that will be part of the IT-OT integration world. Cyber experts need to look at the specific nature of the risk at each layer of the OT system and make sure that the protective measure that will be employed inside that system is going to support each particular mission. They will need to deeply understand the protocols that are used to connect these systems together, speed of data, and information transferred and not introduce any unintended latency or jitter as such inefficiencies can bring the OT systems down. As an example, the patching cycles often tend to be more rapid on the IT side than they are on the OT side of the house. Many OT systems may take years or months to put a patch or protection in place simply because of the operational mission of the particular OT system. From a purpose-built technology perspective, the main difference we see here is that there is a whole host of standardized protocols on the IT side. In the OT side there are a lot of pieces of equipment that have been built around proprietary technology and proprietary protocols which glue the OT systems together and connect them to allow machine-to-machine interaction. The protective measures that are employed in an IT world are often based on standardized protocols whereas on the OT side, we will get into all kinds of esoteric and proprietary protocols that are the systems used to communicate with each other. It is essential for enterprises to utilize technologies that are built purposefully for each specific OT system.

Cybersecurity Solutions for IT-OT Integration

In most enterprises the way IT-OT integration needs to be managed seems to be same from a top-down perspective, but once you get into the details, it becomes apparent that each organization has to deal with IT-OT integration differently. This means that a tailored fit for purpose approach needs to be created by each enterprise.

DEFINITION

Packet is formatted units of data. A packet consists of control information and user data.

The Table 14.1 provides a view on the traditional IT and OT security solutions and how a combination of these two can secure enterprises after IT-OT integration. This is a partial list which provides a starting point for enterprises to manage their security posters in an IT-OT integrated world. Each enterprise needs to tailor its own cybersecurity solutions based on the operational systems in use currently.

In the Table 14.1, we have discussed the different types of security measures to be adopted across the IT layer, the OT layer, and a combination of both.

Table 14.1 Traditional IT and OT Security Solutions

Service	Description	Traditional IT	Traditional OT	IT-OT Integration
Firewall	Acts as a gatekeeper between a network and the wider Internet. Filters incoming and in some cases outgoing traffic by comparing data packets against predefined rules and policies.	✓		✓
Intrusion prevention service & intrusion detection service	Deep packet inspection; protects against malware entry into the network.	✓		✓
Access controls	Controls which users have access to the network or to sensitive sections of the network.	✓		✓
Antivirus and anti-malware software	A software used to prevent, detect, and remove malware.	✓		✓
Application security	Refers to the combination of hardware, software, and best practices used within an enterprise to monitor security issues and risks during application development and operations.	✓		✓
Behavioral analytics	A method by which abnormal behaviors are identified and resolved.	✓		✓
Data loss prevention	A technology which prevents an employee from sharing valuable company information or sensitive data, unwittingly or with ill intent, outside the network.	✓		✓

(Continued)

Table 14.1(Continued) Traditional IT and OT Security Solutions

Service	*Description*	*Traditional IT*	*Traditional OT*	*IT-OT Integration*
Network monitoring and visibility	A technology to automatically generate views into all network communication, enabling policy creation and automated enforcement.		✓	✓
Network segmentation	A capability to manage data flow between IT networks and OT environments.		✓	✓
ICS vulnerability intelligence	A platform that automatically detects industrial malware, including zero-day vulnerabilities. A zero-day vulnerability is a software security flaw that is known to the software vendor but does not have a patch in place to fix the flaw.		✓	✓
OT firewalls	A technology that offers policy-driven and centralized management capability and puts enterprises in control of their industrial environments.		✓	✓

As an example, the firewall acts as a gatekeeper between a network and the wider Internet and is used to track what is going on between personnel inside and outside of the enterprises to make decisions on which access paths need to be opened, which addresses can access services within the enterprise, and so on. On the other side, it is not enough in an OT environment to just open up a connection. It is important to see how somebody is using that connection and gain a deeper understanding on how that protocol is being used. In the IT world there is a lot of discussion on intrusion prevention detection systems that do packet inspection to protect IT systems against malware entry into the network. From the OT side however, network packets are not that important. The key in the OT world is to bring together a string of network packets from a long-lived conversation between two different people to understand network protocols. In OT there is less focus on deploying a tool that carries out network packet inspection on the OT network. Alternatively, the focus is on deploying a tool that really understands and inspects the protocol and recreates the conversation that provides an indication to operators that will prevent certain conversations from ever happening.

IT-OT Integration Reference Architecture

IT-OT integration has not yet become mainstream because the domain is evolving and at the same time complex. In an IT-OT integration enterprise needs to determine and choose the hardware device platform, decides on which operating system to run, which networks to use, which devices to use, and so on. And then finally integration needs to be done in the most secured way. Good news is that by paying attention to security early, enterprises can design security upfront, rather than act reactively.

An IT-OT reference architecture has primarily three major components as depicted in Figure 14.3.

The first one is the device, which is the physical object that is located on the shop floors. The second is the gateway, which is responsible for collecting data from devices and relaying it to the systems, and third is the IoT platform, which is like the nervous system of enterprise business where the IoT data coming from devices are to be combined with other non IoT data to derive useful insight using analytics systems or applications.

IoT Devices

IoT devices are the computing devices that connect wirelessly to a network and have the ability to transmit data. These can be large turbines or oil rigs or can be small and simple tiny sensor located inside a door hinge.

Fundamentally an IoT device, is composed of hardware and software with an operating system, a compute, storage, and connectivity. The big difference between device and a computer is that the inputs and outputs for an IoT device is very different from a traditional computer. As an example,

■ Sensor inputs can be wide variety, such as heat, gas, or infrared, or as simple a button press event.

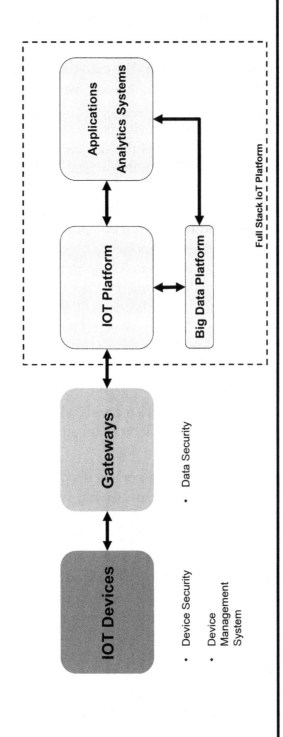

Figure 14.3   IT-OT integration reference architecture

Not all IoT devices are going to have outputs. Ones which has outputs can perform actions for an event. As an example, an event could be pressing a button and corresponding action could be dimming the light. An IoT device has four major components:

Metadata—this is unique information that can identify the device such as device identifier, a firmware version, date of installation of a software, and location of the device.

State—the second component of a device is the state of the device. This is information about the condition of the device such as read only state or read-write state or a setpoint for a thermostat or some sample rate for frequency.

Commands—Commands are a type of input which indicates an action to be taken by a device and is the third component of an IoT device.

Telemetry—the fourth and final component of a device is called the Telemetry which is the most important component of device. Data collected by the device is called telemetry. This is the eyes-and-ears data that IoT devices provide to applications. Telemetry is read-only data about the environment, usually collected through sensors. Telemetry data might be preserved as a stateful variable on the device or sent to applications without storing data on the device.

Verified Boot is a concept that ensures all executed codes come from a trusted source (usually device OEMs) rather than from an attacker or corruption.

In an IT-OT integrated environment, enterprises need to ensure that they deploy devices in their OT estate which are having security built into the device and this is a must. Not only security needs to be built into the device but there should also be a way to fix any security issues as they come up via software updates or upgrades. A number of security features need to be built into the device such as verified boot. The device should also make sure that access to the device, and all the data that is produced through these devices is controlled by the authorized users or systems. And any data that is stored on the device or transmitted across the communication pathways are all encrypted and secure. We are going to discuss the role of a Security advisor in next section as part of IT-OT core team. This role needs to ensure that appropriate devices are chosen that satisfy the security postures we discussed in this section. In an IT-OT environment device security is more important aspect to consider apart from application security.

Device Management System

Within an IT-OT integrated world there will be several devices that enterprise needs to connect and exchange information. This brings in the importance of device management systems. Device management systems broadly addresses the tasks required to make these devices functional and useful in an integrated world.

The key function of a device management system is described here.

Device Provisioning—Device provisioning means making device available on the enterprise network. The device should be able to connect to the local networking environment so that it can start communicating with the enterprise systems.

Device Registration—Device registration is all about registering the device on some sort of registry so that enterprises can keep a track of which devices they have under management.

Device Authorization—Using device authorization IT systems will be able to make sure that they are only speaking to devices that are part of their fleet. At the same time authorization ensures that devices are reaching only those specific systems that they are supposed to.

Fleet Operations—Fleet operations ensure that enterprises are able to monitor and perform operational management of all the devices that are part of their IT-OT estate, so that they know that collectively the entire fleet is performing as they expect to.

Software Updates—And finally, devices need to be having the latest software updates. This is not only important for making sure the device is gaining new functions over time and new features are being added but it is also important for security. Software updates ensure that devices are always maintained with the latest security updates.

An example of device management software is Brillo and Weave toolkits which are part of Google Cloud Platform (GCP) for IoT management. Apart from commercial tools such as GCP, there are numerous open source solutions to perform device management.

Gateways

The second most important layer in the IT-OT integration is the IoT Gateways. An IoT Gateway is a solution for enabling communication between device to device or device to IoT platform.

A key point to note that there are lots of devices on the OT side that cannot communicate with the IoT platforms. One of the main reasons for this is because these devices do not have the in-built capabilities to connect to the Internet e.g., Bluetooth cannot be directly connected to the Internet. Other reason could be that the device does not have the power capacity to support networking since many IoT devices are very low power.

Let me explain this with an example of Philips Lighting. Hue color bulbs are color changing light bulbs controlled with a smart device. The bulb can turn on and off, adjust tone and contrast to create the ideal lighting mood. This is one of the more familiar and sort of widely deployed IoT devices in the market. However, this light bulb by itself cannot reach the IoT platforms since it does not support Wi-Fi connectivity.

To overcome the challenge of devices not being able to connect with the IoT platforms, IoT Gateways have come into existence. IoT Gateways can communicate to any of the devices using device proprietary protocols and transmit data to the IoT platform.

An IoT Gateway is a device that connects its client devices to IoT platforms to perform several tasks on their behalf, such as:

- communicating with IoT platform
- connecting to the Internet when the device cannot directly connect itself, e.g., ZigBee and Bluetooth devices cannot connect to Internet
- authenticating to IoT platform when the device cannot send its own credentials, or when you want to add a layer of security by using the credentials of both the device and the gateway
- publishing telemetry events, getting configuration data, or setting device state
- storing and processing data
- translating protocols

Intel IoT Gateways is a gateway from Intel that enable enterprises to seamlessly interconnect industrial infrastructure devices and secure data flow between devices and the Cloud.

Full Stack IoT Platform

A full stack IoT platform constitutes of a platform that received device data from the IoT Gateway, transforms, standardizes, and stores the data in a big data platform. The second element of full stack IoT platform is the analytics engine that derives insights from the data.

A full stack IoT platform is also called as a multi-layer technology platform that enables straightforward provisioning, management, and automation of connected devices within the IoT universe and finally provides insights based on the data gathered from different devices.

Any IoT platform should be able to follow data through the journey from gathering data from devices to generating insights from the data. The key to transform data from a device into an IoT platform begins with very specific data that comes from a machine specific industrial protocol or health-care device and as it ingested into the platform, data is processed, normalized, and standardized to a structure that is well suited for the analytics platform to generate insights.

One case study is for a multi-store retail customer where an IoT solution was developed to provide digital inventory visibility and accuracy. The solution works by putting RFID tags on every item in the store. Readers placed on the ceiling scans the store and generate a live inventory feed of how much stock is there in the store and how much is present in the storeroom. The application then generates steady stream of the real-time view of the inventory to IoT platform where data is processed and analyzed and then made available to store associates via an application. Using this data store associates can boost their visibility into the accuracy of their inventory in the store upward of 95%, compared to the 60% to 70% typically gained through standard point of sale system. With this data, store associates can track inventory in the storeroom and front of the store and make sure that product is always present where customer needs it, thereby ensuring out of stock situation never occurs. Using this data, corporate office was able to change and adapt their marketing campaigns based on the inventory and also change store hours and staff working hours. This is a classic case study of a store being able to improve revenues by 22% in just 1 year by ensuring customer are able to find the items at the place when they need and avoiding out of stock scenario. A survey by IHL Group has shown that retailers are missing out on nearly $1 trillion in sales because they do not have on hand what customers want to buy in their stores, according to a study of about 600 households.[4]

When to Get Started on IT-OT Integration

The main challenge in an integrated IT and OT world is that an attack on the OT systems cannot be easily determined with the current security strategies which are in place for most enterprises. As an example, if you were an operator, and a specific asset such as a television stops working in your home, you may not even know if the asset has stopped working due to a cyber incident. Once the equipment stops working, your first reaction would be to check the plugs for power output, since this is the way we all think. Alternatively, you would go through a checklist of things that would be more physical rather than looking at the possible malware infection of the device that you are using to control the television.

This is how current cyber postures are, and there is a lot of security awareness, security controls, and training that needs to be delivered to make IT-OT integration a reality. This is because many OT systems have been designed and deployed for the primary mission of operations and have not considered cyber threats as a focus area. The reality of the world today is cyber threats are increasing as connectivity increases with IT-OT integration. Much of the world's critical infrastructure today actually has a problem from a cyber-attack perspective.

All the challenges discussed so far should not stop enterprises for IT-OT integration, and it must start immediately. There are two core focus areas for enterprises to enable IT-OT integration. The first one is to create the right IT-OT integration assessment team and the second is to follow a methodical process to enable IT-OT integration within an enterprise.

Formula 4.0 IT-OT Core Team

Traditionally, OT teams are instrumental in maintaining and scaling lean factory operations. They ensure that all control and automation technologies enable seamless production and operation processes. OT has been intentionally separated from IT and they have different people, goals, policies, and projects. This independence drives OT teams to be agile and efficient on the shop floor. In recent years, IT-OT integration has taken several industries by storm and represents a new source of data that can be leveraged to increase factory efficiency. This new era of connectivity presents the OT team with many opportunities to further manage, automate, and optimize the shop floor and production processes. Unfortunately, without IT-OT integration, these opportunities cannot be capitalized upon. Consider this: if shop floor data is not integrated with data from IT systems and this data is then not processed accurately nor displayed to key decision-makers, operational excellence and production optimization are impossible to achieve.

This brings in a new perspective in terms of the operating model to make IT-OT integration a success, where data and security play a major role. As we discussed earlier, security is one of the major concerns in

IT-OT integration but this cannot stop an enterprise toward the integration. Enterprises need to find out ways to improve security postures both from IT and OT perspectives.

On the other side, there is an enormous amount of data that is pumped from the OT devices, and traditional data management systems simply cannot handle such a load. Using traditional IT systems for real-time decision-making is impossible. With IT-OT integration, enterprises will have interconnected machines and these machines generate a lot of data that need to be analyzed in real-time to give a full picture of what is happening on the floor or even in a single machine. For example, in a shoe manufacturing plant, the machine creating soles can notify the team responsible for sole stitching when there is an unexpected delay or backlog, allowing them to switch to other tasks while maintenance is carried out. This facility-wide visibility is simply impossible without data connectivity, and as such having a big data platform is a must for enterprises embarking on an IT-OT integration. With a big data platform enterprises will be able to bring in all kinds of data from the operational equipment and create a centralized IT-OT network. Subsequently, this network can be connected with the existing IT to generate insights.

Based on the discussion above, the four key roles that are required to make an IT-OT integration successful are listed here.

Operational Technology Lead—The OT lead brings in the shop floor expertise and has complete understanding of the machineries and production processes used within the shop floor. To integrate an OT system into the IT world one needs to understand the ins and outs of things IT has typically not considered, such as:

- – Automation technologies on the shop floor
- – Environmental factors (temperatures, chemical exposure, etc.)
- – Real-time intelligence systems
- – Redundancy protocols
- – Regulatory requirements
- – Shop floor setup and infrastructure

An enterprise can only embark on IT-OT integration if the team planning and performing the integration understands how operations and business issues work and discover ways that IT can help OT to deploy new technology to improve operations. This is one of the main reasons why an OT lead is required in the team. An OT lead forms part of the core team in an IT-OT integration journey.

Information Technology Lead—The IT lead is typically an enterprise architect who comes from the IT organization. The IT lead understands the nuances of the OT systems and by working alongside the OT lead is able to define a technology roadmap for the integration. This role needs to have a complete handle on IT compliance, governance, security, data center or Cloud requirements, types of IT systems used within an enterprise, their integrations, and so on.

Another important capability that an IT lead needs to possess is understanding of the end-to-end IoT reference architecture and the different tools that can enable an IT-OT integration based on which tools and platforms can be identified for the enterprise.

Big Data Lead—The big data lead has never been considered as an important role within the IT-OT integration world. However, enterprises need to understand that IT-OT integration can only be successful if data from OT systems are captured, filtered, and analyzed in a way that can provide useful insights for enterprises to make decisions. Big data leads therefore form part of the core team in an IT-OT integration scenario.

Security Advisor—Security in the IT-OT world is of paramount importance. Any OT system that needs to be integrated with IT systems needs to be analyzed thoroughly from a cybersecurity perspective. Security in context of IT-OT integration means how IT systems will interact with the sensors and devices that are part of the OT systems and the security pertaining to these systems, sensors, and devices. Choosing devices that have in-built security features is another important role a security advisor performs. As an example, in one of the case studies for a large manufacturing company, there were challenges in connectivity between devices and the IoT platforms since many of the devices that this company had were not enable to connect over Internet. This was the time when new devices were brought from Particle IO which is a widely used IoT company that has released the powerful IoT devices with built in cellular connectivity and this gives the ability to have device connect to the IoT platform over Cloud.

Decades ago, when corporations first started leveraging client/server networks and the Internet, they did not think about security until criminals realized they could hack into IT systems to manipulate them and steal money and data. OT environments today face similar challenges when connecting ICS technologies to the network. Until recently, OT was interconnected with proprietary, vendor-based closed connections and protocols that could not be accessed remotely. Now that ICS technologies are moving toward standard IT communications protocols, IT security challenges have become part of OT environments. This is one of the reasons why security considerations should be planned from day one in an IT-OT integration, and a security advisor is the one who plays this role.

> ### DEFINITION
>
> ***Industrial control system (ICS)*** *is a general term that encompasses several types of control systems and associated instrumentation used for industrial process control.*
>
> *Such systems can range in size from a few modular panel-mounted controllers to large interconnected and interactive distributed control systems with thousands of field connections.*

IT-OT Integration Champion—This is an individual who is able to communicate with and relate to both IT and OT groups. The IT-OT integration
champion understands how to convey information in a way that encourages cooperation and collaboration between all the parties involved in
the integration, including OT leads and shop floor staff. It is an important
role which is about defining and re-defining the goals and success criteria
of OT departments to foster collaboration. The challenge is that IT and
OT have different goals, philosophies, and working cultures. The IT-OT
integration champion is the one who brings all these goals and people
together to achieve a common objective of IT-OT integration success.

Planning IT-OT Integration

It is not necessary that all OT systems need to be integrated with the IT systems and it is also not the recommended model as per Formula 4.0 methodology. IT-OT integration is a journey rather than a fixed time project.

Secondly, in the OT world there are hundreds of OT systems that are part
of the shop floor and a benefit analysis needs to be performed to determine
which OT processes and associated systems need to be integrated with IT.
All OT processes within an enterprise need to be analyzed by the IT-OT
core team and each process should be classified into one of the four quadrants of the IT-OT integration toolkit, as depicted in Figure 14.4.

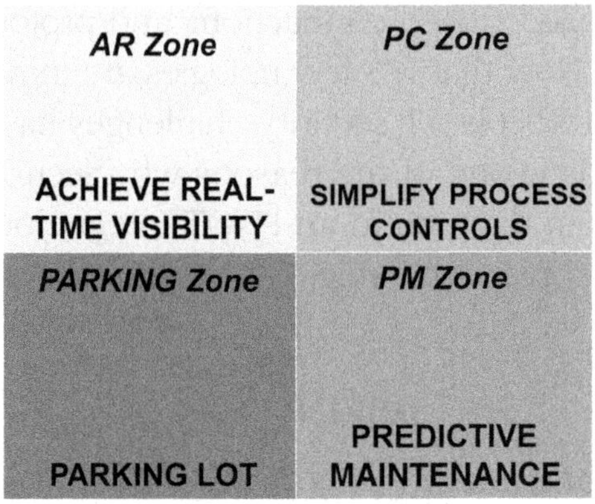

Figure 14.4 IT-OT analysis toolkit

Achieve Real-Time Visibility (AR Zone)—The first quadrant is for processes that needs to achieve real-time visibility on a business process that can enable enterprises either to save costs or improve efficiency. This is one of the important areas where IT-OT integration brings in a lot of value. An IT-OT integration can enable data sharing and reporting in real-time allowing enterprises to make quick decisions. As an example, imagine the cost of parts used in a manufacturing process increases overnight. If shop floor leads and finance teams are notified of this price increase immediately, they along with other stakeholders can take a decision to use parts from other vendors or slowdown production based on the demand. Another example is for a food retailer to receive real-time insights on a specific product expiry date or when a product is going out of stock or is low in stock.

Simplify Process Controls (PC Zone)—The second quadrant is for processes which need to reduce manual interventions to enable a seamless integration starting from product design until the product is ready for consumption. In most of the OT environments today data from one system is manually fed into another system to complete a business process. The goal of IT-OT integration under this quadrant is to reduce manual interventions by digitizing the OT operations wherever possible. As an example, imagine a car manufacturing process in which the shop floor staff have to measure the size of a hole to identify the right screw that goes into it. This is a manual process in most shop floors currently. With IT-OT integration sensors can read the size of each hole and provide the correct description of the size and number of screws required for each unit. This reduces significant manual interventions and improves production efficiency. The same data can then be sent to the procurement systems for new orders even before the screw goes out of stock, and finally the finance systems can be updated with the future cost projections. Another example is where heavy execution systems are expected to be simplified. In the manufacturing sector replacing manufacturing execution systems (MES) and their related applications which are used for inventory tracking, production maintenance, and quality controls can lead to production efficiencies. MES are computerized systems used in manufacturing to track and document the transformation of raw materials into finished goods.

Enabling Predictive Maintenance (PM Zone)—The third quadrant is for business processes that benefits from predictive maintenance. One of the reasons why IT-OT integration is becoming popular is because it can predict failures in equipment that is part of the production process. This helps enterprises combat the issues associated with unplanned downtime, including equipment failure and profit losses.

Parking Zone—The fourth quadrant is for processes which is not planned for IT-OT integration, but has the potential to be utilized in the future. It is essential that all processes within the shop floor are analyzed for applicability toward IT-OT integration and the ones which do not qualify for IT-OT integration are placed in the Parking Zone quadrant.

Once processes are identified for IT-OT integration, IBT needs to be applied to all processes that are part of the AR, PC, and PZ zone.

IT-OT core team teams up with the IBT team to define the problem and opportunities for the processes part of these three zones and arrive at solutions to make the process efficient, cost effective, and automated.

IT-OT Integration with Formula 4.0

IT-OT integration forms an integral part of Formula 4.0 methodology, and the Formula 4.0 foundation platform allows enterprises to utilize the full potential of IT-OT integration in their journey toward digital transformation. Data and analytics and Cloud are key pillars for Formula 4.0, which allows enterprises to achieve maximum mileage from IoT. This is because, enterprises can utilize the support of Cloud providers to rapidly adopt IT-OT integration, and with already created data ecosystems enterprises can import the IoT generated data into their enterprise to perform actions and analytics.

As an example, enterprises that choose Amazon Web Services (AWS) as their Cloud provider can utilize AWS IoT device developer kit which helps to easily and quickly connect hardware device or mobile application to the AWS IoT core. The AWS IoT core is a managed Cloud service that lets connected devices securely interact with Cloud applications and other devices. It can support billions of devices and trillions of messages and can process and route those messages to AWS endpoints and to other devices reliably and securely. With AWS IoT core, applications can keep track of and communicate with all devices, all the time, even when they are not connected. The AWS IoT device SDK enables devices to connect, authenticate, and exchange messages with AWS IoT core. It also supports C language, JavaScript, and Arduino, and includes the client libraries, the developer guide, and the porting guide for manufacturers.

Another example is for enterprises that chose Azure as their Cloud provider. The Azure IoT is a collection of Microsoft-managed Cloud services that connect, monitor, and control billions of IoT assets.

Data and analytics is one of the key elements of Formula 4.0 methodology. With this, IT-OT integration becomes a reality.

IT-OT integration data is a subset and a special case of big data and consists of heterogeneous streams that must be combined and transformed to yield consistent, comprehensive, current, and correct information for business reporting and analysis and business decisions. The convergence of IT-OT integration and big data promises tremendous new business value and opportunities for enterprises across all major industries. Critical to unlocking the value from all this newly created IT-OT integration data is IT-OT integration analytics, which is also sometimes known as IoT analytics.

Some enterprises tend to use existing data analytics platforms to capture data from IT-OT integration and perform analytics, whereas some wish to create a separate platform. There is no right or wrong answer and this varies on a case-by-case basis.

More than one-third of companies in a recent Gartner survey said they are using or are planning to use new, separate data management capabilities to support IT-OT integration. Sixty-one percent of those surveyed expect to leverage and expand an existing data management infrastructure. This is likely because many of the same data management infrastructure tools and technologies applied to more traditional use cases can be leveraged in some fashion to support IT-OT integration.[5]

Enterprises should however evaluate the suitability of existing capabilities for dealing with the scale and distribution requirements of the specific IT-OT integration deployment. They also need to consider the unique governance issues of IT-OT integration data by assessing whether those technologies can deliver to the level required.

Notes

1. https://www.gartner.com/en/newsroom/press-releases/2019-08-29-gartner-says-5-8-billion-enterprise-and-automotive-io#:~:text=Gartner%2C%20Inc.,a%20 21%25%20increase%20from%202019.&text=Utilities%20will%20be%20the%20 highest,to%20reach%201.37%20billion%20endpoints
2. https://www.gartner.com/en/newsroom/press-releases/2019-08-29-gartner-says-5-8-billion-enterprise-and-automotive-io
3. https://451research.com/blog/1934-survey-finds-security-continues-to-be-top-priority-in-deploying-iot-projects
4. https://www.retaildive.com/news/out-of-stocks-could-be-costing-retailers-1t/526327/
5. https://www.gartner.com/smarterwithgartner/how-iot-impacts-data-and-analytics/

Chapter 15

Enterprise Governance

The success of a project is often dependent on people, processes, and capabilities that cut across multiple disciplines. To be successful across other projects that are of similar nature, consistent people, processes, technologies, and capabilities need to be adopted across all functions in an organization. However, leaping from a small success to an organization-wide success is of course never easy, and businesses that have tried big bang adoptions often tend to fail in their attempts. The reason for this is a lack of proper and consistent integration among defined disciplines and processes. The result is suboptimization and confusion, as well as potentially unnecessary expenditure. There is a need for collaborative efforts with incremental and planned adoption to integrate any new methodologies or processes across an organization.

Many individuals who adapt innovative methodologies or processes successfully are happy with the value they have achieved, and they will then try to replicate this success across the organization as extensively as possible. Without the right organization-wide framework or enterprise governance for adopting new trends, turning small scale victories into large-scale success does however tend to be incredibly complex. Many times, organizations will lose the essence of value along the way, which derails even the most wisely developed policies.

In the context of digital transformation, governance can be best viewed as the formal structure for aligning IT strategy with the overall corporate business strategy. Creating and utilizing a formal enterprise governance allows organizations to produce measurable results toward achieving their overall strategic objectives and goals. Additionally, a formal enterprise-wide digital transformation framework managed by a governance at enterprise level takes stakeholder interests into account. This includes the needs and requirements of their staff and the processes they engage in.

An organization that considers all of their stakeholder's needs are better equipped to maximize the value of corporate information while protecting and driving enterprise value.

Technology of course plays a critical role in many processes across an organization. With the invention of new technologies, tools, and techniques on a daily basis, having a formal structure and framework to manage digital transformation is of utmost importance. This allows an organization to optimize the cost of IT services while ensuring that the right choices are being made on technology adoption. Aside from helping to maintain IT and business-related risks at acceptable levels, it also prevents value leaks.

If you ask any executive from any industry their top ten investments over the next 5 years, nine out of ten times digital technologies will be on that list. Investment in digital is seen as being vital in today's dynamic marketspace and is at an all-time high. Executives expect to achieve business value by investing in IT and digital transformation.

Although budgets are being allocated to technology procurement, many executives are left frustrated because the benefits do not materialize. This leaves decision-makers confused. Every business headline they read recommends investing in more digital technology because the ROI is there, yet their businesses are in the red and have not progressed since they invested in more technology.

The example above highlights the term known as "digital transformation fallacy," which means investing more on technology rather than the right technology and in the right way. Right way means performing digital transformation based on a business need rather than a technology need. Executives and decision-makers within the enterprise need to ask whether their organization has the right resources and capabilities to make the right investments in technology based on the business need, that align with their current enterprise strategy, operating model, and their future state business aspirations. This first step is what we call the alignment challenge. It is possible to integrate your business strategies with your IT strategy while being in alignment with your organization's current and future operating models? Secondly, is the organization making the right choices in the most consistent manner that can assure success?

So, how can enterprises realize this level of integration between business and IT? The only way to achieve this alignment with digital transformation is to understand and organize digital assets around the enterprise level business drivers. As an example, a hotel chain in UK, which operates as a low-cost hotel brand has an aspiration to utilize technology to compete in their marketspace, but at the same time does not wish to invest heavily in branding and marketing using external agencies. They also have the vision to bring their operational costs down and pass all such savings to their customers. Translating this vision into an IT strategy using digital transformation as a lever is what constitutes a successful business strategy for this enterprise. This concept is the Formula 4.0 digital transformation strategy.

Formula 4.0 Guidance on Digital Transformation Governance

From my experiences in the field, one of the main challenges enterprises face when discussing governance in context of digital transformation is identifying a suitable enterprise level governance framework that fully captures their organization's structure.

My general feedback has been to select any externally available enterprise level governance framework(s) and start with it, assuming that the framework supports the following:

■ A mechanism where technology choices for digital transformation is made at an enterprise level. This could be the choice of a tool, software package, programming language, or a Cloud provider
■ A mechanism where principles, policies, frameworks, and processes are defined at an enterprise level
■ People, skills, and competency characteristics can be aligned from a digital transformation needs perspective
■ Finally, the framework should allow the monitoring of all the above at an enterprise level

Any governance framework should enable information and related technology to be governed and managed in a holistic manner for the whole enterprise, taking in the full end-to-end business responsibility, including considering the IT-related interests of the enterprise. Irrespective of the governance framework adopted, enterprises should ensure that the framework assists them in achieving their business goals via technology and is able to deliver value through effective governance and management of enterprise IT.

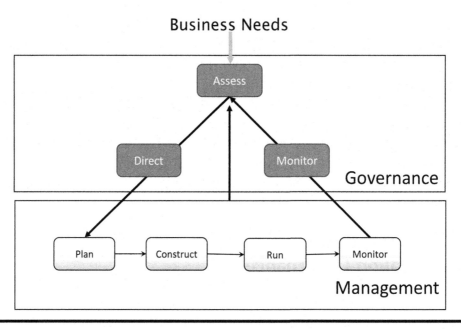

Figure 15.1   Governance approach

As depicted in Figure 15.1, any strong enterprise governance ensures that management is separated from the actual governance. At a governance level based on the business needs, a strategy is devised on how the enterprise needs to transform itself which is then directed to the management team for planning and execution.

Governance ensures that enterprise objectives are achieved by evaluating stakeholder needs, conditions, and options, setting direction through prioritization, decision-making and monitoring performance, compliance, and progress against agreed direction and objectives. Management will plan, build, run, and monitor activities in alignment with the direction set by the governance body to achieve the enterprise's objectives.

As part of Formula 4.0 we are not going to discuss how an enterprise governance should be set up, since there are several frameworks in the market such as Cobit 5 (C5), which provide guidance on enterprise governance. Although C5 is not a framework specifically addressing the digital transformation journey, it does provide guidance that can be further customized to make digital transformation successful at an enterprise level. As an example, many enterprises today have an objective to be cheaper, achieve faster time to market, achieve better customer satisfaction rates, and be competitive in the market using digital as the lever. This objective is further broken down at the governance level by evaluating different areas of implementation to arrive at the enterprise charter, three of which are listed below:

∎ Identify business processes which differentiate enterprise in their market space
∎ Use data and analytics to analyze market and competitor trends and develop new products
∎ Use automation and Cloud to become faster and cheaper

A Formula 4.0 management team constitutes of key leaders from each capability area, such as security, DevOps, Cloud, data, tools, processes, and methodologies. This team is formed based on the strategic objective of the enterprise which is determined by business process changes enterprise want to make. The business process changes will determine the technologies to be adopted and related investments. Based on the enterprise size, one or multiple individuals in respective capability areas are identified which is finally lead by governance team members at the highest level in the organization. This includes positions such as the Chief Information Officer, Chief Digital Officer, and Chief Technology Officer.

The objective of management teams is to ensure appropriate guidelines and processes are defined in each of the respective area that adheres to the Formula 4.0 framework. These are to be defined during plan and build phases. The management team next ensures that agreed objectives are monitored for performance, compliance, and progress during the run and monitor phases.

Figure 15.2 depicts the key capability areas within an enterprise governance. These are applicable for enterprises that are in the process of transforming themselves to digital using Formula 4.0.

The Enterprise-Architecture (EA)—this department plays a central role in reducing the complexity associated with digital transformation. Most companies have a dedicated EA group embedded within the larger IT organization. This group typically

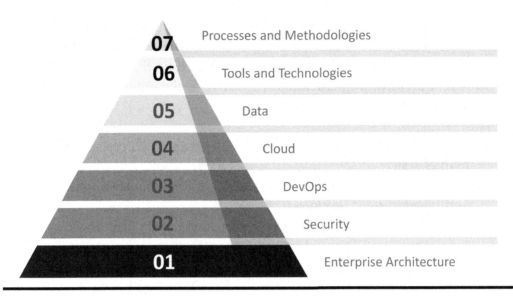

Figure 15.2   Enterprise governance key capabilities

oversees the entire systems architecture, defining design principles, including IT infrastructure. It helps to establish rules and processes around technology usage to ensure consistency across business units and functions. As such, this group can help the CEO and others on the senior leadership team redesign their company business and IT architectures so that they can compete more effectively in a digital era.

Enterprise Security—this plays a vital role in protecting enterprise intellectual property, assets, and overall business operations. Enterprises recognize security as one of the key elements toward digital transformation. Given the complexity of security architectures, enterprises often struggle to understand what it is they need to do in order to enable their secure digital transformation. Enterprises need to build digital resilience into the fabric of their enterprise, ensuring they can gain all the advantages of the digital age while minimizing associated risks. Critical to aligning security strategies with the business is security architecture, a framework of strategies, tactics, and capabilities that provide a common language, consistent approach, and a long-term vision. A security architecture should include a set of high-level architectural principles that can be understood by executives and specialists alike. This function defines the security framework and monitors adherence of these functions, be it in product development, product operations, data security, or Cloud security.

DevOps—this is about automation, technology, and communication. It is about making communication between development and operations non-adversarial and less formal. Enterprise DevOps also shifts some of the infrastructure automation requirements out of the Dev side and into the Ops side of DevOps. With efficient enterprise DevOps governance, development teams within an enterprise are delivering early and often, using automated deployment tools, which includes taking extra effort to address the information requirements of the IT group. In an enterprise lead DevOps approach, application teams are standardizing on a common set of automation tools and approaches across the enterprise. The role of the DevOps department is to ensure that principles and policies are defined in this capability area including identifying and deploying the right tools and techniques.

Cloud—the adoption of Cloud services is fast becoming mainstream among large corporations. An increasing number of enterprises are seeking to reduce cost, accelerate their speed to market, and enable innovation by eliminating traditional data center constraints. Cloud governing functions at an enterprise level becomes far more essential and will determine whether an organization needs to choose a private or public Cloud or go for a multi Cloud strategy. It also looks at which Cloud provider they should choose and why, and so on.

As soon as organizations choose Cloud and start to increase the size of their public Cloud footprint, the complexity of managing the cost, compliance, and health of Cloud increases. While existing corporate governance models can be leveraged to provide oversight, they often lack the integrated Cloud engineering expertise to manage this function properly. To overcome this challenge Cloud function needs to be created at an enterprise level which will ensure that both "build" and "run" are defined and monitored to achieve maximum benefits from moving to Cloud.

Data Governance—data is one of the most important functions for any organization. Data governance (DG) is the process of managing the availability, usability, integrity, and security of the data in enterprise systems, based on internal data standards and policies that also control data usage. Effective DG at enterprise level ensures that organization data is consistent and trustworthy and does not get misused. It is increasingly critical as organizations face new data privacy regulations and rely more and more on data analytics to help optimize operations and drive business decision-making.

A well-designed DG program typically includes a governance team, a steering committee that acts as the governing body, and a group of data stewards at enterprise level. They work together to create the standards and policies for governing data, as well as implementation and enforcement procedures that are primarily carried out by the data stewards.

Tools and Technologies—managing tools and technologies at an enterprise level is another important function which typically gets missed from governance. The pace at which new tools and technologies are evolving in the marketspace is creating immense risk from security, cost leakage, and vendor lock-in perspectives. This is because the decision to introduce a tool or technology is made in business unit silos resulting in a lot of duplication at enterprise level. Many tools and technologies creep into the IT estate of the enterprise over time without proper verification and validation. The end result usually leads to desperate tools and technologies and in many cases multiple tools doing the same job, thereby leading to a cluttered IT tools and technologies estate. Tools and technology governance is a function within an enterprise that should ensure that the right set of tools are deployed across the organization with zero duplication and similar functionalities. This will not only keep the IT estate clean but will also be cost effective.

Processes and Methodologies—product-based organization structure is the need of every organization which is aspiring to improve their business with digital technology. Formula 4.0 mandates every organization to follow a software development life cycle that will allow them to deliver new features to the market in shorter intervals and achieve faster time to market. It is essential that a consistent and singular development methodology is followed across the enterprise with new capabilities added at periodic intervals. Any chosen framework or methodology should encompass a set of principles, processes, and best practices. Agile methodology is the recommendation of Formula 4.0 to develop and deliver high-quality products and services faster which can scale from small to multiple large teams at the project, program, and portfolio levels. The methodologies should support enterprises to successfully navigate digital disruption and effectively respond to volatile market conditions, changing customer needs, and emerging technologies. Some examples of agile methodologies are the Design for Hybrid Agile Adoption framework, SCRUM framework, and Scaled Agile framework.

Companies across the globe and across a wide range of industries are applying increased efforts in digitally transforming their organization and to achieve this an enterprise-wide governance is mandatory. Enterprises across various sectors are in different stages of implementation, with the banking sector making the most changes and stringent developments to digitally transform themselves. Despite the various levels of progress made between companies and industry sectors there is a general consensus that a number of fundamental foundation steps are central to an effective enterprise-wide governance and more importantly for organizations with a desire for digital transformation.

The first step in developing a successful enterprise-wide governance with an aspiration toward digital transformation is to fully understand and map out the current state of the governance framework in place within the enterprise. The next step would then be to determine what changes are required based on the enterprise-wide set objectives of digital, with a vision of how this will be executed. Based on this vision, new disciplines or capability areas need to be altered or newly set-up at an enterprise level that will enable organizations to be successful in their digital transformation journey.

BRINGING THE PIECES TOGETHER

In this section, we will discuss a step-by-step approach to transform enterprises into a digital organization by following the guidelines of the Formula 4.0 methodology, which have been discussed so far in this book.

Overall, Formula 4.0 is an enterprise digital transformation framework that enables organizations to become truly digital.

Chapter 16

The Formula 4.0 Methodology: Bringing All Capabilities Together for Digital Transformation

Many organizations are undergoing digital transformation to take advantage of all the benefits of new digital technology. IDG Communications, Inc. state that:[1] "89% of companies are either in the process of implementing or have already executed a digital-first approach to business processes, operations, and customer engagement." Despite these advances, there are several enterprises that have failed in their digital transformation journey. The reason for these failures is due to several reasons. A digital transformation is not about technology, applications scope, or people scope; it revolves around the business landscape of the enterprises including people and processes. Successful enterprises have ensured that digital transformation is not confined to an area within the organization and they do not embark on a digital transformation journey in business unit silos. Digital transformation is an enterprise wise initiative drive by a business need which then cuts across applications, networks, infrastructure, security, people, and everything that is part of the enterprise landscape. This means that the Chief Information Officer (CIO) is not the one responsible for digital transformation. An enterprise can only achieve a successful digital transformation if all the pillars within the enterprises are brought together and transformed. For this to happen all function or capability heads need to come together, which includes the CIO, Chief Business Officer (CBO), Chief Technology Officer (CTO), Chief Security Officer (CSO), Chief Marketing Officer (CMO), amongst others. Digital transformation is a broad subject that requires competency across strategy and vision, people and culture, process and governance, and technology and capabilities. While there are perennial capabilities and skills that are required for business success (e.g., investment, leadership, culture, change management, and governance), digital transformation requires new capabilities that organizations need to acquire and develop mastery around. These include capabilities related to business models, disruptive technology enablers, platform architectures, digital services mastery, and digital innovation. Formula 4.0 brings all these different capabilities together and provides a powerful methodology by which enterprises can successfully transform themselves to digital and achieve maximum success and benefits from technology.

So far in this book we have discussed different horizontal and vertical capability areas of the Formula 4.0 methodology. This chapter will bring together all these capabilities and explain the end-to-end implementation of Formula 4.0.

Understand the Goals and Objectives of an Enterprise

The first and foremost step in any digital transformation journey is to understand the overall goals and objectives that the enterprise has. There are a variety of reasons why enterprises want to transform to digital, such as:

- To ensure that they create a future state IT architecture that can support them in adopting any new future business models and technologies
- To enhance the user experience for their clients
- To achieve faster time to market i.e., release new products to the market in short intervals
- To use data for making business decisions
- To save costs

Formula 4.0 is a framework that addresses all these goals together and is a business drive digital transformation framework. Any enterprise which is aspiring to utilize technology as their backbone to solve business problems and be competitive in their market needs to adopt Formula 4.0 in full rather than in parts.

Based on the goals of the enterprise, prioritization can be made on specific focus areas. This does not mean that any capability area within Formula 4.0 can be ignored, it just means that prioritization can be made within specific areas to achieve faster results in those which are considered a priority. As an example, assume the first business process selected by an enterprise for transformation has problems and opportunities identified that can be solved by introducing a big data platform. In this instance thought all Formula 4.0 capability areas needs to be implemented; however, higher focus and priority is given to implement big data platform to achieve the desired benefits faster for the selected business processes.

Any enterprise which needs to digitally transform itself should understand that investing more time in planning their digital transformation journey based on business needs is extremely important and will undoubtedly save a lot of time during the implementation.

The digitalization of enterprises is not a matter of developing and improving on technological capabilities, but the reorganization and redesign the business models, including metrics, culture, roles, tools, technologies, and processes.

One of the biggest mistakes that many enterprises make is to set themselves a goal that is too far away or not well thought out and at the same time try to achieve this goal as quickly as possible. The second mistake is that the foundation is not set properly before embarking on their digital transformation journey. Setting up a foundation for digital transformation is essential but at the same time complicated. This is because enterprises need to set a foundation on an already existing enterprise landscape which has likely been in place for many years, if not decades. The planning phase therefore plays a critical role in implementing Formula 4.0 within an enterprise.

The end goal of Formula 4.0 is to enable an enterprise to adopt to any new business models in the shortest time possible in the most agile way using technology as the level.

A central team known as the "taskforce" needs to be formed that will be in-charge of digital transformation for the enterprise. The head of all departments are equally responsible for the success of digital transformation, and implementing Formula 4.0 is an enterprise-wide top-down initiative.

The taskforce needs to assess business challenges and opportunities, people characteristics, processes used within the enterprise, technologies and tools used, inventory of applications, infrastructure, networks, level of automation achieved within the enterprise, and so on. This will help determine the transformation approach to be followed for the enterprise, including timeliness and budgets required for implementing Formula 4.0.

Defining Business Strategy and Identifying Business Processes for Digital Transformation

The first step for any enterprise to embark on their digital transformation journey is to understand the business strategy behind the transformation. Enterprises need to choose from one of the two business strategies, one is the Customer Engagement Strategy and second is Business Transformation Strategy.

Once a business strategy is defined business processes for transformation that can differentiate the enterprise in the market or can improve the customer engagement needs to be identified and placed in one of the four quadrants of BT model. The four quadrants of BT model are Hot Zone, Warm Zone, Cold Zone, and Parking Zone.

IBT model is applied on selected business processes categorized within the Hot and Warm Zone and business solutions are identified.

The next step is to identify all IT systems that are part of the business processes and identify technology solutions to enable digital transformation for systems that are part of the Hot and Warm Zone.

BT model recommends two types of treatments to IT systems that are identified for digital transformation. One is called "digital from core" and the second is "digital from surround." All systems identified for transformation for the business processes within the Hot and Warm Zone are either digitally transformed from core or surround. Systems part of the Cold Zone can be digitally transformed from surround on a need basis.

Setting up the Foundation

The Second step for an enterprise to embark on a digital transformation journey is to set up the right foundation. Cloud infrastructure, Atomic architecture, and API platforms are the digital triplets which form the foundation for enterprises to become digital.

Cloud Infrastructure

Infrastructure forms the foundation of any enterprise. Across industries around the world, digital transformation is changing the way organizations of all sizes do business. Harnessing the power of the technology with Cloud, big data, and analytics as the foundation, organizations are trying to leverage new digital competencies to transform every step of the value chain. This leads to the creation of new revenue streams, the elimination of inefficient and redundant processes, and a shift away from repetitive day-to-day tasks to more strategic, future-looking work. For organizations to remain competitive in this super dynamic market, IT must embrace digital transformation and must have the right infrastructure in place to achieve this. Infrastructure is therefore a key enabler and forms the foundation layer for any digital transformation.

Outdated infrastructure characteristics such as lengthy and manual configuration and management processes have longer lead times to procure new infrastructure, they allow lower flexibility to adopt to newer technologies and are less secure. Overall this can hinder the enterprise's ability to further the goals of digital business.

In a traditional enterprise, valuable IT staff time is spent "keeping the lights on" instead of aligning infrastructure and network capabilities with strategic initiatives that improve operational efficiency and enhance the customer experience. An infrastructure that is truly digital ready can dynamically align with the ever-changing needs of the enterprise. That means allowing more agility and faster time to innovation, better security, and greater operational efficiency and simplicity.

Although digital transformation with Formula 4.0 is not purely a technology initiative, new business models will be underpinned by technologies. To a large extent, over the past 5 years, infrastructure has taken the lead in adopting faster, more agile, and automated approaches to supporting digital transformation with private, public, and hybrid Cloud strategies. With Formula 4.0, there is lot of emphasis on Cloud and networks that connect private and public Clouds.

Most of the networks currently existing within an enterprise are built to provide fast, reliable connectivity but not to meet the new demands of digital. The demands of digital in context of Formula 4.0 include the elements listed below:

Scale—the investment in digital platforms will form the basis of delivering new customer experiences and optimized operating models. With investments in technologies such as mobile and Internet of Things (IoT) (which are substantial components of Formula 4.0) networks will be made up of 10–100 times more endpoints. Securely connecting these massively distributed networks will require advances not readily available in traditional infrastructure and networks.

Speed—organizations with digital initiatives need to move fast and adapt to change in the new normal. New innovative applications, services, and business processes need an IT infrastructure that can be agile, and most organizations' infrastructure has not been built to cope with this constant need to support change and ensure continuous service assurance throughout.

Cloud—the modernization of existing critical business systems will involve the migration of applications to a hybrid Cloud deployment model. This transition puts renewed emphasis on the network and connectivity, not just to ensure performance from site to site but also to ensure that the performance of specific applications is reliable and satisfactory for the end user.

Security—adoption of digital initiatives that rely on technologies such as data, AI and Machine Language, Cloud and IoT opens up new threats and opportunities for attack. A digital-ready network must be the first line of defense and provides a unique platform for rapid detection and response to threats.

The taskforce needs to analyze the current infrastructure to define the future state of the enterprise platform.

Moving to an architecture that is heavily based on Cloud and virtualization raises alarms for many IT enterprises. Concerns about data privacy, security, and the need to defend the network against external threats have long been at the center of many conversations. Many of these concerns have however already addressed by Cloud providers. In addition, Formula 4.0 addresses some of the application level security and compliance concerns with embedded security in infrastructure, application development, and operations cycles.

Formula 4.0 mandates that Cloud infrastructure is adopted for an enterprise embarking on their digital transformation journey, as discussed in Chapter 6.

DEFINITION

Cloud Interconnect *provides low latency, highly available connections that enable enterprises to reliably transfer data between On-Premises and Cloud networks.*

Although Cloud is the preferred model in Formula 4.0, this does not necessary mandate the use of a public Cloud. A hybrid Cloud could be the way forward for many enterprises. This brings a new perspective on the networks and connectivity to enable systems to interact sitting on private and public Clouds. It is therefore essential that enterprises plan for Cloud interconnect fabrics that will ensure servers are maintained and managed regionally. As an example, ECX Fabric (Equinix Cloud Exchange Fabric) is a service that enables any business to connect private and public Clouds including the world's largest network service and Cloud providers, on the Equinix platform.

Selecting the Right Cloud Strategy

Having the right Cloud strategy is key to success. The public Cloud let enterprises access compute resources through the Internet or dedicated connections. A private Cloud keeps data within the data center and uses a proprietary architecture. The hybrid Cloud model mixes public and private Cloud models and transfers data between the two. Finally, in a multi-Cloud scenario, enterprises operate from more than one public Cloud provider.

Aside from considering where applications should live, it also needs to be considered how they will perform once they are migrated to Cloud and what are the cost considerations and strengths of each of the Cloud providers. Many organizations have seen vendor lock-in with a single Cloud provider; however, the benefits of multi-Cloud need to be analyzed very carefully before making a choice.

As discussed in Chapter 6, it is essential that we determine the stack of applications that need to move to Cloud. This is determined by several factors, such as:

■ Will migrated applications use all features of Cloud, as it is a waste to pay to migrate if it is not essential?
■ Stale data is another concern with Cloud migration. Without a good reason, it is probably unwise to move historical data to the Cloud.
■ How well will an application perform once it is migrated? Is there adequate bandwidth for optimal application performance? It also needs to be investigated whether an application's dependencies may complicate a migration.

The steps or processes an enterprise follows during a Cloud migration vary based on factors such as the type of migration it wants to perform and the specific resources it wants to move. That said, common elements of a Cloud migration strategy include the following:

- Evaluation of performance and security requirements
- Selection of a Cloud provider
- Selection of a single or multi-Cloud strategy i.e., choose one Cloud service provider or multiple
- Selection of which Cloud type suits them i.e., Private or Public or Hybrid Cloud
- Calculation of costs
- Understanding why and when applications need to move to Cloud

There is also a need to address nonfunctional requirements before embarking on a Cloud migration journey, such as:

- **Interoperability**—the ability of different information systems, devices, and applications to access, exchange, integrate, and cooperatively use data in a coordinated manner, within and across organizations.
- **Data Security**—refers to the protection of data against unauthorized access or corruption and is necessary to ensure data integrity. Data integrity is a desired result of data security, but the term data integrity refers only to the validity and accuracy of data rather than the act of protecting it.

Without proper planning, a migration could degrade application performance and lead to higher IT costs thereby negating the main benefits of Cloud computing.

In summary, a careful analysis needs to be performed on which Cloud provider to close, the type of Cloud to be adopted, which applications need to move to Cloud and when, and their associated benefits. An appropriate network strategy should be defined to ensure that data and applications residing on Cloud can seamlessly integrate with other applications, irrespective of location.

Atomic Architecture

As discussed in Chapters 5 and 9, product development with Formula 4.0 needs to follow Atomic architecture patterns. These are patterns in which applications are separated into loosely coupled services. With detailed services and lightweight protocols, Atomic architecture offers increased modularity, making applications easier to develop, test, deploy, and, more importantly, to change and maintain without being dependent on other functions within the application.

Enterprises should ensure that all product developments adapt to an Atomic architecture pattern and any exceptions need to be considered on a case-by-case basis.

API Platform

As discussed in Chapter 8, an API platform is an organization which brings together two or more distinct but interdependent groups through a program-matically consumable service or an API, creating a foundation for automated interactions between them.

It is mandatory that enterprise embark on API led transformations to realize the benefits of digital transformation. However, introducing an API platform into an enterprise needs to be carefully planned and taskforce teams need to validate the existing enterprise systems to understand how systems interact with each other, the kind of systems in place and the technologies in use. In the end, bringing in an API platform means that existing system to system interaction needs to change which may require changes to the existing code. Introducing API into an organization is a journey rather than a onetime activity and the taskforce needs to define the approach toward APIfication. APIfication is the process in which APIs are introduced into the enterprise with the goal of ensuring that each and every system interaction is enabled only via APIs.

Tools and Software Consolidation

Today's CIOs are under pressure to ensure that they not only adopt to the digital trends that are prevailing in the market to be competitive, but also at the same time there is huge pressure on cost optimization and ensuring that IT estate within their enterprise is at the right optimized level that will enable them to adapt to any changing business needs in the most agile way. This poses a very strong need for standardization and consistency in the IT estate of every enterprise.

Unnecessary IT adds complexity and high costs, reduces effectiveness, and stalls innovation which ultimately slows down an enterprise in their digital transformation. The answer to this issue lies, according to Forrester research, in strategic and ongoing consolidation to eliminate redundant capabilities. There are many compelling reasons why an enterprise should consider technology consolidation as their first priority.

The past decade has seen the rise of many technologies. Enterprises have acquired them, trying to understand and take advantage of new technology trends for their organizations. Many enterprises which had siloed and departmental level governance have cluttered their IT estate with duplicate tools and technologies since IT was not governed at the enterprise level.

During my career I have seen many organizations that have more than a 30% duplication in tools and technologies within their IT estate, and such organizations not only end up spending a lot of money on licenses but they spend an equal amount of money in retaining these resources catering to technology stacks. Such situation has also led to several security concerns because in a large enterprise where IT is not governed centrally, old versions of software continue to prevail and become vulnerable to cybersecurity attacks.

Identifying and standardizing technologies that are required to run IT business is the first step for any organization in their digital transformation journey, after which consolidation becomes the core. Consolidation is the process of simplifying the technology environment. As an example, an enterprise named ABC Lodge had been traditionally using four different reporting tools across four different departments. Since each department was using a different tool, the enterprise has employed several resources to generate reports using these four tools. A consolidation exercise across these departments reduced the tools from four to one and the resource count was reduced by 75%.

Today, companies like Microsoft are building solutions that have a wider range of capabilities in a single product stack, allowing departments to reduce the level of complexity that exists in their environments. This results in improved efficiencies, reduced cost, and innovation.

Most organizations do however still have many distinct tools and technologies providing duplicate capabilities. Consolidating all such tools can benefit organizations in three ways, which are discussed below.

Tactical Benefits

Tactical benefits are reduced licensing costs, centralized storage, streamlined operations, and the management of software, workstations, servers, and networks.

Consolidation increases productivity by reducing the maintenance and management of technology. Most tools and software platforms require time for upkeep. By cutting down on the number of tools to be supported and managed, organizations can save between 25% and 50% on costs and resourcing hours, per my own experiences.

Operational Benefits

Operational benefits are the time saved through increased system availability, reduced downtime and optimal disaster recovery. To achieve these, enterprises need to consider standardizing assets and processes, reducing workarounds, and removing inefficiencies generated by moving between different tools and technologies.

The other operational benefit is that the team will be able to become experts in their domain, allowing more efficient use of training budgets. A more focused team with a deeper understanding of the singular should result in innovation by freeing up time and focusing their attention.

Strategic Benefits

Strategic benefits emerge in improved organizational responsiveness via a flexible and scalable IT environment that can quickly adapt to future growth.

Forrester's 2010 report found that "companies that took a holistic rather than a piecemeal approach to their virtual infrastructure were able to dramatically increase infrastructure consolidation gains and improve their flexibility, responsiveness, and resiliency, at a cost they could afford. The incremental cost saving achieved through tactical deployments will not save nearly as much as those who take a strategic approach to virtualization and consolidation."

A well planned and executed IT consolidation strategy can provide an enterprise with the ability to continuously evaluate new, possibly beneficial technologies. Aligning technologies to enterprise goals and capabilities will drive clear and compelling value to the organization and the end user, as well as assist in becoming innovative.

Formula 4.0 Tools Consolidation Approach

In traditional enterprises, multiple tools and software are in use. Many enterprises have been operating in business unit silos, and therefore several duplicate tools and software have been introduced within the enterprise knowing or unknowingly.

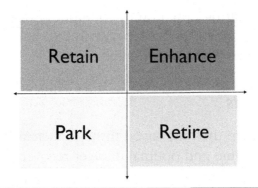

Figure 16.1   Formula 4.0 treatment types

An inventory of all tools and technologies across all the business units within an enterprise needs to be collected by the taskforce. Subsequently, the taskforce needs to place them in one of the four quadrants of the Formula 4.0 treatment types as depicted in Figure 16.1 and following actions need to be taken based on the quadrants.

Retain—this is a quadrant where tools and software that need to continue to exist within the enterprise are placed.

Retire—these are the tools and software that need to be retired because they are either duplicates or there is a need to replace existing tools with alternate ones.

Enhance—these are tools and technologies that need an upgrade. There are many enterprises which have introduced several tools and technologies but have not been able to upgrade them to the latest versions. Old version of tools and technologies create vulnerabilities that online criminals take advantage of to breach systems. Therefore, enterprises are at high risk if they are using outdated version. Another side effect of using old version of tools and technologies is that support from the tool vendors are no longer available, which expose an enterprise to unknown risks and compliance issues.

Park—all tools and technologies that cannot be placed in retain, retire, or enhance go here. Over time, tools and software from parking quadrants will move to one of the other three quadrants.

The end goal of the enterprise is to have one single source of inventory truth across the organization. This means the avoidance of any duplication of tools and software existing in an enterprise, and ensuring that all tools and software are the latest versions.

Product Organization and People Transformation

To succeed in digital transformation, enterprises need to reorganize themselves into a product-based structure, which is cross-functional and organized around customer issues.

The most well-known and often touted example of a product-driven business is Apple. Steve Jobs and his team successfully created products that the market did not even initially know that it needed or wanted. They operated on the "build it and they will come" strategy when creating the iPod, without necessarily identifying the market or customer; they just knew that there was going to be a market for the product once it was out.

First, Apple developed a team to create the iTouch. Another team was separately working on building the iPhone. The iTouch team focused solely on developing their product, and the iPhone team did the same. Although the products have similarities, this did not become a constraint for Apple, as they solely focused on the product instead of the competition. As a result, Apple was able to build these products in a shorter time than expected, each of them complementing one another.

With a product-based organization, enterprises can achieve what Apple has achieved and will have the ability to perform similar stunts as Apple if they so wish. This cannot be achieved in a project-based structure. This is one of the reasons why Formula 4.0 recommends a product-based organization structure for any enterprise embarking on digital transformation. At the end, the reason why enterprises want to become digital is because they want to be nimble with very short release cycles. This typically means that the software development methodology should transition from project-based structure to a Product Organization.

The taskforce needs to analyze the current operating model to define the transformation approach for a product-based organization. Typically, this involves assessing HR and reporting structures as well as the goals and objectives of individuals. In many cases, the IT organization undergo a major shift from a technology centric operating model to a business centric operating model.

Measurement processes across the enterprise also need a radical shift in a Product Organization as enterprises move from a technology centric metrics to a business centric measurement. Using Formula 4.0, teams are measured on metrics such as product margins, monthly recurring revenues, customer churn rate, customer retention rate, new customer acquisition index, and so on.

People Transformation aka Workforce

Digital transformation has made potential market entry for companies a lot easier than it was in the past. Modern technology now means you can launch a product or service quickly and with few resources.

Genuine digital transformation involves technology enabling different ways of working for people to transform their organizations and what they do for their customer. Transformation offers something more significant than technology alone and this type of wholesale enterprise shift is huge, as nothing in the existing business model is left untouched.

To achieve digital transformation, talent is critical. Without the right talent or without focusing on employees, any enterprise will struggle to progress with digital transformation.

Formula 4.0 Product Organization provides a clear guidance on the kind of individuals required who can make the enterprise successful. Once the Product Organization structure is defined, the next step in the process is to transform the enterprise from a pyramid to a diamond shape as per the guidance provided in Chapter 10. Moving to a diamond cannot be an overnight exercise and needs to be carefully planned. This involves changes to the existing team and the hiring and firing of personnel. The taskforce needs to understand existing people characteristics within the enterprise, such as their skillsets, their operating model, and their strengths and weaknesses, based on which a workforce strategy needs to be devised. The taskforce will assess the current resources within the enterprises and define the changes required from both skill and pyramid perspectives. The first step is to map the product structure of each department with the resourcing needs and then apply the Hackfest model of Formula 4.0 to identify the product engineering team.

Hackfest follows a step-by-step process starting from shortlisting individuals for a Product Organization until the time they are trained and deployed into individual teams.

Setting Up DevSecOps for Product Development

DevOps is a union of process, people, and working products that is enabled via tools and technology, with continuous integration and delivery. DevOps accelerate the process of delivering applications and software services at a high speed and high velocity. Introducing security into the DevOps process is called DevSecOps, and all modern enterprises today use a variety of tools and technologies for their development, operations, and to manage their security.

Introducing DevSecOps into an enterprise with Formula 4.0 will mean that existing processes need to be validated by the taskforce to come up with a gap analysis. It is essential that a DevSecOps pipeline is created for the enterprise and while creating this, pipeline tools and technologies existing within the enterprise should be validated for fitment. The end goal is to create a state-of-the-art DecSecOps platform that can provide maximum automation to the development and operations process. This will also enable automation monitoring and self-healing capabilities by adopting to AI and ML capabilities, as per the Formula 4.0 guidelines, laid out in Chapter 11.

Data First

Many enterprises are embarking on their data first journey and this has become extremely important for everyone. For an enterprise to be relevant in the market, they need to adopt a data first strategy. This means that business decisions are made based on insights which an enterprise gets from analyzing the data. As an example, a food retailer may wish to reduce the price of their products based on the pricing insights it receives on its competitors.

The Formula 4.0 taskforce needs to understand the enterprise business context and its needs before embarking on a data first approach.

Today's economic climate is forcing companies to become more and more data-driven in order to compete and survive. Companies that are data-driven are those that are ahead in the market, but the good news is that adopting a data first strategy is neither difficult nor expensive. Several enterprises depend on making business decisions based on data patterns of their competitors or customer buying patterns. For example, enterprise A decided to do more sales online. With such a need this enterprise forces customers down the digital path but not all customers are ready to go the online way. After a few months the enterprise understands that it cannot force all its customers to follow the digital channels, and during these months millions of dollars are lost in revenue for this enterprise. Based on the data analysis of their customers, the enterprise understands that only selected customers in a specific age range will adopt to digital channels and the enterprise business strategy changes based on this new insight.

Another example is for retailers, which are enterprises, who embark on their data first strategy since the majority of their business decisions are happening based on the data of their competitors. Examples could be a food retailer who changes their product prices every day based on their competitor, to remain competitive and retain customers who may be considering moving to another retailer.

Creating a data platform is the first step for all such enterprises. Using Formula 4.0, enterprises can transform themselves to maturity level 2 of the data maturity framework which means the traditional pyramid is reversed by automating the data pipelines and data operations. The end state is an enterprise with less money spent on data operations and more time spent on insights to make business decisions, as discussed in Chapter 12.

Companies that have become data-driven are successful because they adopt a data first strategy that permeates their entire organization.

Enterprise Governance

Digital transformation is imperative for all businesses. That message comes through loud and clear from every keynote, panel discussion, article, or study related to how businesses can remain competitive and relevant as the world becomes increasingly digital.

Formula 4.0 mandates that process tool and technologies and operating models are standardized and governed at an enterprise level, moving away from business unit silos. This brings in the most important aspect which is to understand the current processes which are in place within an enterprise that can enable the transformation agenda. The need from Formula 4.0 is a product-based organization with governance managed at an enterprise level; this is defined in Chapters 9 and 15, respectively.

Enterprise Governance within Capability Areas

It is mandatory that key capability areas within an enterprise are introduced at the enterprise level during the foundation phase, and all department or business unit level governances are dissolved as per the guidance provided in Chapter 15. Formula 4.0 enterprise governance capabilities spans across:

- Enterprise-architecture
- Security

- DevOps
- Cloud
- Data capability
- Tools and technologies
- SDLC methodologies

It is essential that the taskforce understands the current governance and defines a transformation journey with the end state being centralized governance at an enterprise level.

And Finally—Enabling Automation with RPA, AI, and ML

The key to digital transformation is getting the basics right. Once the basics are set, enterprises can achieve enormous benefits from technology, be it with an existing known technology or an unknown future technology. Adopting the Formula 4.0 framework not only helps to set the foundation for transformation, but also provides a platform for the future.

Automation using RPA, AI, and ML needs to be applied consistently across all areas of IT within the enterprise which will bring in maximum speed and efficiency in almost any initiative that the enterprise embarks on. As an example, bringing in automation within the data management processes will inverse the data pyramid. Bringing in automaton in DevSecOps will enable enterprises to achieve maximum productivity and eliminate manual interventions thereby improving quality. Bringing automation into testing will reduce manual testing efforts. Automation is another area where several enterprises have seen exceeding benefits, not only from a cost reduction perspective but also in efficiency improvement and business satisfaction. Automation is the core to achieving maximum mileage from digital and should be applied consistently across all areas in the enterprise.

IT-OT Integration as the Last Capability Area

With all the above capability areas set up, enterprises are ready to adopt to any new digital technology. With a data platform using Cloud, Atomic architecture, and API platforms, IT-OT Integration becomes a reality for enterprises. The Formula 4.0 methodology allows enterprises to utilize the full potential of IoT in their journey toward digital transformation. Enterprises can also utilize the support of Cloud providers to rapidly adopt IoT, and with already created data ecosystems enterprises can import the IoT generated data into their enterprise to perform actions and analytics.

Note

1. https://cdn2.hubspot.net/hubfs/1624046/Digital%20Business%20Executive%20 Summary_FINAL.pdf?t=1534365095051

Index

Printed in the United States
by Baker & Taylor Publisher Services